Images in Our Souls:
Cavell, Psychoanalysis, and Cinema

Psychiatry and the Humanities, Volume 10

Assistant Editor
Gloria H. Parloff

Published under the auspices of the
Forum on Psychiatry and the Humanities,
The Washington School of Psychiatry

Images in Our Souls

Cavell, Psychoanalysis, and Cinema

Edited by
Joseph H. Smith, M.D.
William Kerrigan, Ph.D.

The Johns Hopkins University Press
Baltimore and London

©1987 Forum on Psychiatry and the Humanities of the
Washington School of Psychiatry

The Johns Hopkins University Press, 701 West 40th Street,
Baltimore, Maryland 21211
The Johns Hopkins Press Ltd., London

♾ The paper used in this publication meets the mini-
mum requirements of American National Standard for Information Sciences—Permanence of Paper for Printed Library Materials, ANSI Z39.48-1984.

Library of Congress Cataloging-in-Publication Data

Images in our souls.

(Psychiatry and the humanities ; v. 10)
Includes index.
1. Moving-pictures—Psychological aspects.   2. Moving-
picture plays—History and criticism.   3. Psychoanalysis.
I. Cavell, Joseph, 1926–   . II. Smith, Joseph H.,
1927–   . III. Kerrigan, William, 1943–   .
IV. Series.
RC321.P943   vol. 10   .   616.89 s   87-3879
[PN1995]   [791.43'01'9]
ISBN 0-8018-3511-9 (alk. paper)

Contributors

Stanley Cavell
Walter M. Cabot Professor of Aesthetics and the
General Theory of Value, Harvard University

Micheline Klagsbrun Frank
Psychologist, Washington, D.C.

Timothy Gould
Assistant Professor, Department of Philosophy,
Metropolitan State College, Denver

Karen Hanson
Associate Professor, Department of Philosophy,
Indiana University

Stanley R. Palombo
Clinical Associate Professor of Psychiatry, George
Washington University Medical School

William Rothman
Director, International Honors Program on Film,
Television and Social Change, Boston

Irving Schneider
Clinical Associate Professor of Psychiatry,
Georgetown University Medical School; Faculty,
Washington School of Psychiatry

Bruce H. Sklarew
Faculty, Baltimore–District of Columbia Institute for
Psychoanalysis; Clinical Associate Professor of
Psychiatry, Howard University

Stephen M. Weissman
Clinical Associate Professor of Psychiatry, George
Washington University Medical School

Robert Winer
Chair, Psychoanalytic Family Therapy Training
Program, Washington School of Psychiatry

Contents

Introduction 1
Joseph H. Smith

1 Psychoanalysis and Cinema: The Melodrama of the Unknown
  Woman 11
  Stanley Cavell

2 Hitchcock's *Vertigo:* The Dream Function in Film 44
  Stanley R. Palombo

3 *Vertigo:* The Unknown Woman in Hitchcock 64
  William Rothman

4 Witnessing and Bearing Witness: The Ontogeny of Encounter in
  the Films of Peter Weir 82
  Robert Winer

5 Stanley Cavell and the Plight of the Ordinary 109
  Timothy Gould

6 The Shows of Violence 137
  Irving Schneider

7 *Kiss of the Spiderwoman* 150
  Micheline Klagsbrun Frank

8 Ingmar Bergman's *Cries and Whispers:* The Consequences of
  Preoedipal Developmental Disturbances 169
  Bruce H. Sklarew

9 Chaplin's *The Kid* 183
  Stephen M. Weissman

10 Being Doubted, Being Assured 187
  Karen Hanson

Index 203

Images in Our Souls:
Cavell, Psychoanalysis, and Cinema

Introduction

Joseph H. Smith

This, more than any other volume in the Psychiatry and the Humanities series, is a book about America. It is, more than any other, a book on women and on gender identity and difference. It is a philosophic and psychoanalytic exploration of the ordinary. It is a book on movies.

This diverse range of subject matter reflects the intensity of Stanley Cavell, whose Weigert Lecture introduces and sets the theme of this volume. Cavell views psychoanalysis from "a perspective in which our culture appears as having entered on a path of radical skepticism (hence on a path to deny this path) from the time of, say, Descartes and Shakespeare—or, say, from the time of the fall of Kings and the rise of science and the death of God—[with] late in this history, the advent of psychoanalysis." From this perspective, skepticism, regardless of its status or validity as a philosophic position, can be read as symptomatic of an insecurity and thus a new need for security.

The insecurity arose along with several questions that, if accepted, also interpret or at least mark off skepticism as quandary. They are questions that can be seen as endlessly enabling—or disabling, depending upon the direction from which one sees answers as likely to come. Is skepticism the consequence of a loss that befell humanity, to be grieved or repaired, or is it to be seen as the result of an achieved catastrophe, a catastrophe in which human finitude is revealed? Or is skepticism, rather than being a *response* to passively experienced or actively achieved catastrophe, itself the cause of such catastrophe? Is skepticism a cloud of doubt that mushroomed over the world at the end of the medieval period, competing with the antiskeptical thrust of the Renaissance, or is skepticism itself one of the fruits of the Renaissance? Is skepticism a way of undermining

1

the ordinary or, as such, a necessary step in providing antiskeptical access to the ordinary as an exceptional achievement? Cavell calls it "the achievement of the human" (1979, 463).

In part 4 of *The Claim of Reason: Wittgenstein, Skepticism, Morality, and Tragedy* (1979), Cavell does not wholly reject any of these questions, but neither does he seek answers to any of them along lines laid down by Descartes, Locke, Hume, or Kant (cf. Rorty 1982, 187–88). In the spirit of the title of the first chapter of part 4, "Between Acknowledgment and Avoidance," he undertakes a study of doubt and resistance to doubt as part of our being, of our history, of behavior taken as "hieroglyph of the soul" (1979, 475), and of our capacity to doubt also that view of behavior.

The move from "the skeptic's picture of intellectual limitedness" to Wittgenstein's "picture of human finitude" (Cavell 1979, 431) is central in this study. Cavell identifies a passive wish at the heart of "active" skepticism, "a wish for the connection between my claims of knowledge and the objects upon which the claims are to fall to occur without my intervention, apart from my agreements" (351–52). If skepticism concludes (but maybe it also begins) "with the conditions of human separation, with a discovering that I am I" (389), this "I am I" does not convey information; it is not an answer to the question "Who am I?" as a piece of self-knowledge in the sense of taking the self to be identified with the mind. Self-doubt, in fact, "is not overcome by any set of beliefs I may have about myself, any more than skeptical doubt about the existence of the world is overcome by any set of beliefs I may acquire about the world" (393).

In the "I am I" one affirms, acknowledges, appropriates finitude in the act of owning oneself. The discovery comes not as new knowledge but in a yielding to what was already known. Cavell argues for "an understanding of the having of a self as an acceptance of the idea of being by oneself, and an understanding of being by oneself in turn in terms of being [in a sane sense] beside oneself. . . . It [is] . . . an understanding of self-possession as a certain achievement of aloneness (call it oneness, or wholeness; Thoreau spells it holiness and says that it seeks expression)" (367).

It is this achievement of aloneness that precedes any full capacity to be *with* another. Furthermore, if the path of radical skepticism was entered from the time of the fall of Kings, the rise of science, and the death of God, it was a path that led to realizing that "the other now bears the weight of God" (482) in showing that one is not alone in the universe. With the late medieval catastrophe, humanity, thrown back on its own resources, was called upon to find new ways to know the world, self, and other—new ways of being in the world, of being oneself, and of acknowledging one's relation to and need of the other. In that context, differences and samenesses previously unattended, including differences and samenesses between men and women, would come to light. The essential sameness would be that of man and woman being equally called upon, each—not without the help of the other—to assume his or her own subjecthood.

The older understanding of selfhood in terms of "the right of the subject's particularity, his right to be satisfied . . . the right of subjective freedom . . . [as] the pivot and center of the difference between antiquity and modern times" (from Hegel's *Philosophy of Right,* as quoted in Cavell 1979, 467) took on a new secular and political urgency. This led, notwithstanding persisting slavery and discrimination against women, to the American experiment, in which subjecthood, glossed as the right to life, liberty, and the pursuit of happiness, was attributed as being in-alienable to each individual. The attribution of subjecthood (in later, Kierkegaardian terms) is based on the assumption that every individual is in possession of that which it essentially is to be an individual. In America, this attribution left room for Emerson's conviction that each individual is called upon to assume his or her part in creating a more perfect human community but also is free to develop his or her own idea about what a more perfect community might be.

This Emersonian idea is the constant context of Cavell's thought in his study and teaching of film. The philosophers and poets who are promi-nent among his heroes (they all regularly attend movies with him) are those who attended the ordinary—Wordsworth, Coleridge, Emerson, Thoreau, Kierkegaard, Austin, Wittgenstein, Heidegger. His allegiance to the critics Robert Warshow and Walter Benjamin is based, first of all, on their both refusing "to exempt themselves from the mass response elicited by film."

Though he hastens to add "(by some films, by some good films)" (1981a, 268), he does not refer to a narrow sector of films made by and for an elitist audience. He means good movies, in fact, scandalously popular movies such as *The Philadelphia Story* and *It Happened One Night.* This refusal to exempt himself from the popular response elicited by film is entirely in accord with the philosophical position not only of *Pursuits of Happiness* (1981a) and his contribution to the present vol-ume, but also of *Must We Mean What We Say?* (1976), *The World Viewed* (1979), *The Claim of Reason* (1979), *The Senses of Walden* (1981b), and *Themes out of School* (1984).

In his writing on remarriage comedy, Cavell defines marriage—and especially remarriage—as the transformation of incestuous knowledge "into an erotic friendship capable of withstanding, and returning, the gaze of legitimate civilization." Cavell can quickly relate this putting together of night and day, of the covert and the overt, to Kierkegaardian repetition, Nietzsche's eternal recurrence (for which the wedding ring is the symbol), and a particularly apt vision of Freud's *Beyond the Pleasure Principle*.

Failures in marriage, failures in the ongoing task of remarriage or of achieving again the capability of marital intimacy, failures in faithful and willing repetition forward, failures in attunement to eternal recurrence, failures to create a happy life together in the face of death, are the concerns of melodrama, one species of which Cavell here names the melodrama of the unknown woman. In recurrently becoming married again, attunement to woman's unknownness, which could otherwise turn treacherous, is as vital as overcoming man's unknowingness, which could otherwise turn villainous. Of course, woman's unknownness is an aspect of every man and man's unknowingness of every woman, and that, too, needs to be mutually acknowledged. These are the tasks that prove to be of unending interest, leading as they do toward love and wisdom on the one hand or, on the other, toward revenge (self- or other-directed) rooted in nihilism and envy. It is from these dramas of everyday life that questions at once philosophical, psychoanalytic, historical, and aesthetic arise.

One of the ways in which Cavell links philosophy and psychoanalysis is by virtue of their shared (male) skepticism, and one of the ways in which he links psychoanalysis and film is by virtue of their both beginning with the overt suffering and the covert wisdom of women. The suffering of women, Cavell believes, is of a different register than the skepticism, nihilism, or doubts of men. Cavell sees psychoanalysis, cinema, and ultimately philosophy as asking woman how it is that she escapes doubt and what it is that she knows. The urgency of the questions presumably derives from an anxious conviction that an answer would explain her lack of doubt, shadowed by a horror that it would not—or, even if it should, that it would not touch the doubt that assails man.

The first loss of an other is beyond all beginnings—always instead a discovery that the other was always already other. And every subsequent losing is also a relosing—a relosing vital to that to be gained in each instance of refinding. One could equally well say that each instance of refinding is a prelude vital to that to be gained in each relosing.

Men and women assist each other in finding themselves by each being the means of the other's losing themselves. Men and women each assist the other in losing themselves by each being the means of the other's finding themselves again. But what is lost and what is found in each is different, in some dimension, different beyond all knowing of the other or by the other. I read this as spiritual equality. Woman is created and educated by man no more than man's awakening, education, and creation is by woman.

Cavell speaks of "reading" a film. To view and appropriate a film, to take an interest in a film, he reminds us, is to take an interest in one's experience of a film. In his words, "to examine and defend my interest in . . . films is to examine and defend my interest in my own experience, in the moments and passages of my life I have spent with them" (1981a, 7).

I here turn to "readings" of Cavell and to readings of film in the light of Cavell's thought.

Both Stanley Palombo, a psychoanalyst, and William Rothman, a humanist, write on Hitchcock's *Vertigo*. Palombo extends his prior work on the construction of dreams and the meaning of dreaming to an analysis of a dream within a film and a comparison of the meaning of dreaming and that of viewing a film. Like reading a book or looking at a work of art, viewing a film *can* be the passive, voyeuristic experience it is often taken to be. In addition, it can be, as suggested in Palombo's concluding paragraphs, in Robert Winer's concepts of witnessing and bearing witness, and in the discussions of defensive and nondefensive passivity that appear in virtually every essay included here, an act of imaginative synthesis and working through. Reading is always a weak or strong misreading or rewriting, and the same order of complexity is assumed throughout this volume for viewing a film.

This is to say that voyeurism and exhibitionism have more than each other as opposites. An opposite of the defensive activity of voyeuristic looking is to really look—to look at the object but to look also in awareness of the subject looking, which is to say, to look in a way that calls for rethinking one's experience in the light of such seeing. Similarly, exhibitionism marks an at least transient foreclosure of the possibility of either genuine self-revelation or genuine awareness of the other.

All viewing confronts the viewer, at some level, with the question of his or her mode of viewing. Is the looking simply to uncover the facts of the case so that they may be beheld, or is it to look both outwardly and inwardly in such a fashion as to allow for change? Hitchcock can be taken to mean that the truth will make one free, but he can also be taken, in *Vertigo* at least, to be saying that truth perceived as merely the facts of the case can impose the opposite of freedom.

If Ferguson's (James Stewart's) unraveling of the case were limited only to finding out what happened in Judy's (Kim Novak's) story, we could imagine him left more fundamentally unraveled than he had been while hospitalized and, in the final scene, ready himself to jump from the tower. Indeed, during most of the film he pursues facts. While so doing he is foreclosed from seeing that Judy, as Rothman suggests, was no longer just Judy, and also foreclosed from any inner looking that could have led to a needed rewriting of his own narrative. But at the end of the film, and at the end of Palombo's article, we are permitted to imagine him profoundly shaken but not unraveled.

Rothman's contribution is a meditation on unknownness. Like Louis Jourdan at the end of *Letter from an Unknown Woman,* Stewart at the end of *Vertigo* awakens—too late—to the realization that he has failed to acknowledge a woman. Although Rothman reads the final kiss as emblematic of Stewart's forgiveness of Judy, I think it truer to Rothman's insight into the tortuousness of Hitchcock's own fated unknownness to read the kiss as tribute to a love doubly tragic in that it could not have been realized even had Stewart awakened earlier.

At the end of his article, Rothman touches on an approach to the study of film in the question as to whether "every authentic authorship discovers its own story." Such an approach is fully spelled out in the essay by Robert Winer, "Witnessing and Bearing Witness: The Ontogeny of Encounter in the Films of Peter Weir." Winer traces modes of participation and encounter that correspond to critical developmental tasks from early adolescence to mature adulthood in five major films directed by Weir. In the developmental sequence, Winer demonstrates a crucial shift from witnessing to bearing witness. In the concluding paragraph, he speculates that filmographies might recapitulate ontongeny on a broad scale and that analogous studies might delineate similar recapitulations in the work of any artist.

Winer also undertakes a consideration of witnessing and bearing witness in the psychoanalytic situation. "No witnessing can be simply naive; every witnessing requires bearing witness. The patient's discovery that this is so is the heart of the analytic process."

Timothy Gould reflects on Cavell's conclusions about skepticism, film, and the ordinary as exemplified in another Hitchcock film, *Shadow of a Doubt.* In taking Cavell's work as one way of inheriting Wittgenstein's understanding of his methods as therapies, Gould notes how Cavell links resistances internal to philosophy with resistances in thinking about film.

A central resistance to that which calls for thinking when viewing movies—a resistance displayed in disdain and in derogatory statements (not just by intellectuals) that the movies are an escape or a fetish or something to be apologized for—manifests itself as an intolerance for the passivity of viewing movies. We learn about ourselves and about movies in acknowledging this aspect of witnessing. In viewing, for instance, the "unreal" events of the film, we are faced with our own uncertainty as to what our conviction in reality turns on. More important, Gould shows (and shows how Cavell has shown) that acknowledging and thinking about the passivity of the viewer (of ourselves as viewers) opens thought also to the issue of passiveness in philosophy and thus to accounts of the place and import of passivity in human existence.

Gould proceeds to Cavell's account of Wittgenstein as providing the means for undoing philosophy's efforts to repudiate the world of the ordinary, and to Hitchcock's depiction of a parallel effort of repudiation. The belief that Gould sees at the center of Cavell's vision is that "the willingness to repudiate the ordinary world is at once the most common and the most intellectual (or intellectualized) form of the wish to repudiate the world as such."

These themes are tracked in *Shadow of a Doubt,* in which Gould finally lets Charlie's (Teresa Wright's) silent declaration of knowledge and isolation stand as echoing ambiguities and uncertainties in his own reflections on Cavell's work. But not quite. Although it strikes me as a statement with which Cavell would agree, Gould goes on (in a passage reminiscent of Rorty's [1982, 108–9] account of Derrida's efforts to save us from the fate of "a last word") to write, "To banish the skeptic's banishment of the ordinary is finally to accommodate the knowledge that we had already been willing to banish the world. We must let go of the wish to respond to the skeptic's provocation, accepting instead what there remains to be instructed by. This will take silence as well as resolve."

In "The Shows of Violence," Irving Schneider reviews current thinking on the relation between mass media and personal fantasy and behavior. His emphasis is on studying the motivations and satisfactions of the audience, or "consumers" of film, as understood in the light of the social, economic, and political contexts of their lives.

At one level, the issue of whether violence depicted evokes violence enacted turns on the individual's capacity for sublimation of a thirst for revenge—say, along Nietzschean lines as discussed herein by Gould—as opposed to a tendency to directly enact revenge after witnessing a portrayal of it. For example, one suicide in a psychiatric hospital sometimes precipitates an epidemic of suicides. That may not be preventable. But if researchers discovered incontrovertibly that a television or film portrayal of adolescent suicide could precipitate suicide in an adolescent viewer, the issue of whether or not the film should be shown would become wrenching indeed.

In that instance, the competing issues would be a specific threat to life versus the less specific, but powerful, threat posed by censorship. People do need affirmation, as Schneider mentions, that even the most deeply repressed impulse is still within the range of the human. Those not counted in the statistics of violent response to portrayals of violence and suicide are those who respond by achieving the peace of a more solid inner commitment to life and to nonviolence.

The issue is easier to consider in less extreme and more ordinary instances, such as in the fictive dimension, or at any rate, in the fictive interludes of everyday life. If a father pretends to be a grizzly bear to the delight of his three-year-old son, he could, depending on a multitude of other factors, be contributing to episodes of violence in his son's adult behavior. But in the main, he is affirming an already established tacit knowledge that the son can love his father (and his father him) notwithstanding any aggression that he has noted in or projected upon the father. Imagine the result if, instead of easily and unconsciously risking the symbolic enactment, the father had refrained or had been constrained to explain to the child—perhaps out of fear of frightening him or of inciting the seeds of violence, or out of the wish to enlighten him—the nature of father-son ambivalence or the meaning of the son's games. Kierkegaard long ago lamented that the child would go quite mad.

In adolescence, peers, teachers, and fictional accounts, rather than parents, would more likely mediate this kind of integration. But even shows of violence in the real world can foster such integration by virtue of benevolent internalized parental imagoes. One of the points Schneider documents is that violent shows can lose their power of inciting violence in children if they are seen with or discussed with adults. A major point of his article is that acknowledgment of the propensity to violence is an aspect of healthy parent-child relatedness and probably an essential element in the development of ordinary controls and necessary sublimation.

Micheline Frank finds in *Kiss of the Spiderwoman* an intimate exploration of male and female, self and other. She here considers issues of passivity and activity, of confusion between internal and external, of regression, and of the similarities and dissimilarities between dreaming and viewing a movie, in the context of Winnicott's potential or transitional space and of Stoller's studies on symbiotic anxiety and gender identity. Frank sees the power of this film to be in a doubling of passivity. There is the passivity of viewing, but there is also the passivity of what is viewed—in Molina's yearning for the all-too-gratifying intimacy of an unending symbiosis, partly gratified by his own addiction to movies and to fantasies of making movies.

In one paragraph Frank aligns the thought of Cavell, the thought of Lacan, and a description of intercourse from a woman's point of view into a passage that is as convincing as any in the volume of a link between skepticism and maleness. In her conclusion she states that, as an instance of feminine writing, hers is not an argument toward closure but "an exploration, a loosening of boundaries, a bringing-together of diverse ideas, 'risking contamination' through interpenetration."

In a discussion of preoedipal developmental disturbances as revealed in Bergman's *Cries and Whispers,* Bruce Sklarew traces the efforts of three sisters to survive the effect upon them of their mother. The mother emerges as vain, narcissistic, isolated, cold, and uncaring, yet also as gentle, beautiful, and, in words from Agnes's diary, "so alive and so present."

Bergman's account of the play to his cast bears some resemblance to Frank's conclusion on feminine writing: "As I turn this project over in my mind, it never stands out as a completed whole . . . it resembles a dark, flowing stream: faces, movements, voices, gestures, exclamations, light and shade, moods, dreams. Nothing fixed, nothing really tangible other than for the moment, and then only an illusory moment. A dream, a longing, or perhaps an expectation, a fear, in which that to be feared is never put into words."

Although Sklarew denies that they are accepted by contemporary psychoanalysis as descriptive of the feminine, the traits emphasized as feminine in the older psychoanalytic literature apply to the three sisters. Perhaps these traits could be thought of as their styles of coping. Masochism is dominant in Karin, passivity in Agnes, and narcissism in Maria. With the exception of Agnes's belief that she is like the father, which is perhaps more indicative of a wish to be unlike her mother, there is a striking absence of mention of the father.

Here again, the regressive pull of film viewing is taken to the second power by the often nonverbal encounters and the symbiotic yearning of the characters in the scenes viewed, notwithstanding (or maybe because of the fact) that the intimacy and intimate touching portrayed are strangely evocative of ships passing in the night. But as the death of Agnes nears, images of yearning for symbiosis shift, or are refocused, and are revealed as also images of a longing for the highest form of love, ultimately unconditional and sacrificial.

Stephen Weissman's brief but telling tribute, a part of his larger work in progress on Chaplin, reminds us that the force of *The Kid* is derived not only from the immediacy of a personal loss, but also from a loss that taps into and is framed by an archetypal myth.

The discussion throughout the volume of skepticism, activity and passivity, difference, and gender difference, culminates in Karen Hanson's closing essay, "Being Doubted, Being Assured." With the aim of elucidating the passive form of the skeptical worry "Am I known to the other?" (echoing the recognition that Hegel and Lacan take as the term of desire), she discusses Descartes in the dialogue with Princess Elizabeth that led to his last major work, *The Passions of the Soul.*" Princess Elizabeth had confessed that she would not find it so difficult to attribute physicality to the soul. Descartes replied that it was possible to conceive of the soul as material (which could strike one as unduly ponderous since she had just done it), but intellect alone was inadequate to grasp such a conception.

The next woman Hanson brings up against Descartes is Greta Garbo, in whom, she believes, the lineaments of a supreme example of the passive version of the *cogito* can be seen. "Gazing at this unknown woman, we are assured of human existence, not by any action of our own, or any special action of hers, but by her passionate revelation of distance and depth." The evocation of such images by Hanson, Cavell, and others here who address the theme may more clarify the meaning of woman as unknown than all our words.

After tracing out the intricacies of her own ideas and Cavell's ideas on activity and passivity and gender difference, Hanson ends with a note on the moral hazards that pervade the communication of psychoanalytic and philosophic ideas.

I have emphasized points of philosophic and psychoanalytic import unifying these essays with hardly a glimpse of the artistry and magic of the particular films described. But the play here, and probably the more intimate unity, is in the accounts of the films themselves, beginning with Cavell's depiction of Ophuls's *Letter from an Unknown Woman.*

References

Cavell, Stanley. *Must We Mean What We Say?* Reprint. Cambridge: At the University Press, 1976.

———. *The World Viewed.* Cambridge, Mass.: Harvard University Press, 1979.

———. *The Claim of Reason: Wittgenstein, Skepticism, Morality, and Tragedy.* New York: Oxford University Press, 1979.

———. *Pursuits of Happiness.* Cambridge, Mass.: Harvard University Press, 1981a.

———. *The Senses of Walden.* San Francisco: North Point Press, 1981b.

———. *Themes out of School: Effects and Causes.* San Francisco: North Point Press, 1984.

Rorty, Richard. *The Consequences of Pragmatism.* Minneapolis: University of Minnesota Press, 1982.

1   Psychoanalysis and Cinema: The Melodrama of the Unknown Woman

Stanley Cavell

When the man in Max Ophuls's' film *Letter from an Unknown Woman* reaches the final words of the letter addressed to him by the, or by some, unknown woman, he is shown—according to well-established routines of montage—to be assaulted by a sequence of images from earlier moments in the film. This assault of images proves to be death-dealing. His response to finishing the reading of the letter is to stare out past it, as if calling up the film's images; and his response to the assault of the ensuing repeated images is to cover his eyes with the outstretched fingers of both hands in a melodramatic gesture of horror and exhaustion. Yet he sees nothing we have not seen, and the images themselves (as it were) are quite banal—his pulling the veil up over the woman's hat, the two of them at the Prater amusement park in winter, her taking a candied apple, their dancing, his playing a waltz for her on the piano in an empty ballroom. An apparently excessive response to apparently banal images—it seems a characterization of a response to film generally, at least to certain kinds of film, perhaps above all to classical Hollywood films. But since Max Ophuls is a director, and this is a film, of major ambition, the implication may be that this man's response to the return-ing images of the film and of his past—his horror and exhaustion—somehow underlies our response to any film of this kind, perhaps to major film as such, or ought to. It seems a particular mode of horror that these hands would ward off, since we may equally think of the images looming at this man not as what he has seen but as what he has *not* seen, has refused to see. Then are we sure that we have seen what it is up to us to see? What motivates these images? Why does their knowledge consti-tute an assault? If *Letter from an Unknown Woman* were merely the high-class so-called woman's film, or tearjerker, it is commonly taken to

11

Stefan Brand (Louis Jourdan) and his servant John (Art Smith) in Max Ophuls's
Letter from an Unknown Woman (1948).

be—as the bulk of the melodramas I will refer to here are taken to be—it and they could not justify and satisfy the imposition of such questions of criticism. The only proof that any of them can do so is, of course, to provide a convincing reading in which one or another of them does so. That is not what I want to attempt here, but instead to do less and more than that. Less, because the passages of reading I provide here concern only certain isolated moments of any film. But more, because I will adduce moments from two groups of films designed at once to suggest the range and detail of their relations as a whole and to sketch the intellectual palette that convincing readings will, for my taste, have to support. Here I am looking for a sense of the ground on which any reading I would be moved to offer will succeed or fail.

In accepting the assignment to give this year's Weigert lecture on the topic of psychoanalysis and cinema, I knew that I would want to use the occasion to take further the work represented in my book *Pursuits of Happiness*. That book defines a genre of film—a genre I name the comedy of remarriage—on the basis of what I call reading the individual members of a set of films, which is meant to prove them to constitute a genre, where proving this constitution turns in part on showing the group as a whole to enact, and, I hope, to illuminate, Freud's early vision (in *Three Essays on the Theory of Sexuality*) that "the finding of the object is in fact the refinding of it," together with a surprising conjunction of preconceptions in what can be called philosophy. In re-marriage comedy, unlike classical comedy, happiness, such as it is, is arrived at not by a young pair's overcoming social obstacles to their love, but instead by a somewhat older pair's overcoming obstacles that are between, or within, themselves (facing divorce, being brought *back* to-gether, and finding one another *again*). A remarkable sequence of conse-quences flows from this shift of emphasis, segments of which will be rehearsed in what follows.

Remarriage comedy, in effect enacting what Freud calls the diphasic character of human sexuality, displays the nostalgic structure of human experience. Since these films, being major achievements of the art of film, thus reveal some internal affinity of the phenomenon of nostalgia with the phenomenon of film, the popular nostalgia now associated with movies stands to be understood as a parody, or avoidance, of an inherent, treacherous property of the medium of film as such. The drama of the remarriage genre, the argument that brings into play the intellectual and emotional bravery of the beautiful, lucid pairs whose interactions or conversations form the interest of the genre—Irene Dunne and Cary Grant, Barbara Stanwyck and Henry Fonda, Katharine Hepburn and Spencer Tracy—turns on their efforts to transform an intimacy as be-tween brother and sister into an erotic friendship capable of withstanding, and returning, the gaze of legitimate civilization. They conduct, in short, the argument of marriage. In *The Philadelphia Story* (directed by George Cukor in 1940) this ancient intimacy—here between Katharine Hepburn and Cary Grant—is called, twice, having grown up together. In *The Awful Truth* (directed by Leo McCarey in 1937) the woman (Irene Dunne) actually, climactically, enacts a role as her husband's sister (the husband is again Cary Grant), in which this high-minded society lady blatantly displays her capacity for low-down sexiness.

The transformation of incestuous knowledge into erotic exchange is a function of something I call the achievement of the daily, of the diurnal, the putting together of night and day (as classical comedy puts together the seasons of the year), a process of willing repetition whose concept is the domestic, or marriage, however surprising the images of marriage become in these films. "Repetition" is the title Kierkegaard gives to his thoughts about the faith required in achieving marriage (*Repetition*); and repetition, or rather eternal recurrence, is the recipe Nietzsche discovered as the antidote for our otherwise fated future of nihilism, the thing Nietzsche calls "the revenge against time and its 'It was'"—a revenge itself constituting a last effort not to die of nostalgia. Nietzsche explicity invokes the concept of marriage in his prophetic cry (in *Thus Spoke Zarathustra*) for this redemption or reconception of time. He says it is "high time" for this, and in German the literal translation of "high time" is *Hochzeit* (wedding); moreover, his symbol of eternal recurrence is the (wedding) ring. These ideas of repetition may be said to require of our lives the perpetual invention of the present from the past, out of the past. This seems to be the vision of Freud's *Beyond the Pleasure Principle,* in which death—I take it to be psychological death—comes either through the success of this invention, that is, the discovery of one's own death (hence, surely, of one's own life, say, of one's willingness to live), or else through the relapse of the psychological into the biological and beyond into the inorganic, which may be viewed as counter modes of repetition.

In writing *Pursuits of Happiness* I incurred a number of intellectual debts that I propose here not to settle but somewhat to identify and organize—in effect, to rewrite certain of my outstanding promissory notes. My initial business will be to confirm a prediction of *Pursuits of Happiness* to the effect that there must exist a genre of film, in particular some form of melodrama, adjacent to, or derived from, that of remarriage comedy, in which the themes and structure of the comedy are modified or negated in such a way as to reveal systematically the threats (of misunderstanding, of violence) that in each of the remarriage comedies dog its happiness. I am calling the new genre the melodrama of the unknown woman. My next main business will be to say how I cloak my debt to the writing of Freud, which means to say what I conceive certain relations of psychoanalysis and philosophy to consist in. My concluding piece of business, as a kind of extended epilogue, will be to produce a reading of the moment I invoked in opening these remarks, a man's melodramatic covering of his eyes, from the Ophuls film from which I have adapted the title of the new genre.

The prediction that some form of melodrama awaited definition was based on various moments from each of the comedies of remarriage. In the earliest of the definitive remarriage structures, *It Happened One Night* (directed by Frank Capra in 1934, with Clark Gable and Claudette Colbert), the pair work through episodes of poverty, theft, blackmail, and sordid images of marriage; in *The Awful Truth* the pair face distrust, jealousy, scandal, and the mindless rumoring of a prospective mother-in-law; in *His Girl Friday* (from 1940, directed by Howard Hawks, with Cary Grant and Rosalind Russell) the pair deal with political corruption, brutal moralism, and wasting cynicism; in *The Lady Eve* (from 1941, directed by Preston Sturges, with Fonda and Stanwyck), with duplicity and the intractableness of the past; in *The Philadelphia Story*, with pretentiousness, perverseness, alcoholism, and frigidity.

But it is in the last of the remarriage comedies, *Adam's Rib* (from 1949, directed by George Cukor, with Hepburn and Tracy), that melodrama threatens on several occasions almost to take the comedy over. The movie opens with a sequence, in effect a long prologue, in which a wife and mother tracks her husband to the apartment of another woman and shoots him. Played by the virtuoso Judy Holliday, the part is continuously hilarious, touching, and frightening, so that one never rests content with one's response to her. An early sequence of the film proper (so to speak) consists of the screening of a film-within-a-film, a home movie that depicts the principal pair's coming into possession of their country house in Connecticut, in which Spencer Tracy twice takes on comically the postures and grimaces of an expansive, classical villain, threatening, with a twirl of his imaginary mustache, to dispossess Katharine Hepburn of something more precious than country houses. These passing comic glimpses of the man's villainous powers recur more disturbingly toward the end of the film, when he in turn tracks his spouse and confronts her in what he might conceivably take to be a compromising situation, and for all the world threatens to shoot her and her companion (David Wayne). What he is threatening them with soon proves to be a pistol made of licorice, but not too soon for us to have confronted unmistakably a quality of violence in this character that is as genuine—such is the power of Spencer Tracy as an actor on film—as his tenderness and playfulness. I say in the chapter on *Adam's Rib* in *Pursuits of Happiness* that Tracy's character as qualified in this film declares one subject of the genre as a whole to be the idea of maleness itself as villainous, say sadistic. (Having made his legal point, Tracy turns the candy gun on himself, into his mouth, and proceeds to eat it—a gesture that creates its comic effect but that also smacks of madness and of a further capacity for violence and horror hardly less frightening on reflection than the simple capacity for shooting people in anger.) The suggestion I drew is that if the male gender as such, so far in the development of our culture, and in so beautifully developed a specimen of it as Spencer Tracy, is tainted with villainy, then the happiness in even these immensely privileged marriages exists only so far as the pair together locate and contain this taint—you may say domesticate it, make a home for it—as if the task of marriage is to overcome the villainy in marriage itself. Remarriage comedies show the task to be unending and the interest in the task to be unending.

The taint of villainy leaves a moral cloud, some will say a political one, over these films, a cloud, that my book does not try, or wish, to disperse. It can be pictured by taking the intelligent, vivid women in these films to be descendants of Nora in Ibsen's *A Doll's House,* who leaves her husband and children in search of what she calls, something her husband has said she required, an education. She leaves saying that he is not the man to provide her with one, implying both that the education she requires is in the hands of men and that only a man capable of providing it, from whom it would be acceptable, could count for her as a husband. Thinking of the woman of remarriage comedy as lucky to have found such a man, remarriage comedy studies, among other matters, what has made him, inescapably bearing the masculine taint, acceptable. That she can, with him, have what the woman in *The Awful Truth* calls "some grand laughs" is indispensable, but not an answer; the question becomes how this happens with him.

This prompts two further questions, with which we are entered into the melodrama of unknownness. What of the women who have not found, and could not manage or relish a relationship with such a man, Nora's other, surely more numerous, descendants? And what, more particularly, of the women of the same era on film who are at least the spiritual equals of the women of remarriage comedy but whom no man can be thought to educate—I mean the women we might take as achieving the highest reaches of stardom, of female independence so far as film can manifest it—Greta Garbo and Marlene Dietrich and, at her best, Bette Davis?

The price of the woman's happiness in the genre of remarriage comedy is the absence of her mother (underscored by the attractive and signal presence, whenever he is present, of the woman's father) together with the strict absence of children for her, the denial of her as a mother—as if the woman has been abandoned, so far, to the world of men. Could remarriage comedies achieve their happiness in good faith if they denied the possibility of another path to education and feminine integrity? It would amount to denying that the happiness of these women indeed exacts a price, if of their own choice, affordable out of their own talents and tastes, suggesting instead that women without these talents and tastes are simply out of luck. Such an idea is false to the feeling shown by these women toward women unlike themselves—as, for example, Rosalind Russell's toward the outcast woman in *His Girl Friday*, or Irene Dunne's toward the nightclub singer whose identity she takes on in *The Awful Truth*, or Claudette Colbert's toward the mother who faints on the bus in *It Happened One Night*. It is as if these moments signal that such films do not stand in generic insulation from films in which another way of education and integrity is taken.

With one further feature of the way of education sought by Nora's comedic progeny, I can formulate the character I seek in a melodrama derived from the comedy of remarriage that concerns those spiritually equal women (equal in their imagination of happiness and their demand for it) among those I am calling Nora's other progeny.

The demand for education in the comedies presents itself as a matter of becoming created, as if the women's lives heretofore have been nonexistent, as if they have haunted the world, as if their materialization will constitute a creation of the new woman and hence a creation, or a further step in the creation, of the human. This idea has various sources and plays various roles as the theory of remarriage develops in *Pursuits of Happiness*. Theologically, it alludes to the creation of the woman from Adam in *Genesis*, specifically its use by Protestant thinkers, impressive among them John Milton, to ratify marriage and to justify divorce. Cinematically, it emphasizes the role of the camera in transforming human figures of flesh and blood into psychic shadows of themselves, in particular in transforming the woman, of whose body more than is conventional is on some occasion found to be revealed (today such exposure would perhaps be pointless), so that Katharine Hepburn will be shown pointedly doing her own diving in *The Philadelphia Story*, or awkwardly crawling through the woods in a wet, clinging dress, or having her skirt torn off accidentally on purpose by the man in *Bringing Up Baby*, or being given a massage in *Adam's Rib*. The most famous of all such exposures, I guess, is that of Claudette Colbert showing some leg to hitch a ride in *It Happened One Night*. Dramatically, the idea of creation refers to a structure Northrop Frye calls Old Comedy—he is, however, thinking primarily of Shakespearean drama—in which the woman holds the key to the happy outcome of the plot and suffers something like death and resurrection: *All's Well That Ends Well* and *The Winter's Tale* would be signal examples. I take Hermione in *The Winter's Tale* to be the other primary source (along with Ibsen's Nora) of the woman in remarriage comedy, understanding that play as a whole, in the light of the film genre, as the greatest of the structures of remarriage. *The Winter's Tale* also proves (along with *A Doll's House*) to underlie the women of the derived melodrama of unknownness, since while Hermione's resurrection at the close of the play (which I interpret as a kind of marriage ceremony) is a function of Leontes's faith and love, it is before that a function of Paulina's constancy and effectiveness, and the ceremony provides Hermione not just with her husband again (to whom she does not at the end speak) but as well with her daughter again (to whom she does speak).

In remarriage comedy the transformation of the woman is accomplished in a mode of exchange or conversation that is surely among the glories of dialogue in the history of the art of talking pictures. The way these pairs talk together I propose as one perfect manifestation of what Milton calls that "meet and cheerful conversation" (by which he means talk as well as more than talk), which he, most emphatically among the Protestant thinkers so far as I have seen, took to constitute God's purpose in instituting sexual difference, hence marriage. But now if deriving a genre of melodrama from remarriage comedy requires, as I assume, the retaining of the woman's search for metamorphosis and existence, it nevertheless cannot take place through such ecstatic exchanges as earmark the comedies; which is to say that the woman of melodrama, as shown to us, will not find herself in what the comedies teach us marriage is, but accordingly in something less or conceivably more than that.

Then the sense of the character (or underlying myth) of film I was to look for in establishing a genre of melodrama may be formulated in the following way: a woman achieves existence (or fails to), or establishes her right to existence in the form of a metamorphosis (or fails to), apart from or beyond satisfaction by marriage (of a certain kind) and with the presence of her mother and of her children, where something in her language must be as traumatic in her case as the conversation of marriage is for her comedic sisters—perhaps it will be an aria of divorce, from husband, lover, mother, or child. (A vast, related matter, which I simply mention here, is that what is normally called adultery is not to be expected in these structures, since normally it plays no role in remarriage comedies—something that distinguishes them from Restoration comedy and from French farce. Thus, structures such as *Anna Karenina* and *Madame Bovary* are not members of what I am calling the melodrama of the unknown woman. In this genre it will not be the threat of social scandal that comes between a woman and a man, and no man could recover from participation in the special villainy that exercises the law to separate a woman irrevocably from her child.)

The films I begin from that seem to obey these intuitive requirements, together with guesses as to their salient roles within the genre, are, in summary, these seven or eight: *Blonde Venus,* with Marlene Dietrich, directed by Josef von Sternberg in 1932, which particularly emphasizes that the woman has nothing to learn from the men there are; *Stella Dallas,* directed by King Vidor in 1937, with Barbara Stanwyck and John Boles, which emphasizes the woman's business as a search for the mother, perhaps carrying a shame of the mother; *Showboat,* the Oscar Hammerstein–Jerome Kern operetta (literally a melodrama), directed by James Whale in 1936, which, as it were, mythically prepares Irene Dunne, because of the supporting or grounding presence in it of Helen Morgan and Paul Robeson, for her lead in the *The Awful Truth,* thus establishing an inner connection between this comedy and this melodrama; *Random Harvest,* with Ronald Colman and Greer Garson, directed by Mervyn LeRoy, in 1942, which most purely underscores the persistence of the feature in this genre of melodrama of the goal of remarriage itself; *Now Voyager,* also from 1942, which elaborates most completely the feature of metamorphosis as Bette Davis is transformed from Aunt Charlotte into the mysterious, magnetic Camille Vale, unforgettably helped by Paul Henreid and Claude Rains; *Mildred Pierce,* directed by Michael Curtiz in 1945, in which Joan Crawford emphasizes the theatricality in this melodrama, although one may decide that the feel of this feature in the film is too crazy to link it to the other members, so that it becomes rather a link to some further genre; *Gaslight,* directed by George Cukor in 1944, with Ingrid Bergman and Charles Boyer, which portrays in full length, no doubt with melodramatic or operatic exaggeration, the villainous, mind-destroying mode of marriage that both the comedy and the derived melodrama of remarriage set themselves against; *Letter from an Unknown Woman,* 1948, which emphasizes, by failure, fantasies of metamorphosis and fantasies of perfect communication and of the transcendence of marriage. I add to the list Eric Rohmer's *The Marquise of O,* made in 1977 with startling faithfulness to the Heinrich von Kleist tale of 1805. The odd dates of origin and cinematic transcription are not the only respects in which Kleist's tale plays a special role in relation to the genre of unknownness. This tale most hideously expresses the villainy of the husband of the genre (he has, under the signs of impeccable honor, raped the woman he wants to marry while she is in a drugged sleep), and it also finds an ending of the most secure conjugal happiness, of the comedy of existence truly achieved, of any member of the genre. It is as if this tale undertakes all by itself to redeem the violence and ugliness that will cling to sexual hunger and satisfaction at their best—as if to prepare the soul for what Jacques Laplanche, in his *Life and Death in Psychoanalysis,* calls the traumatic nature of human sexuality, thus harking all the way back to Breuer and Freud's *Studies on Hysteria.*

This list of candidates for membership in this genre of melodrama that I propose to derive from remarriage comedy is bound to seem less perspicuous than the list of films from which I began in defining the comic genre. While the melodramas were all made in Hollywood and all within the same two decades as the comedies (except for *The Marquise of O*), they lack the overlapping of directors, actors and actresses, and of that critical sound—of high and embattled wit—that gives a sensuous coherence to the group of comedies. And, of course, individually the melodramas are less ingratiating and, perhaps partly for that reason, less famous, or rather less beloved, than the comedies. (This difference in coherence may go to show, after all, something Tolstoy did not exactly say: that only happy remarriages are alike.) But if I am right that the melodramas belong together as I say they do, that will serve to justify my concept of the genre, which is used not primarily to establish a classification of objects but to articulate, let me say, the arguments among them. This is a significant matter, which I pass here with two remarks: (1) The list of members is in principle never closed, membership always being determined experimentally, which is to say, in specific acts of criticism, on the basis of a work's participation in the genre's argument; (2) if the case for the genre is good enough, it ought itself to suggest some understanding of its films' relative unknownness, or lack of love.

But what is all this about unknownness? What does it mean to say that it motivates an argument? And what has the argument to do with nihilism and diurnal recurrence? And why is it particularly about a woman that the argument takes place? What is the mystery about her lack of creation? And why should melodrama be expected to "derive" from comedy? And what is it that makes the absence of a woman's mother a scene of comedy and the presence of her mother a scene of melodrama? And— perhaps above all—what kinds of questions are these? Philosophical? Psychoanalytic? Historical? Aesthetic? If, as I hope, one would like to answer "All of these!" then one will want to say how it is that the same questions can belong to various fields that typically, in our culture, refuse to listen to one another.

The questions express further regions of what I called the intellectual debts incurred in writing *Pursuits of Happiness,* ones I had the luxury then of mostly leaving implicit. The debt I have worked on most explicitly in the past several years concerns the ideas of the diurnal, and of eternal repetition, and of the uneventful, as interpretations of the ordinary or everyday.

The concept of the ordinary reaches back to the earliest of my debts in philosophy. The first essay I published that I still use—"Must We Mean What We Say?" (1958)—is a defense of so-called ordinary language philosophy as represented by the work a generation ago at Oxford of J. L. Austin and at Cambridge of the later Wittgenstein. Their work is commonly thought to represent an effort to refute philosophical skepticism, as expressed most famously in Descartes and in Hume, and an essential drive of my book *The Claim of Reason* (1979) is to show that, at least in the case of Wittgenstein, this is a fateful distortion, that Wittgenstein's teaching is on the contrary that skepticism is (not exactly true, but not exactly false either; it is) a standing threat to the human mind, that our ordinary language and its representation of the world *can* be philosophically repudiated and that it is essential to our inheritance and mutual possession of language, as well as to what inspires philosophy, that this should be so. But *The Claim of Reason,* for all its length, does not say, any more than Austin and Wittgenstein do very much to say, what the ordinary is, why natural language is ordinary, beyond saying that ordinary or everyday language is exactly not a special philosophical language and that any special philosophical language is answerable to the ordinary, and beyond suggesting that the ordinary is precisely what it is that skepticism attacks—as if the ordinary is best to be discovered, or say that in philosophy it is only discovered, in its loss. Toward the end of *The Claim of Reason,* the effort to overcome skepticism begins to present itself as the motivation of Romanticism, especially its versions in Coleridge and Wordsworth and in their American inheritors Emerson and Thoreau. In recent years I have been following up the idea that what philosophy in Wittgenstein and Austin means by the ordinary or everyday is figured in what Wordsworth means by the rustic and common and what Emerson and Thoreau mean by the today, the common, the low, the near.

But then *Pursuits of Happiness* can be seen as beginning to pay its philosophical debts even as it incurs them. I have linked its films' portrait of marriage, formed through the concepts of repetition and devotion, with what, in an essay that compares the projects of Emerson and of Thoreau with—on an opposite side of the American mind—those of Edgar Allan Poe and of Nathaniel Hawthorne, I called their opposite efforts at the interpretation of domestication, call it marriage. From this further interpretation of the ordinary (the ordinary as the domestic) the thought arises that, as in the case of literature, the threat to the ordinary that philosophy names skepticism should show up in film's favorite threat to forms of marriage, namely in forms of melodrama. This thought suggests that, since melodramas together with tragedy classically tell stories of revenge, philosophical skepticism will in return be readable as such a story, a kind of violence the human mind performs in response to its discovery of its limitation or exclusion, its rebuff by truth.

The problem of the existence of other minds is the formulation given in the Anglo-American tradition of philosophy to the skeptical question whether I can know of the existence (not, as in Descartes and in Hume, of myself and of God and of the external world, but) of human creatures other than myself, know them to be, as it were, like myself, and not, as we are accustomed to asking recently with more or less seriousness, some species of automaton or alien. In *Pursuits of Happiness,* I say explicitly of only two of the comedies that they are studies of the problem of the existence of the other, but the overcoming of skeptical doubt can be found in all remarriage comedy: in *It Happened One Night* the famous blanket that empirically conceals the woman and thereby magnifies her metaphysical presence dramatizes the problem of unknownness as one of splitting the other, as between outside and inside, say between perception and imagination (and since the blanket is a figure for a film screen, film as such is opened up in the split); in *The Lady Eve* the man's not knowing the recurrence of the same woman is shown as the cause of his more or less comic, hence more or less forgivable, idiocy; in *The Awful Truth* the woman shows the all-knowing man what he does not know about her and helps him find words for it that take back the divorce; in *Adam's Rib* the famously sophisticated and devoted couple demonstrate in simple words and shows and in surrealistic ordinariness (they climb into bed with their hats on) that precisely what neither of them knows, and what their marriage is the happy struggle to formulate, is the difference between them; in *The Philadelphia Story* the man's idea of marriage, of the teaching that the woman has chosen to learn, is his willingness to know her as unknown (as he expresses it, "I'll risk it, will you?").

Other of my intellectual debts remain fully outstanding, to Freud's work before all. A beholdenness to Sigmund Freud's intervention in Western culture is hardly something for concealment, but I have until now on the whole left my commitment to it fairly implicit. This has happened not merely out of intellectual terror at Freud's achievement but in service of an idea and in compensation for a dissatisfaction I might formulate as follows: psychoanalytic interpretations of the arts in American culture have, until quite recently, on the whole been content to permit the texts under analysis not to challenge the concepts of analysis being applied to them, and this seemed to me to do injustice both to psychoanalysis and to literature (the art that has attracted most psychoanalytic criticism). My response was to make a virtue of this defect by trying, in my reading of film as well as of literature and of philosophy, to recapitulate what I understood by Freud's saying that he had been preceded in his insights by the creative writers of his tradition—that is, to arrive at a sense (it was my private touchstone for when an interpretation had gone far enough) for each text I encountered that psychoanalysis had become called for, as if called for in the history of knowledge, as if each psychoanalytic reading were charged with rediscovering the reality of psychoanalysis. This still does not seem to me an irrelevant ambition but also no longer a sufficient response in our altered environment, in which some of the most interesting and useful criticism and literary theory being produced is in decisive part psychoanalytic in inspiration, an alteration initiated for us most prominently by the past two or so decades of work in Paris and represented in this country by—to pick examples from which I have profited in recent months—Neil Hertz on the Dora case and on Freud's "The Uncanny," Shoshana Felman on Poe and on Henry James's *The Turn of the Screw,* and Eve Kosovsky Sedgwick on homophobia in *Bleak House.*[1] And now my problem has become that I am unsure whether I understand the constitution of the discourses in which this material is presented in relation to what I take philosophy to be, a constitution to which, such as it is, I am also committed. So some siting of this relation is no longer mine to postpone.

I content myself here with saying that Freud's lifelong series of dissociations of his work from the work of philosophy seems to me to protest too much and to have done harm (however necessary, and to whatever good) whose extent is only now beginning to reveal itself. I call attention to one of these dissociations in which Freud's ambivalence on the matter bleeds through. It comes in chapter 4 of *The Interpretation of Dreams,* just as he has distinguished "the operations of two psychical forces (or we may describe them as currents or systems)" (*S.E.* 4:144). Freud goes on to say: "These considerations may lead us to feel that the interpretation of dreams may enable us to draw conclusions as to the structure of our mental apparatus which we have hoped for in vain from philosophy" (145). Given that this feeling is followed up by Freud in the extraordinary chapter 7, which ends the book, a piece of theoretical speculation continuous with the early, posthumously published "Project for a Scientific Psychology," the ambiguity of the remark seems plain: it can be taken—and always is, so far as I know—to mean that our vain waiting for *philosophy* is now to be replaced by the positive work of something else, call it psychoanalysis (which may or may not be a "scientific" psychology); but the remark can equally be taken to mean that our *waiting* for philosophy is at last no longer vain, that philosophy has been fulfilled in the form of psychoanalysis. That this form may destroy earlier forms of philosophizing is no bar to conceiving of psychoanalysis as a philosophy. On the contrary, the two thinkers more indisputably recognized as philosophers who have opened for me what philosophy in our age may look like, such as could interest me—Wittgenstein in his *Philosophical Investigations* and Martin Heidegger in such a work as *What Is Called Thinking?*—have both written in declared opposition to philosophy as they received it. Heidegger has called philosophy the deepest enemy of thinking, and Wittgenstein has said that what he does replaces philosophy.

The idea of "replacing" here has its own ambiguity. It could mean what the logical positivists roughly meant, that philosophy, so far as it remains intelligible, is to become logic or science. Or it could mean what I take Wittgenstein to mean, that the impulse to philosophy and the consequences of it are to be achieved by replacing, or reconceiving, the ground or the place of the (thus preserved) activity of philosophizing. And something like this could be said to be what every original philosopher since at least Descartes and Bacon and Locke has illustrated. It is as if in Wittgenstein and in Heidegger the fate to philosophize and the fate to undo philosophizing are located as radical, twin features of the human as such. I am not choosing one sense of replacement over the other for Freud's relation to philosophy. On the contrary, my sense remains that the relation is so far ambiguous or ambivalent. Such matters are apt to be discussed nowadays in terms of Freud's preoccupation with what is called priority or originality—issues differently associated with the names of Harold Bloom and of Jacques Derrida. So it may be worth my saying that Bloom, in "Freud's Concepts of Defense and the Poetic Will," the essay of his that constituted the annual lecture to the Forum on Psychiatry and the Humanities for 1978 (published 1980), strikes me as unduly leveling matters to speak of Freud's crisis in *Beyond the Pleasure Principle* as obeying the structure of a poet's demand, against his precursors, for equal immortality. Freud's problem there was less to establish his originality or uniqueness than to determine whether the cost or curse of that *obvious* uniqueness might not itself be the loss of immortality. I find that I agree here with what I understand to be Derrida's view (of chapter 2 anyway) of *Beyond the Pleasure Principle,* that in it, and in anticipation of his own death, Freud is asking himself whether his achievement, uniquely among the sciences (or, for that matter, the arts) in being bound to the uniqueness of one man's name, is inheritable: this is the question enacted by the scenes of Freud the father and grandfather circling the *Fort/Da* game of repetition and domination, looking so much like the inheritance of language itself, of selfhood itself. What is at stake is whether psychoanalysis is inheritable—one may say repeatable—as science is inheritable, our modern paradigm for the teachable. If psychoanalysis is not thus inheritable, it follows that it is not exactly a science. But the matter goes beyond this question. If psychoanalysis is not exactly (what we mean by) a science, then its intellectual achievement may be lost to humankind. But if this expresses Freud's preoccupation in *Beyond the Pleasure Principle* and elsewhere, then the preoccupation links his work with philosophy, for it is in philosophy that the question of the loss of itself is internal to its faithfulness to itself.

This claim reveals me as one of those for whom the question whether philosophy exists sometimes seems the only question philosophy is bound to, that to cease caring what philosophy is and whether it exists— amid whatever tasks and in whatever forms philosophy may appear in a given historical moment—is to abandon philosophy, to cede it to logic or to science or to poetry or to politics or to religion. That the question of philosophy is the only business of philosophy is the teaching I take from the works of Wittgenstein and of Heidegger that I have claimed the inheritance of. The question of inheritance, of continued existence, appears in their work as the question whether philosophy can be taught, or, say, the question how thinking is learned, the form the question takes in *Beyond the Pleasure Principle*. It is perhaps primarily for this reason that my philosophical colleagues in the Anglo-American profession of philosophy still, on the whole (of course, there are exceptions), hold Wittgenstein or Heidegger at a distance, at varying distances from their conceptions of themselves.

What would be lost if philosophy, or psychoanalysis, were lost to us? One can take the question of philosophy as the question whether the life of reason is (any longer) attractive and recognizable, or as the question whether by my life I can and do affirm my existence in a world among others, or whether I deny this—of myself, of others, and of the world. It is some such question that Nietzsche took as the issue of what he called nihilism, a matter in which he had taken decisive instruction from Ralph Waldo Emerson. I persist, as indicated, in calling the issue by its, or its ancestor's, older name of skepticism, as I persist in thinking that to lose knowledge of the human possibility of skepticism means to lose knowledge of the human, a possibility I envision in *The Claim of Reason,* extending a problematic of Wittgenstein's, under the title of soul-blindness.

It is from a perspective in which our culture appears as having entered on a path of radical skepticism (hence on a path to deny this path) from the time of, say, Descartes and Shakespeare—or, say, from the time of the fall of Kings and the rise of the new science and the death of God— that I see, late in this history, the advent of psychoanalysis as the place, perhaps the last place, in which the human psyche as such (the idea that there is a life of the mind, hence a death) receives its proof. And it receives proof of its existence in the only form in which that psyche can (any longer) believe it—namely, as essentially unknown to itself, say unconscious. As Freud puts it in the closing pages of *The Interpretation of Dreams:* "The unconscious is the true psychical reality" (*S.E.* 5:613). This can seem a piece of mere rhetoric on Freud's part, arbitrarily underrating the reality of consciousness and promoting the unconscious out of something like a prejudice that promotes the reality of atomic particles over the reality of flesh and blood and its opposable things—and certainly on less, or no, compelling intellectual grounds. Whereas, seen in its relation to, or as a displacement of, philosophy, Freud's assertion declares that for the mind to lose the psychoanalytic intuition of itself as unconscious would be for it to lose the knowledge that it exists. (One may feel here the need for a dialectical qualification or limitation: this loss of proof, hence of human existence, is specific to the historical and political development in which the individual requires such a proof before, as it were, his or her own eyes, a private proof. The question may then be open whether, in a further development, the proof might be otherwise possible, say, performed before the answering heart of a community. But in that case, would such a proof be necessary? Would philosophy?)

How easy this intuition is to lose (the mind's [psychoanalytic] intuition of its existence as unconscious), how hard the place of this intuition is to find—the place of the proof of existence constituted in the origin of psychoanalysis as a fulfillment of a philosophy—is emblematized by how obscure this or any relation of philosophy and psychoanalysis is to us, an obscurity our institutions of learning serve to enforce. (I do not just mean that psychoanalysis is on the whole not a university subject and only questionably should become one; I mean as well that philosophy is, or should become, only questionably such a subject.)

The tale to be told here is as yet perhaps untellable by us and for us in America—the tale of Freud's inheritance (inescapable for an ambitious student of German culture of Freud's time) of the outburst of thinking initiated by Kant and then developed continuously by Fichte, Schelling, Hegel, Schopenhauer, and Nietzsche. One possible opening passage of this story is from the same closing pages I was just citing from *The Interpretation of Dreams:* "What I . . . describe is not the same as the unconscious of the philosophers" (*S.E.* 5:614). "In its innermost nature it [i.e., psychical reality, the unconscious] is as much unknown to us as the reality of the external world, and it is as incompletely presented by the data of consciousness as is the external world by the communications of our sense organs" (*S.E.* 5:613). Freud allows himself to dismiss what he calls "the unconscious of the philosophers" (no doubt referring to what some philosophers have referred to with the word "unconscious") without allowing himself to recognize that his connecting in the same sentence the innermost nature of psychic reality and the innermost nature of external reality as equally, and hence apparently for the same reasons, unknown, is pure Kant, as Freud links the unknown ground of both inner and outer to a realm of an unconditioned thing-in-itself, which Kant virtually calls the It (he spells it X) (cf. *Critique of Pure Reason,* A109).[2]

Kant's linking of the inner and the outer sounds like this: "The conditions of the *possibility of experience* in general are at the same time the *possibility of the objects of experience"* (A158, B197). Heidegger, in *What Is Called Thinking?,* quotes this passage from Kant and from it in effect rapidly derives the tradition of German so-called Idealism. He adduces some words of Schelling, in which the pivot of inner and outer sounds this way: "In the final and highest instance, there is no being other than willing. Willing is primal being and to [willing] alone belong all [primal being's] predicates: being unconditioned, eternity, independence of time, self-affirmation. All philosophy strives only to find this highest expression" (90–91). The predicates of being unconditioned and of independence of time will remind us of Freud's predicates of the unconscious. Schelling's lectures in Berlin in 1841 were, as noted in Karl Lowith's *From Hegel to Nietzsche,* attended by Engels, Bakunin, Kierkegaard, and Burckhardt. And 1841 is also the year of Emerson's first volume of essays. It sounds this way: "Permanence is a word of degrees. Every thing is medial" (404). "It is the highest power of divine moments that they abolish our contritions also . . . for these moments confer a sort of omnipresence and omnipotence, which asks nothing of duration, but sees that the energy of the mind is commensurate with the work to be done, without time. . . . I unsettle all things . . . I simply experiment" ("Circles," 411–12).

Compared with the philosophical culture of Schelling's audience, Emerson's mostly had none; yet his philosophizing was more advanced than Schelling's—if Nietzsche's is (since Emerson's transcendental realm is not fixed, the direction or height of the will is in principle open). Heidegger claims for his quotation from Schelling that it is the classic formulation of the appearance of metaphysics in the modern era, an appearance that is essential "to understand[ing] that—and how— Nietzsche from the very start thinks of revenge [the basis of nihilism] and the deliverance from revenge in metaphysical terms, that is, in the light of Being which determines all beings" (90). However remote the fate of such a claim may seem to us here and now, it will, if nothing else, at any time stand between us and our desire, however intermittent, yet persistent, for an exchange with contemporary French thought; since Heidegger's interpretation of Nietzsche is one determinant of the Paris of, say,

Derrida's Plato and Rousseau and of Lacan's Freud. (It may be pertinent to cite the effort in recent decades to bring Freud within the orbit of German philosophizing, in particular within that of Heidegger's thought, an effort made by the existential-analytic movement [*Daseins-analyse*]. This is not the time to try to assess that effort, but I may just note that my emphasis on Freud as, so to speak, an immediate heir of German classical philosophy implies that establishing his relation to philosophy does not require mediation [or absorption] by Heidegger. The point of this emphasis is that Freud's is to be understood as an alternative inheritance, a competing inheritance, to that of Heidegger's. Otherwise, Freud's *breaking* with philosophy, his [continued] subjection to it and its subjection to him, will not get clear. Then Wittgenstein's is a third inheritance, or path, from Kant.)[3]

In these paths of inheritance, Freud's distinction is to have broken through to a practice in which the Idealist philosophy, the reigning philosophy of German culture, becomes concrete (which is roughly what Marx said socialism was to accomplish). In Freud's practice, one human being represents to another all that that other has conceived of humanity in his or her life and moves with that other toward an expression of the conditions that condition that utterly specific life. It is a vision and an achievement quite worthy of the most heroic attributes Freud assigned himself. (And it is perhaps the vision that most intuitively backs my thought that Freud's claim to philosophy lies not [directly] in his sympathy with science and its philosophy but in his struggle with, or against, German Idealism.) But psychoanalysis has not surmounted the obscurities of the philosophical problematic it inherits of representation and reality. Until it stops shrinking from philosophy (from its own past), it will continue to shrink before the derivative question, for example, of whether the stories of its patients are fantasy merely or (also?) of reality, and it will continue to waver between regarding the question as irrelevant to its work and as of the essence of it.

It is hardly enough to appeal here to conviction in reality, because the most untutored enemy of the psychological, as eagerly as the most sophisticated enemy, will inform you that conviction is one thing, reality another. The matter is to express the intuition that fantasy shadows anything we can understand reality to be. As Wittgenstein more or less puts an analogous matter: the issue is not to explain how grammar and criteria allow us to relate language to the world but to determine what language relates the world to be. This is not well expressed as the priority of mind over reality or of self over world (as, among others, Bloom expresses it [1980, 7]. It is better put as the priority of grammar—the thing Kant calls conditions of possibility (of experience and of objects), the thing Wittgenstein calls possibilities of phenomena—over both what we call mind and what we call the world. If we call grammar the Logos, we will more readily sense the shadow of fantasy in this picture.

From the reassociation of psychoanalysis with philosophy in its appearance on the stage of skepticism, as the last discoverer of psychic reality (the latest discoverer, its discoverer late in the recession of that reality), I need just two leaps in order to get to the interpretation I envision of the moment I began with from *Letter from an Unknown Woman*. The two leaps I can represent as questions that together have haunted the thoughts I am reporting on here. The first is: Why (granted the fact) does psychic reality first present itself to psychoanalysis—or, why does psychoanalysis first realize itself—through the agency (that is, through the suffering) of women, as reported in the *Studies on Hysteria* and in the case of Dora, the earliest of the longer case histories? The second question is: How, if at all, is this circumstance related to the fact (again, granted the fact) that film—another invention of the last years of the nineteenth century, developing its first masterpieces within the first decades of the twentieth century—is from first to last more interested in the study of individual women than of individual men? Men are, one could say, of interest to it in crowds and in mutual conflict, but it is women that bequeath psychic depth to film's interests. (It is to my mind a question whether certain apparently obvious exceptions [Chaplin, Keaton, Gary Cooper, for example] are exceptions to the contrast with the masculine.) My conviction in the significance of these questions is a function, not surprisingly, of my speculations concerning skepticism, two junctures of it especially. The one is a result of my study of Shakespeare's tragedies and romances as elaborations of the skeptical problematic; the other concerns the role of the human body in the skeptical so-called problem of other minds. I will say something about each of these junctures.

Since we are about to move into speculations concerning differences in the knowing of women from that of the knowing of men, I just note in passing that I am not leaping to but skipping over the immensely important matter of determining how it is that the question of sexual difference turns into a question of some property that men are said to have that women lack, or perhaps vice versa—a development that helps to keep us locked into a compulsive uncertainty about whether we wish to affirm or to deny difference between men and women. As *Adam's Rib* ends, Tracy and Hepburn are joking about this vulgar error of looking for a *thing* that differentiates men and women. (It is my claim that they are joking; it is commoner, I believe, to assume—or imagine, or think, or opine—that they are perpetuating this common error. Here is a neat touchstone for assessing the reception of these comedies; perhaps their endings form the neatest set of such touchstones.)

In Lacan, the idea of the phallus as signifier is not exactly a laughing matter. The reification, let me put it, of sexual difference is registered, in the case of knowledge, by finding the question of a difference in masculine and feminine knowing to turn into a question of some fixed way women know that men do not know, and vice versa. Since in ordinary, nonmetaphysical exchanges we do not conceive there to be some fact one gender knows that the other does not know, any more than we conceive there to be some fact the skeptic knows that the ordinary human being does not know, the metaphysical exchanges concerning their differences are apt to veer toward irony, a sense of incessant false position, as if one cannot know what difference a world of difference makes. No one exactly denies that human knowledge is imperfect; but then how does that become the skeptic's outrageous removal of the world as such? No one exactly denies that there are differences between men and women; but then how does that become an entire history of outrage? It is from this region that one must expect an explanation for climactic passages of irony that characterize the melodrama of the unknown woman.

When in *Blonde Venus* Marlene Dietrich hands a derelict old woman the cash her husband has handed her, repeating to the woman, in raging mockery, the self-pitying words her husband had used to her in paying her back, to be quits with her, the money she had earlier given him to save his life, the meanness of the man's gesture is branded on his character. When toward the end of *Letter from an Unknown Woman* the man calls out smoothly to the woman, whose visit he interprets as a willingness for another among his endless dalliances, having disappeared to get some champagne, "Are you lonely out there?" and she, whose voice-over tells that she came to offer her life to him, replies, mostly to the camera, that is, to us, "Yes. Very lonely," she has taken his charming words as her cue for general death.

The state of irony is the negation, hence the equivalent in general consequence, of the state of conversation in remarriage comedy. Some feminists imagine that women have always spoken their own language, undetected by men; others argue that women ought to develop a language of their own. The irony in the melodrama of unknownness develops the picture, or figuration, for what it means idiomatically to say that men and women, in denying one another, do not speak the same language. I am not the only male of my acquaintance who knows the victimization in this experience, of having conversation negated, say, by the male in others. The finest description known to me of ironic, systematic incomprehension is Emerson's, from "Self-Reliance": "Well, most men have bound their eyes with one or another handkerchief and attached themselves to some one of these communities of opinion. This conformity makes them not false in a few particulars, authors of a few lies, but false in all particulars. Their every truth is not quite true. Their two is not the real two [as in the idea of two genders? or of just two Testaments?]; their four is not the real four [as in the idea of four corners of the earth? or of just four Gospels?]: so that every word they say chagrins us, and we know not where to begin to set them right'' (264).

The first of my concluding leaps or questions about the origination of psychoanalysis and of film in the sufferings of women concerns the most theoretically elaborated of the studies I have so far produced of Shakespeare, on *The Winter's Tale*. It has raised unforgettably for me, I might say traumatically, the possibility that philosophical skepticism is inflected, if not altogether determined, by gender, by whether one sets oneself aside as male or female. And if philosophical skepticism is thus inflected then, according to me, philosophy as such will be. The issue arises as follows: Leontes obeys the structure of the skeptical problematic in the first half of *The Winter's Tale* as perfectly as his forebear Othello had done, but in the later play jealousy, as an interpretation of skeptical, world-removing doubt, is a cover story not for the man's fear of female desire (as Othello's story is) but for his fear of female fecundity, represented in Leontes's doubt that his children are his. Leontes's story has figured in various talks of mine in the past two or three years, and more than once a woman has afterward said to me in effect: If what Cartesian skepticism requires is the doubt that my children are mine, count me out. It is not the only time the surmise has crossed my mind that philosophical skepticism, and a certain denial of its reality, is a male business; but from the dawning of *The Winter's Tale* on me the business seems to me to be playing a role I know I do not fathom in every philosophical move I make. (It is the kind of answer I can contribute to the question who or what Shakespeare is to say that it is commonly in texts associated with this name that the bearing of a philosophical issue, or rather the issue of modern philosophy, is established.)

From the gender asymmetry here it should not be taken to follow that women do not get into the way of skepticism, but only that the passion of doubt may not express a woman's sense of separation from others or that the object of doubt is not representable as a doubt as to whether your children are yours. The passion is perhaps another form of fanaticism, as in part Leontes's is. (*Letter from an Unknown Woman* suggests that the fanaticism is of what you might call love.) And the object of doubt might be representable as one directed not toward the question of one's children but toward the question of the father of one's children.

(This is the pertinence of Kleist's *The Marquise of O,* the main reason in its content for what I called its specialness in relation to the melodrama of unknownness.) But how can one know and show that this other passion and this other object create equivalents or alternatives to masculine skepticism?

It is at this juncture of the skeptical development that psychoanalysis and cinema can be taken as asking of the woman: How is it that you escape doubt? What certainty encloses you, whatever your other insecurities, from just this torture? At an early point in my tracking of the skeptic, I found myself asking: Why does my search for certainty in knowing the existence of the other, in countering the skeptic's suspicion concerning other minds, come to turn upon whether I can know what the other *knows?* So the formulation of what we want from the woman as an access to her knowledge would record the skeptical provenance of the woman's presence at the origin of psychoanalytic and of cinematic discovery. But then we must allow the question: But *who* is it who wants to know? A natural answer will be: The man wants the knowledge. This answer cannot be wrong; it is the answer feminists may well give to Freud's handling of the case of the woman he called Dora. But the answer might be incomplete.

This is the point at which two sources of material bearing on psychoanalysis and feminism warrant being prominently brought into play, which I can now barely name. The first is represented in two texts of Jacques Lacan's entitled "God and the *Jouissance* of the Woman" and "A Love Letter," which when I came upon them twelve months ago struck me at several points as having uncanny pertinence to the considerations that arise here. When Lacan announces, "There is no such thing as The woman" (144) (sometimes paraphrased or translated as "The woman does not exist" [137]) I was bound to ask myself whether this crossed the intuition I have expressed as the task of the creation of the woman. I find that some of Lacan's followers react to the remark as obvious and as on the side of what women think about themselves, while others deny this reaction. I take it to heart that Lacan warns that more than one of his pupils have "got into a mess" (144) about the doctrines of his in which his view of the woman is embedded; clearly I do not feel that I can negotiate these doctrines apart from the painful positions I am unfolding here.

My hesitations over two further moments in Lacan's texts—moments whose apparent pertinence to what I am working on strikes me too strongly to ignore—are hesitations directed less to my intellectual difficulties with what is said than to the attitude with which it is said. When Lacan says, "I believe in the *jouissance* of the woman in so far as it is something more" (147), he is casting his view of women as a creed or

credo ("I believe"), as an article of faith in the existence and the difference of the woman's satisfaction. So he may be taken as saying: What
there is (any longer?) of God, or of the concept of the beyond, takes
place in relation to the woman. It matters to me that I cannot assess the
extent or direction (outward or inward) of Lacan's mock heroism, or
mock apostlehood here, since something like this belief is in effect what I
say works itself out, with gruesome eloquence, in the case of Othello,
who enacts Descartes's efforts to prove that he is not alone in the universe by placing a finite, feminine other in the position assigned by
Descartes to God. Moreover, letting the brunt of conviction in existence, the desire of the skeptical state, be represented by the question of
the woman's orgasm, is an interpretation of Leontes's representation of
the state of skepticism by the question of the woman's child (following a
familiar equation in Freud's thinking of the production of the child with
the form of female sexual satisfaction, an equation present in Shakespeare's play). So skeptical grief would be represented for the man not
directly by the question "Were her children caused by me?" but by the
double question "Is her satisfaction real and is it caused by me?"

The other source of material (still within my first leap) that I can do
little more than name here is the excellent recent collection of essays,
subtitled *Freud-Hysteria-Feminism* (Bernheimer and Kahane 1985), on
the Dora case. Here I lift up one consideration that speaks to both of the
leaps or questions at hand: How does the problem of knowing the
existence of the other come to present itself as knowing what the other
knows? And: Who is it who wants to know of the woman's existence?
The former seems—in the light of the Dora collection—a way of asking
what the point is of the "talking cure" (the name of psychoanalytic
therapy that Anna O., the woman whose case was reported by Breuer in
Studies on Hysteria, was the first to use); and the answer to the latter
seems routinely assumed to be Freud the man. The contributors to the
volume are about equally divided between men and women, and it
seems to me that while the men from time to time are amazed or
appalled by Freud's assaults upon Dora's recitations, the women, while
from time to time admiring, are uniformly impatient with Freud the
man. The discussions are particularly laced with dirty talk, prompted
generally by Freud's material and drawn particularly by a remark of
Lacan's on the case in which, in an ostentatious show of civilization, he
coolly questions the position of the partners in Freud's fantasy of Dora's
fantasy of oral intercourse. It is in their repetition of Lacan's question,
not now coolly but accusingly, that the women's impatience is clearest; it
is a kind of structural impatience. To talk to Freud about his talking cure
is to be caught up in the logic expressed by Lacan (in "A Love Letter") in
the formula: "Speaking of love is in itself a *jouissance*." Feeling the

unfairness in thus being forced to talk love to Freud, a woman may well accuse him of ignorance in his designs upon Dora, upon her knowledge, not granting him the knowledge that his subject is the nature of ignorance of exactly what cannot be ignored. She may well be right.

The consideration I said I would lift from the discussions of Dora takes on the detail of Freud's choice of the fictitious name Dora in presenting his case. Freud traces his choice to the paradigm of a change of name his sister had required of, and chosen for, her maidservant. The women represented in this collection on the whole use this information to accuse Freud of treating the woman he called Dora like a servant, of thus taking revenge on her for having treated him in this way. It is an angry interpretation, which seeks to turn the tables on the particular brilliance Freud had shown in calling Dora's attention to her angry treatment of him in announcing her termination of treatment by giving him two weeks' notice. A less impatient interpretation would have turned Freud's act of naming around again, taking it not as, or not alone as, a wish to dominate a woman, but as a confession that he is thinking of himself in the case through an identification with his sister. As if the knowledge of the existence of a woman is to be made on the basis of already enlisting oneself on that side.

This takes me to the other of my concluding leaps or questions, now concerning not generally the genderedness of the skeptical problematic, but specifically concerning the role of the body in the problem of other minds. To counter the skeptical emphasis on knowing what the other doubts and knows, I have formulated my intuition that the philosophical recovery of the other depends on determining the sense that the human body is expressive of mind, for *this* seems to be what the skeptic of other minds directly denies, a denial prepared by the behaviorist sensibility in general. Wittgenstein is formulating what behaviorism shuns—and so doubtless inviting its shunning of him—in his marvelous remark: "The human body is the best picture of the human soul" (178). One can find some such idea expressed in the accents of other thinkers—for example, in Hegel's *Philosophy of Fine Art:* "The Human shape is the sole sensuous phenomenon that is appropriate to mind" (186); or again in Emerson's essay "Behavior": "Nature tells every secret once. Yes, but in man she tells it all the time, by form, attitude, gesture, mien, face and parts of the face, and by the whole action of the machine" (1039). Freud is expressing the idea in one of his reasonably measured, yet elated, Hamlet-like recognitions of his penetration of the secrets of humanity. In the middle of his writing of the Dora case he turns aside to say: "He that has eyes to see and ears to hear may convince himself that no mortal can keep a secret. If his lips are silent, he chatters with his finger-tips; betrayal oozes out of him at every pore" (*S.E.* 7:77–78). Freud's twist on the philosophers here is registered in his idea of our expressions as betraying ourselves, giving ourselves (and meaning to give ourselves) away—as if, let us say, the inheritance of language, of the possibility of communication, inherently involves disappointment with it and (hence) subversion of it.

Expression as betrayal comes out particularly in Freud's phrase from his preceding paragraph, in which he describes one of what he calls Dora's "symptomatic acts" as a "pantomimic announcement" (specifically in this case, an announcement of masturbation). Freud and Breuer had earlier spoken of the more general sense of human behavior as pantomimic—capable of playing or replaying the totality of the scenes of hidden life—in terms of the hysteric's "capacity for conversion," "a psycho-physical aptitude for transposing very large sums of excitation into the somatic innervation" ("The Neuro-Psychoses of Defence," *S.E.* 3:50), which is roughly to say, a capacity for modifying the body as such rather than allowing the excitation to transpose into consciousness or to discharge into practice. While this capacity is something possessed by every psycho-physical being—that is, primarily human beings—a particular aptitude for it is required for a given sufferer to avail herself or himself of hysteria over other modes of symptom formation, as in obsessions or phobias. The aptitude demands, for example, what Freud calls "somatic compliance," together with high intelligence, a plastic imagination, and hallucinatory "absences," which Anna O. (in *Studies on Hysteria*) taught Breuer to think of as her "private theater."

It seems to me that Freud describes the aptitude for hysterical conversion with special fascination—as if, for example, the alternative choice of obsession were, though no less difficult to fathom, psychologically rather undistinguished. (See, for example, "The Neuro-Psychoses of Defence," *S.E.* 3:51.) Breuer and Freud's most famous statement of the matter, in their "Preliminary Communication" of 1893, is: "Hysterics suffer mainly from reminiscences," a statement to be taken in the light of the insistence that hysterical motor symptoms "can be shown to have an original or long-standing connection with traumas, and stand as symbols for them in the activities of the memory" ("Frau Emmy von N.," *S.E.* 2:95). Hysterical symptoms are "mnemonic symbols," where this means that they bear some mimetic allegiance to their origins. Freud will say fifteen years later, in the "Rat Man" case, that "the leap from a mental process to a somatic innervation—hysterical conversion . . . can never be fully comprehensible to us" (*S.E.* 10: 157), a claim I find suspicious coming from him, as though he wishes sometimes to appear to know less than he does, or feels he does, about the powers of women.

In place of an argument for this, I offer as an emblem for future argument the figure of the woman who on film may be understood to have raised "the psycho-physical aptitude for transposing . . . large sums of excitation into the somatic innervation" to its highest art; I mean Greta Garbo, I suppose the greatest, or the most fascinating, cinematic image on film of the unknown woman. (Perhaps I should reassure you of my intentions here by noting that Freud's sentence following the one I just repeated about the psycho-physical aptitude in question begins: "This aptitude does not, in itself, exclude psychical health" [S.E. 3:50].) It is as if Garbo has generalized this aptitude beyond human doubting—call this aptitude a talent for, and will to, communicate—generalized it to a point of absolute expressiveness, so that the sense of failure to know her, of her being beyond us (say visibly absent) is itself the proof of her existence. (The idea of absolute expressiveness locates the moment in the history of skepticism at which such a figure appears as the moment I characterize in The Claim of Reason as the anxiety of inexpressiveness.)

This talent and will for communication accordingly should call upon the argument of hysteria for terms in which to understand it. In Garbo's most famous postures in conjunction with a man, she looks away or beyond or through him, as if in an absence (a distance from him, from the present), hence as if to declare that this man, while the occasion of her passion, is surely not its cause. I find (thinking specifically of a widely reprinted photograph in which she has inflected her face from that of John Gilbert's, her eyes slightly raised, seeing elsewhere) that I see her jouissance as remembering something, but, let me say, remembering it from the future, within a private theater, not dissociating herself from the present moment, but knowing it forever, in its transience, as finite, from her finitude, or separateness, as from the perspective of her death. As if she were herself transformed into a mnemonic symbol, a monument of memory. (This would make her the opposite of the femme fatale she is typically said—surely in defense against her knowledge—to be.) What the monument means to me is that a joyful passion for one's life contains the ability to mourn, the acceptance of transience, of the world as beyond one—say, one's other.

Such in my philosophy is the proof of human existence that, on its feminine side, as conceived in the appearance of psychoanalysis, it is the perfection of the motion picture camera to provide.

Here I come upon my epilogue, and a man's hands over his eyes, perhaps to ward off a woman's returning images. Letter from an Unknown Woman is the only film in our genre of melodrama that ends with the woman's apparent failure; but as in Gaslight, her failure perfectly shadows what the woman's success in this genre of human perplexity has to overcome: the failure here is of a woman's unknownness to prove her existence to a man, to become created by a man; a tale the outcome of which is not the transcendence of marriage but the collapse of a fantasy of remarriage (or of perpetual marriage), perhaps in favor of a further fantasy, of revenge, of which the one we see best is a screen; a tale in which the woman remains mute about her story, refusing it both to the man and to the world of woman; and a tale in which the characters' perspective of death is not to know forever the happiness of one's own life but finally to disown it, to live the death of another (as they have lived the other's life). (For some this will establish the necessity of psychology; for others, the necessity of politics; for others, the need of art.)

A reading of the film, in the context I have supplied here, might directly begin with the marks of these fantasies, of their negations of the reality, as it were, of remarriage as established in the genre that explores remarriage. For example, the woman in Ophuls's film is shown to be created through metamorphosis, not, however, by or with the man, but for him, privately—as her voice-over tells him (and us) posthumously: "From that moment on I was in love with you. Quite consciously I began to prepare myself for you. I kept my clothes neater so that you wouldn't be ashamed of me. I took dancing lessons; I wanted to become more graceful, and learn good manners—for you. So that I would know more about you and your world, I went to the library and studied the lives of the great musicians." What is causing this vortex of ironies, the fact of change or the privacy of it? The idea that woman's work is not to converse with men but to allure them is hardly news, and it is laid out for observation in Ophuls's work, in his participation in the world of fashion and glamour. That the intimacy of allure exactly defeats the intimacy of conversation is a way to put the cause of irony in the film, not alone its incessance in its closing sequences ("Are you lonely out there?") but also at the beginning of their reencounter, as the woman tracks the man back in Vienna until he notices her. He says, "I ought to introduce myself" and she interrupts with, "No. I know who you are"—a remark that could not be truer or more false.

Privacy and irony are in turn bound up in the film with the theme and structure of repetitions. Again this feature here negates its definitive occurrences in remarriage comedy, where repetitiveness is the field of inventiveness, improvisation, of the recurrence of time, open to the second chance; in (this) melodrama time is transient, closed, and repetition signals death—whether the repetition is of its camera movements (for example, the famous ironic repetition of the girl's waiting and watching on the stairs) or its words ("I'll see you in two weeks, two weeks") or its imagery (the woman's denial of chance and her weddedness to fate is given heavy symbolization in the film's endless iteration of iterated iron bars, which become less barriers against this woman's desire than the medium of it). Passing these essential matters, the moment I close with is also one of ironic repetitiion, and I ask of the woman's returning images: Why are they death-dealing?

Of course, they must make the man feel guilt and loss; but the question is why, for a man whose traffic has been the sentiments of remorse and loss, the feeling this time is fatal. Surely it has to do with the letter itself, beginning as from the region of death ("By the time you read this I may be dead") and ending in the theme of nostalgia ("If only . . . if only . . ."). And, of course, it has to do with the fact that there is a double letter, the depicted one that ends in a broken sentence, and the one that depicts this one, the one bearing the title *Letter from an Unknown Woman,* this film that ends soon but distinctly after, narrated from the beginning, it emerges, by the voice of a dead woman, ghost-written. The implication is somehow that it is the (ghost) woman who writes and sends the film. What can this mean? That the author of the film is a question for the film is suggested when the man says to his mute servant, who enters as the man has finished reading the letter, "You knew her," and the servant nods and writes a name on a page on the desk on which the letter lies, by the feeling that the servant is signing the letter, and hence the film. No doubt Ophuls is showing his hand here, breaching and so declaring, as it were, his muteness as a director, as if declaring that directing (perhaps composing of any kind) is constantly a work of breaching muteness (how fully, and how well timed, are further questions). But this cannot deny that it is a woman's letter he signs, assigns to himself as a writer, a letter explicitly breaching, hence revealing, muteness.

Moreover, the letter already contained a signature, on the letterhead of the religious order in whose hospital the unknown woman died, of someone styled "Sister-in-charge." Whether or not we are to assume that this is the same locale to which the unknown woman had gone to be delivered anonymously of her and the man's child, her connection with the religious order happens in front of our eyes, as she leaves the train platform after rushing to see the man off for a hastily remembered concert tour. Walking directly away from us, she gradually disappears into blackness at the center of the vacant screen, upon which, at what we might project as her vanishing point, there is a rematerialization, and the figure of the woman is replaced by, or transformed into, walking at the same pace toward us, what turns out as it comes into readable view to be a nun. So the woman is part of the world of religion, of a place apart inhabited, for all we see of it, solely by women, a world Ophuls accordingly also assigns himself, I mean his art, in signing the woman's letter.

(Whether in claiming the mazed position of the feminine the actual director is manifesting sympathy with actual women or getting even with them; and whether in competing with the feminine other the director is silencing the woman's voice in order to steal it and sport its power as his (?) own; and whether positive [or negative] personal intentions could overtake the political opportunism [or political insight] of any such gesture; these are questions that I hope are open, for my own good.)

Granted that forces both lethal and vital are gathered here, and granted that the film is the medium of visible absence, I ask again how these forces, in the form of returning images, deal death. Since I mostly am not considering here the narrative conditions of the woman depicted as writing the letter, I leave aside the question whether the vengeance in this act is to be understood as endorsed or reversed in the director's countersigning of it. I concentrate now on the sheer fact that the images return as exact moments we and the man have witnessed, or perhaps imagined, together. The present instants are mechanically identical with the past, and this form of repetition elicits its own amalgam of the strange and the familiar. I take it as a repetition that Freud cites as causing the sense of the uncanny in his essay to which he gives that title. Then this is also a title Ophuls's film suggests for the aesthetic working of film as such, an idea of some vision of horror as its basis. Freud's essay includes a reading of E. T. A. Hoffmann's romantic tale "The Sand Man," a tale that features a beautiful automaton, something not untypical of Hoffman or more generally of the romantic tale of the fantastic. Freud begins his reading by denying, against a predecessor's reading, that the uncanniness of the tale is traceable to the point in the story of "uncertainty whether an object is living or inanimate" (*S.E.* 17:230). Now that point is precisely recognizable as an issue of philosophical skepticism concerning our knowledge of the existence of other minds. But Freud insists that instead the uncanny in Hoffmann's tale is directly attached to the idea of being robbed of one's eyes, and hence, given his earlier findings, to the castration complex.

I find this flat denial of Freud's itself uncanny, oddly mechanical, since no denial is called for, no incompatible alternative is proposed: one would have expected Sigmund Freud in this context to invoke the castration complex precisely as a new explanation or interpretation of the particular uncertainty in question, to suggest it as Hoffmann's prepsychoanalytic insight that one does not see others as other, acknowledge their (animate) human existence, until the oedipal drama is resolved under the threat of castration. (This is a step, I believe, that Jacques Lacan has taken; I do not know on what ground.) Instead Freud's, as it were, denial that the acknowledgment of the existence of others is at stake amounts, to my mind, to the denial that philosophy persists within psychoanalysis, that the psychoanalytic tracing of traumatically induced exchanges or metamorphoses of objects of love and subjects of love into and out of one another remains rooted in philosophy.

And I think we can say that when the man covers his eyes—an ambiguous gesture, between avoiding the horror of knowing the existence of others and avoiding the horror of not knowing it, between avoiding the threat of castration that makes the knowledge accessible and avoiding the threat of outcastness should that threat fail—he is in that gesture both warding off his seeing something and warding off at the same time his being seen by something, which is to say, his own existence being known, being seen by the woman of the letter, by the mute director and his camera—say, seen by the power of art—and seen by us, which accordingly identifies us, the audience of film, as assigning ourselves the position, in its passiveness and its activeness, of the source of the letter and of the film; which is to say, the position of the feminine. Then it is the man's horror of us that horrifies us—the revelation, or avoidance, of ourselves in a certain way of being feminine, a way of being human, a mutual and reflexive state, let us say, of victimization. The implications of this structure as a response to film, to art, to others, for better and for worse, is accordingly a good question. I guess it is the question Freud raises in speaking, in "Analysis Terminable and Interminable," of "the repudiation of the feminine"—which he named as the bedrock beyond which psychoanalysis cannot go. My thought is that film, in dramatizing Freud's finding, oddly opens the question for further thought.

I leave you with a present of some words from the closing paragraphs of Henry James's "The Beast in the Jungle."

> The creature beneath the sod [the buried woman companion] *knew* of his rare experience, so that, strangely now, the place had lost for him its mere blankness of expression. . . . (T)his garden of death gave him the few square feet of earth on which he could still most live . . . by clear right of the register that he could scan like an open page. The open page was the tomb of his friend. . . . He had before him in sharper incision than ever the open page of his story. . . .
>
> The name on the table smote him . . . and what it said to him, full in the face, was that *she* was what he had missed. . . . Everything fell together . . .; leaving him most of all stupefied at the blindness he had cherished. The fate he had been marked for he had met with a vengeance . . .; he had been the man of his time, *the* man, to whom nothing on earth was to have happened. . . . This horror of waking—*this* was knowledge.

James's tale in theme and quality better measures Ophuls's film than the story of Stefan Zweig's from which its screenplay was, excellently, adapted. Such is the peculiar distribution of powers among the arts.

Notes

This paper is a revised version of the Edith Weigert Lecture, sponsored by the Forum on Psychiatry and the Humanities, Washington School of Psychiatry, October 18, 1985.

1. In this connection I want to reaffirm my continuing indebtedness to the work and friendship of Michael Fried. His extraordinary new book, *Realism, Writing, Disfiguration: On Thomas Eakins and Stephen Crane* (1987), also more explicitly relates itself to Freudian concepts than his past writing has done. I cannot forbear noting specifically, for those who will appreciate the kind of confirmation or ratification one may derive from simultaneous or crossing discoveries in writing that one admires, the light thrown by Fried's breakthrough discussion of Stephen Crane on the passage from James's "The Beast in the Jungle" on which the present essay closes.

2. In a set of editorial notes prepared for my use, Joseph H. Smith, in responding to my claim that Freud here takes on Kant's views exactly at a point at which he wishes to distinguish the psychoanalytic idea of the unconcious from "the unconscious of the philosophers," finds that "it is inconceivable to me that Freud was unaware of being Kantian here." I am grateful, first of all, for the confirmation that the Kantian provenance of Freud's thought seems so patent. But further, as to whether Freud could in that case have been "unaware" of the provenance, I would like to propose the following: if Freud was aware of it, then his omitting of Kant's name just here, where he is explicitly dissociating himself from philosophy, is motivated, deliberate, showing an awareness that his claim to dissociation is from the beginning compromised, say ambivalent; but if, on the contrary, Freud was not aware of his Kantianism just here, say unconscious of it, then he was repressing this fact of his origin. Either of these possibilities, suppression or repression, I am regarding as fateful to the development of psychoanalysis as a field of investigation (supposing this more distinct from psychoanalysis as a therapy than it perhaps can be) and rather in support of my claim that Freud's self-interpretation of his relation to philosophy is suspicious and, contrary to what I know of its reception by later psychoanalysts, ought to be treated.

I cite one piece of positive evidence here to indicate Freud's ambivalent awareness of resistant understanding of the depth of his intellectual debt to Kant (one may press this evidence to the point of suppression or repression). Of the dozen or so references to Kant listed in the general index of the *Standard Edition,* one bears directly on whether Freud saw the Kantianism of his view of the proof and the place of the unconscious. At the end of the first section of "The Unconscious" Freud says this:

> The psycho-analytic assumption of unconscious mental activity appears to us . . . as an extension of the corrections undertaken by Kant of our views on external perception. Just as Kant warned us not to overlook the fact that our perceptions are subjectively conditioned and must not be regarded as identical with what is perceived though unknowable, so psycho-analysis warns us not to equate perceptions by means of consciousness with the unconscious

mental processes which are their object. Like the physical, the psychical is not necessarily in reality what it appears to us to be.[*S.E.* 14:171]

This expression of indebtedness to Kant precisely discounts the debt, since Kant equally "warned us" not to equate the appearance of the psychic with the reality of it, the warning Freud arrogates to psychoanalysis as an "extension" of Kant's philosophical contribution to the study of knowledge. It is the *connection* of the study of inner and outer that my paper claims is "pure Kant."

Now Freud might have meant something further in his arrogation. He might have been compressing, in his discounting of the debt to Kant, a claim to the effect that Kant did not lay out the conditions of the appearance of the inner world with the systematicness with which he laid out the conditions of the appearance of the outer world, the world of objects; in short, that Kant lacked the tools with which to elicit a system of categories of the understanding for the psyche, or the subjective, comparable to the one he elicited for the external, or the objective, world. These tools, unlike those of Aristotle that Kant deployed, came into the possession of Western thought only with psychoanalysis. Something of this sort seems to me correct. But if Freud had claimed this explicitly, hence taken on the obligation to say whether, for example, his "categories" had the same status as Kant's, then the awareness would have been inevitable that his quarrel with philosophy was necessary, was philosophy. Unawareness of his inheritance of Kant would then indeed have been inconceivable.

3. After a conversation with Professor Kurt Fischer, now at the University of Vienna, I realize that I should, even in this opening sketch of the problem of inheriting philosophy, be more cautious, or specific, in speaking of Freud's "inheritance" of classical German philosophy. I do not mean that an Austrian student in the later nineteenth century would have had just the same philosophical education as a German student of the period; nor does my claim require that Freud read so much as a page in one of Kant's works. It would have been enough for my (or Freud's) purposes for him to have received his Kant from the quotations of Kant he would have encountered in his reading of Schopenhauer. My focus—that is, in speaking here of Freud's inheritance of the German outburst—is on who Freud is, on what becomes of ideas in that mind, rather than on what, apart from a mind of that resourcefulness, German philosophy is thought to be. I assume that more or less the same ought to be said of the inheritance of German thought by that other Austrian student, Wittgenstein.

References

Bernheimer, Charles, and Kahane, Claire, eds. *In Dora's Case: Freud-Hysteria-Feminism.* New York: Columbia University Press, 1985.

Bloom, Harold. "Freud's Concept of Defense and the Poetic Will." In *The Literary Freud: Mechanisms of Defense and the Poetic Will,* edited by Joseph H. Smith. Psychiatry and the Humanities, vol. 4. New Haven: Yale University Press, 1980.

Cavell, Stanley. *Must We Mean What We Say?* Reprint. Cambridge: At the University Press, 1976.

———. *The Claim of Reason: Wittgenstein, Skepticism, Morality, and Tragedy.* New York: Oxford University Press, 1979.

———. *Pursuits of Happiness: The Hollywood Comedy of Remarriage.* Cambridge, Mass.: Harvard University Press, 1981.

Emerson, Ralph Waldo. *Essays and Lectures.* Edited by Joel Porte. New York: Library of America, 1983.

Felman, Shoshana. "Turning the Screw of Interpretation." *Literature and Psychoanalysis: The Question of Reading; Otherwise. Yale French Studies* 55/56 (1977):94–207. Reprint. Baltimore: Johns Hopkins University Press, 1982.

Freud, Sigmund. *The Standard Edition of the Complete Psychological Works of Sigmund Freud.* Edited and translated by James Strachey. 24 vols. London: Hogarth Press, 1953–74.

"Project for a Scientific Psychology" (1950 [1895]), vol. 1.

Studies on Hysteria (1893–95), vol. 2 [with Josef Breuer].

"The Neuro-Psychoses of Defence" (1894), vol. 3.

The Interpretation of Dreams (1900–1901), vols. 4, 5.

Fragment of an Analysis of a Case of Hysteria (1905), vol. 7.

Three Essays on the Theory of Sexuality (1905), vol. 7.

Notes upon a Case of Obsessional Neurosis (1909), vol. 10.

"The Unconscious" (1915), vol. 14.

"The 'Uncanny'" (1919), vol. 17.

Beyond the Pleasure Principle (1920), vol. 18.

"Analysis Terminable and Interminable" (1937), vol. 23.

Fried, Michael. *Realism, Writing, Disfiguration: On Thomas Eakins and Stephen Crane.* Chicago: At the University Press, 1987.

Hegel, Georg W. F. *Philosophy of Fine Art: Introduction.* Translated by Bernard Bosanquet. London: Kegan, Paul, Trench, Taübner, 1905.

Heidegger, Martin. *What Is Called Thinking?* Translated by J. Glenn Gray. New York: Harper & Row, 1968.

Hertz, Neil. "Dora's Secrets, Freud's Techniques." In Bernheimer and Kahane (1985).

James, Henry. *The Great Short Stories.* New York: Modern Library, 1945.

Kant, Immanuel. *Critique of Pure Reason.* Translated by Norman Kemp Smith, New York: Humanities Press, 1950.

Lacan, Jacques. *Feminine Sexuality.* Articles selected and translated by Juliet Mitchell and Jacqueline Rose. New York: W. W. Norton, 1982.

Laplanche, Jacques. *Life and Death in Psychoanalysis.* Translated by Jeffrey Mehlman. Baltimore: Johns Hopkins University Press, 1976.

Löwith, Karl. *From Hegel to Nietzsche* (1941). Translated by David E. Green. New York: Holt, Rinehart and Winston, 1964.

Sedgwick, Eve Kosovsky. "Homophobia, Misogyny, and Capital: The Example of *Our Mutual Friend.*" *Raritan* 2, no. 3 (Winter 1983), pp. 126–51.

Wittgenstein, Ludwig. *Philosophical Investigations.* 3rd ed. Translated by G. E. M. Anscombe. London: Basil Blackwell & Mott, 1958.

2   Hitchcock's *Vertigo:* The Dream Function in Film

Stanley R. Palombo

Psychoanalytic interest in film has traditionally fastened on character and dramatic conflict, rather than on the formal and structural aspects of the medium itself.[1] Recent advances in the psychoanalytic theory of dreaming, prompted by the discovery of REM (Rapid Eye Movement) sleep in the laboratory, have opened a new perspective on dreaming as an essential constituent of the adaptive information-processing functions of the mind.[2] This study will examine the dream function as it is incorporated into the psychological structure of film, exemplified in this case by Hitchcock's *Vertigo* (1958).

The realization that what appears on the screen is different from the real world, and therefore a potential substitute for it or alternative to it, had been exploited by Méliès in his earliest fantasy films of the 1890s. The stereotyped dream experience became a natural subject for popular films.[3] Munsterberg (1916) recognized that isolated camera shots, the raw material furnished by the camera, could be assembled and organized into larger and more substantial dramatic structures only by "overcoming the forms of the outer world, namely, space, time, and causality, and by adjusting the events to the forms of the inner world, namely, attention, memory, imagination, and emotion."[4]

Munsterberg's work suggested that all film is inherently fantastic or dreamlike. The *departures* from reality brought about by the technique of film composition, even when "reality" itself is being represented, produce an *intensification* of the viewer's everyday experience.[5] A bridge was needed between the psychological categories Munsterberg had derived from Kant and the material phenomenology of the film image. Dreaming, especially *the mechanism of condensation* described by Freud, might have offered an instructive parallel here. But Freud's the-

44

Detective Scottie Ferguson (James Stewart) eyes a fall in Alfred Hitchcock's *Vertigo* (1958).

ory that dreams are substitute fulfillments for unrealizable wishes suggested that the mechanisms of dream construction could only distort and degrade the representation of "reality."[6]

Condensation appeared in film theory in another, non-Freudian, form. This was provided by Sergei Eisenstein's recognition of *montage* as the central activity of the filmmaker. Montage in its primary meaning is simply the cutting and splicing of individual camera shots to form coherent sequences. Before Eisenstein, it was thought of primarily as a means of creating and maintaining the viewer's sense of psychological continuity in the face of discontinuities in point of view and subject matter in the succession of scenes. In his work as a film director and in his critical and theoretical writings, Eisenstein showed that montage was not merely a device for enhancing narrative sequence, but a method for creating new meanings by combining familiar objects and ideas in unexpected juxtapositions.

Eisentein's great insight was his realization that the persistence of imagery in the mind's eye of the viewer converts a physical sequence of images into a psychological composite or superimposition. This is the effect that creates the basic illusion of motion in the rapid sequence of still frames that passes through the shutter of the film projector. Eisenstein realized that in montage a similar effect is created at a higher level of complexity, with the shot rather than the frame serving as the unit of structure.

Like Freud in his descriptions of the mechanism of condensation in dreaming, Eisenstein thought of the superimpositions of montage in both energic and semantic terms. But unlike Freud, Eisenstein recognized that the process of superimposition was a constructive act that enhanced rather than degraded the meanings of the superimposed images. He wrote of the encounter of the shots brought together in montage as creating a collision of attractive forces in the viewer, compelling him to see each of the elements of the newly formed combination with new insight. Superimposition produced a dialectical synthesis of these contrasting and opposing features.

Eisenstein's favorite analogy for montage was the ancient ideographic writing systems of the Far East (Eisenstein 1929). In those systems, according to Eisenstein, two pictures or picture-signs, each recording a simple fact of nature, were combined to produce an entity of a higher order, a concept that transcended the concreteness of each of the elements that made it up. He felt that a film ought to be like a poem written in Chinese or Japanese.

In his later years, Eisenstein (1938) extended his conception of montage to apply at any level of complexity in the structure of the film drama. Groupings much larger than the single shot could serve as units of higher-level structure. Even the conventional structure of narrative, with exposition followed by disruption and then resolution, is a dialectical movement in which the first two elements are superimposed to form a new composite. In particular, the repetition of a significant image at a later point in the film creates a montage relationship between the two contexts in which the image occurs.

The Dream Function

Modern dream theory brings the close relationship between film technique and psychological processes into much sharper focus. As it can be understood today, dreaming is an essential step in the processing of new experience, linking new events with related events stored in long-term memory. The mechanism of condensation described by Freud is not a defensive intervention for hindering the expression of forbidden wishes but an adaptive procedure that superimposes representations of past and present events in order to discover the *tertium comparationis,* the common element, that determines their associative connections in permanent memory.

Dreaming creates the associative network that brings together the various strands of our individual experience, organizing them to reflect their important cognitive and affective similarities (Rapaport 1942). Film draws its power to move us from its ability to reproduce this associative organization in microcosm.

More directly than any of the other arts, film reconstructs the mental processes through which individual moments of experience are integrated into larger units of stable meaning. Replicated on the celluloid strip, events can be isolated, selected, compounded, arranged, and reordered, just as they are when our interior organizational processes structure our experience in creating our long-term memories.[7]

A successful film recapitulates in microcosm the viewer's acquisition of his or her own memory organization. It establishes itself as it opens with what might be called ''collective memories,'' situations universal to the human condition, memories shared by the viewer and the culture, allusions to literature or to film history, the faces of the stars, the landmarks of a familiar city. Gradually the characters emerge as individuals, their identities established by the pattern of significant details that gathers around them as they disappear and reappear on the screen.

The complexities and vulnerabilities of this process give depth and density to the story. The screen can represent either the world that contains a character or the world contained by the character, the world in which he lives or the world he perceives or imagines, consciously or unconsciously. The irregular succession on the screen of objective and subjective worlds creates the montage effect described by Eisenstein at its most subtle and often most effective. As the camera moves between these worlds the viewer experiences a shock of recognition. More precisely, the viewer registers a configuration of events that, in conjunction with other, earlier or later, configurations, will produce a shock of recognition at the dramatically appropriate moment.[8]

As in dreaming, this effect is produced through a series of superimpositions in which a present event is seen as a new version of something past, though with a difference that enlarges or deepens or even reveals the emotional significance of the original experience for the first time. Montage, understood in its widest sense, applied at all levels of organization, is the technique that replicates the work of condensation in the imaginative reorganization of experience that normally takes place when we dream.

The Film Vertigo

In Alfred Hitchcock's *Vertigo,* the dream function that underlies and informs the structure of every film is brought to the surface of the dramatic action. Hitchcock shows us the disintegration of a character whose dreams are sabotaged by a malevolent adversary. We see his dream world decomposed by apparently chaotic events that call forth his most primitive memories of pain and loss. His struggle to make sense of these events, to comprehend the pattern of his disillusionment and despair, reaches its tragic denouement in the final scene of the film.

Vertigo begins with a rooftop chase across the San Francisco skyline. Detective John Ferguson (Jimmy Stewart) and another policeman are pursuing an armed man over steep gables and across narrow alleys. Ferguson slips and hangs by his fingertips from a loose metal gutter eight stories above the street. His partner tries to pull him back onto the roof, but loses his footing. From Ferguson's viewpoint we watch the partner fall to his death in the street below. No other help is in sight, but Ferguson comes out alive, with nothing more than a sprained back and a case of acrophobia.

The scene leaves the viewer with a bad feeling. Its nightmarish implausibility suggests reckless negligence on Ferguson's part, a willingness to risk danger out of all proportion to possible benefits.

We next see Ferguson visiting his friend Midge (Barbara Bel Geddes) a few weeks later. Rather than accept a "desk job," he has resigned from the police force because of his acrophobia. He tries to hide his anxiety, telling Midge not to be so "motherly." He is not going to "crack up." But he becomes dizzy listening to the music of J. C. Bach and asks to have the phonograph turned off.[9]

There is some banter about a strapless brassiere on display in Midge's studio, where Ferguson has interrupted her work. (She is a painter who works as a clothing designer.) She tells him the bra works on "the cantilever principle," recalling his suspension in midair at the end of the chase scene. He rather casually changes the subject to Midge's love life. She responds by reminding him that he is the only man she ever loved and that they were engaged in college for three weeks until he reneged. He says he is still available, but then asks immediately if she remembers a college classmate named Gavin Elster (Tom Helmore), who has just phoned him.

The personal talk is over. Ferguson tries to demonstrate how much better his acrophobia has become by climbing a kitchen stool. When he reaches the top of the stool he suddenly sees the street far below through the window. In the brief flash allowed the viewer, it looks uncannily like the street over which Ferguson was hanging in the first scene. It appears as if he might be hallucinating the earlier experience. He panics and collapses, fainting into Midge's arms.

The initially unmotivated terror of the opening scene has been placed by the recurrence of this image as a raging fear of his dependence on Midge and her mothering. As in the composite imagery of a dream, Mother's bosom has been revealed as both the parapet to which Ferguson clings for dear life (the cantilevered brassiere) and as the abyss into which he must fall when the crack-up comes (Midge's arms at the bottom of the stool). *Vertigo* traces the repercussions of this infantile conflict in Ferguson's adult sexual life.

This information comes to the viewer through the dreamlike process of the film exposition. The relevance of the detailed action of the scene is not obvious at first viewing. It tends to register outside the onlooker's conscious awareness, but it creates an unconscious template on which all other aspects of Ferguson's relations with women will later be formed in the viewer's mind. For Ferguson the awareness of this pattern will be achieved, if at all, at the last tragic moment of the film.

Unaware of his desire, Ferguson is indifferent to the meaning of his fear. Although he feels the loss of his occupation, his relief at losing it is palpable. He is determined to enjoy his newly sanctioned passivity.

He goes to see Elster, who commiserates with him over his acrophobia and offers him some private detective work. Elster's wife, Madeleine (Kim Novak), seems to be possessed by the spirit of a long-dead great-grandmother. She makes mysterious journeys in a trancelike state. Elster asks Ferguson to find out where she is going. Although he finds the story unbelievable, Ferguson allows himself to be fascinated by the mysterious and morbid turn of events in the mind of this beautiful stranger. He reluctantly agrees to follow Madeleine during her mysterious excursions.

Ferguson watches at the bar in Ernie's as Elster shows Madeleine off to him. She is blond, wearing a green shawl over a black dress. Hermann's score tells us that Ferguson is smitten. He is aroused by Madeleine's beauty, elegance, remoteness. He follows her through a labyrinth of lovely San Francisco streets, straining for glimpses as he tries (rather ineptly, it seems) to stay out of her sight.

She leads him to a flower shop, where she buys a bouquet for the grave of Carlotta, her great-grandmother, at the Mission Dolores. In a long shot of the mission interior we see her leaving through a door at the far end of the church for the cemetery. This shot will be echoed in the climactic scenes of the film, as Madeleine flees Ferguson for the last time.

A long, flowery sequence in the cemetery is filmed in soft focus. Madeleine stares at a grave with Carlotta's name inscribed on the headstone. She drives to the art museum, where she sits in rapt attention in front of a portrait of Carlotta, still holding the bouquet, which is identical to the one held by Carlotta in the painting. Finally, she leads Ferguson to an old hotel, once Carlotta's home, where she appears to have rented a room. Suddenly and mysteriously, she disappears.

Ferguson is in a haze throughout this adventure, letting himself believe Elster's story in order to justify his growing sexual hunger for Madeleine. He rather tactlessly elicits Midge's aid in tracking down Carlotta's background. (She was a courtesan who went mad after being forcibly separated from her only child, Madeleine's grandmother.) The scene fades to green rather than black.

On the next day, Ferguson follows Madeleine to the edge of San Francisco Bay, to the foot of one of the towers of the Golden Gate Bridge. He rushes after her when she leaps into the water. As he fishes the unconscious Madeleine out of the bay, he grazes her prominent breast; then he drives her, still unconscious, in her green Jaguar to his apartment. We next see her awakening in Ferguson's bed, her clothes neatly hung out to dry in the kitchen.

This scene provides the mythical climax of Ferguson's daydream. He imagines he has earned the love of a woman who looks and acts like a goddess. She responds to his tentative advances like a goddess coming to life, then disappears once again while Ferguson is trying to explain her whereabouts to Elster on the telephone. Madeleine has become Mélusine, the sea-nymph who remained faithful to her human lover only as long as he refrained from watching her in her bath, where her composite nature as a mermaid was revealed.[10]

Ferguson neither sees nor smells anything fishy. Madeleine reappears the next morning to thank him for saving her. They go off together, wandering in the redwood forest at Muir Woods. She is agitated, disappears behind trees, lunges toward the water again. He holds and comforts her.

She tells him a recurrent dream that appears to have been sent by Carlotta. There is a mirrored corridor, darkness, death at the end of it, an empty room, an open grave. Then she recalls a new piece of the dream: "a tower in Spain, a garden." She wonders if she is mad, grabs Ferguson, and begs him to stay with her forever.

That evening Ferguson is given his first clear view of a composite female monster. Midge has painted a copy of Carlotta's portrait at the museum, but with her own head replacing Carlotta's. Ferguson misses the point, seeing Midge's jealousy but not the danger she perceives in the double image of Madeleine/Carlotta. He walks out in a rage. Midge tears her hair, curses herself, and defaces the painting after he goes.

The next morning, Madeleine comes to Ferguson's apartment to tell him she has had the dream again. She recalls the Spanish tower, the square, the green, the cloister, the livery stable—then Ferguson adds dramatically, "The hotel, the saloon—it's all there, it's no dream, you've been there before, you've seen it." Madeleine denies this repeatedly, as Ferguson tells her about the Mission San Juan Bautista, a hundred miles south of San Francisco, preserved as a museum as it was in the nineteenth century.

But he continues excitedly, "It's going to be all right. You've given me something to work on. I'm going to take you down there this afternoon. When you see it you'll remember when you saw it before. It'll finish your dream. It'll destroy it, I promise you."

Vertigo has reached what appears to be the same crux as Hitchcock's earlier dream movie, *Spellbound* (1945). If the actual events condensed in the dream imagery can be remembered, then the pathological misidentification of the present with the past can be dissolved and the dreamer's life restored to a normal progressive course.[11] In both films the interpreter leads the dreamer back to the scene of the events of the dream in order to recover their original meaning in the dreamer's experience.

When they visit the mission that afternoon, Ferguson is at his most assertive, putting all his strength into an effort to convince Madeleine that the reality of the dream setting abrogates the power of the dream over her, leaving her free to enjoy and return his love. In the livery stable he says, "Where you are now is all real, not merely as it was six months ago or a hundred years ago. There's the gray horse [she dreamed about]. You see, there's an answer for everything."

But Madeleine remembers only Carlotta's childhood experience of the mission, when she was scolded by a Sister Theresa. (The appearance of a nun will twice foreshadow an unexpected death in *Vertigo*.) Madeleine has no memory of being at the mission as herself, in her own lifetime. She declares her love for Ferguson, but says mysteriously that it wasn't supposed to happen this way, as if her love were still overshadowed by the compulsion connected with the dream. She says there is something she has to do, then rushes into the mission church.

Ferguson goes after her, sees her disappear through the door to the tower, and tries to follow her up the stairs. But as he looks down he sees the floor rising to meet him. (This is the famous shot in which the camera zooms in and tracks out at the same time.) His acrophobia defeats him as his anxiety prevents him from climbing any farther. He hears a scream, then through the window of the tower he sees Madeleine's body hurtle past him to fall heavily on the tiled roof below.

Vertigo is not a repetition of *Spellbound*. Ferguson's attempt to make sense of Madeleine's dream has not "finished it," as he promised. Quite the contrary, it seems only to have led her more certainly into its fatal trap. Hitchcock seems to have given up his belief in the efficacy of dream interpretation. The viewer is shocked both by the sickening fall of Madeleine's body and by Hitchcock's apparent loss of faith in the psychological power of the truth revealed in dreams. The shock reverberates against the narrative structure of the film itself. The death of the heroine halfway through the film forcefully violates the viewer's conventional narrative expectations. The story appears to have ended with Madeleine's death.[12]

The further events of the film unfold in an atmosphere of unreality. Why is Hitchcock dragging it on? The viewer is demoralized and suspicious. But, in fact, Hitchcock is planning a much deeper investigation of the dream substrate of waking life than he attempted in *Spellbound*. And the working out of this investigation will produce even greater shocks to the viewer's sensibility.

At the coroner's inquest Ferguson is all but declared criminally negligent in Madeleine's death. A very composed Elster apologizes for the judge's harshness and for causing Ferguson so much distress by asking him to do more than he was capable of. Ferguson is not comforted by this display of sympathy.

At home Ferguson has a dream of his own, a nightmare incorporating much of the imagery of Madeleine's dream. In fact, it could have been the dream Madeleine described to him, with Madeleine's figure replaced everywhere by his own, including a final scene in which he plunges from the top of the tower. The graphic representation of the dream is unfortunately not of high quality, especially in the two-dimensional swirling disintegration of Carlotta's bouquet that opens it. The contrast with the

Dali images in *Spellbound* and with the brilliant title sequence of *Vertigo* is very prominent.

The poorly realized dream images in *Vertigo* may give the viewer the impression that the nightmare is a decorative rather than a structural element in the architecture of the film. But the nightmare does two things essential to advance the movement of the film.

First, the nightmare shows how closely Madeleine's dream fits Ferguson's inner emotional state, as that state was revealed in the original "acrophobia" scene with Midge. Madeleine's dream could have been designed to order for Ferguson. Second, the nightmare introduces an idea that is entirely new to Ferguson. A "dream idea," of course, is not a logical statement but a composite image that brings together two apparently unrelated elements of experience to form a new configuration of meaning. Elster, as he appeared for the last time in the courtroom, but with a distinctly sinister expression, is aligned in this scene with a living Carlotta, dressed as in the museum portrait. A final shot zooms in on Carlotta's necklace, now in the possession of Madeleine.

Ferguson's dream has made a creative leap—it has linked the haunting of Madeleine by Carlotta with Ferguson's new feeling that he is somehow Elster's victim. It sets Carlotta and Elster together in a conspiratorial stance, the reverse of their earlier relationship as competitors for Madeleine's soul. As in the original scene with Midge, the viewer does not know enough to make rational sense of this new information. But the information adds to the unconscious associative network already set up in the viewer's mind, a network that gives rise to expectations in viewing the remainder of the film of which the viewer is quite unaware.

On the screen, Ferguson reacts to the nightmare and its implications by falling into a profound psychological depression. He is hospitalized for several months, during which he is unwilling to acknowledge Midge or her patronizing (matronizing?) attempts to cheer him up. "Mozart is the boy for you," she says, putting a record on the phonograph she has brought to his hospital room. "You're not lost—Mother's here." When Ferguson fails to respond, Midge blurts out angrily to the doctor that Ferguson is still in love with Madeleine. She walks down the dim hospital corridor and leaves for good.

Ferguson leaves the hospital to begin a pathetic search for Madeleine. Like the eight-month-old child in Piaget's experiment who looks for the missing ball where he *first* saw it, Ferguson returns to the places where he first encountered Madeleine. He is back in his trancelike state of distant and unspoken admiration, this time with the implications of morbidity and madness that accompany his denial of her death.

In front of the flower shop he spots a rather coarse-looking young woman who resembles Madeleine. He follows her to her hotel, where she opens the window of her room with the same gesture Madeleine had used at the hotel in which Carlotta had once lived.

Ferguson goes to the young woman's room. It is filled with the eerie green light of the hotel sign just outside her window. She fends him off, but seems to read his desperate eagerness. "I know," she says, "I remind you of someone, someone who ditched you." And then, "She's dead, isn't she?" Her name is Judith Barton, as she tries to prove with a Kansas driver's license and family photos.

She accepts an invitation to dinner. When Ferguson leaves, she gets out her suitcase and starts to write a letter. As she looks off into the distance, the tower of the mission church fades in. Madeleine reaches the top of the stairs. She screams as Elster throws the body of another woman, dressed identically, over the edge.

For the viewer who has identified himself with Ferguson, the effect of this flashback is extraordinary, almost a personal betrayal. Not only is the dead Madeleine whom Ferguson loved a fraud, but so is the living Judy he is about to fall in love with. The scene was Hitchcock's own addition to the script, inserted over universal opposition from his advisers. Hitchcock believed (the finished film bears him out) that the snapping of the suspense for the viewer was necessary to focus attention on Ferguson's emotional reaction to the doubleness of his situation.

The flashback clarifies the doubleness of the viewer's situation as well. It supplies the missing associations to Madeleine's dream, denied to Ferguson when he questioned her in the livery stable. The completion of Madeleine's associations by Judy confirms Ferguson's belief that the mysteries of the dream imagery (and the dreamer's life) can be resolved when the events incorporated into the dream imagery are actually known. Hitchcock has not abandoned this position, as he had led the viewer to believe earlier in the film. But Ferguson is not the beneficiary of this new information. Hitchcock shows instead that the dream function can be defeated by bad information, that the dreamer is vulnerable to the bad faith of others he depends on, as well as to his own mechanisms of idealization and denial, his own bad faith with himself.

By completing Madeleine's dream for the viewer, the flashback shows how the dream functions differently for the audience and the characters of the film. That is, the dream functions differently as a structural element of the film as a whole, as an experience for the viewer, and as a narrative element in the plot, an event occurring in the lives of the characters. As a structural element the dream is a success. It creates the essential associative links between the earlier and later episodes in the viewer's experience of the film. As an element of the plot it is a false dream, consciously fabricated by one character to obscure the relationships between events critical to the life of another.

The viewer is safe within the dream structure of the film as a whole, but his identification with Ferguson has been violently disturbed. For the film character enmeshed in the plot, the falsifications are real. After the flashback, Ferguson has a chance to discover and assimilate what Hitchcock has already divulged to the viewer. The viewer must watch Ferguson's struggle from a distance—from the viewpoint of a parent, perhaps, but no longer from that of another self.

This effect is created in a different way in Peter Weir's *The Year of Living Dangerously* (1982). In that film the romantic couple is released from control of the master character who scripts their love affair, Billy Kwan. Their narcissistic sparring comes to a halt when Billy loses faith in them and kills himself. Suddenly they must fight to hold each other, and their love becomes real as they struggle to overcome a set of obstacles over which Billy is now powerless to guide them. In *Vertigo*, the disappearing mastermind is Elster. He withdraws from the scene with the real Madeleine's inheritance, and Ferguson and Judy must find their own way.[13]

In the letter, Judy confesses the murder. "Elster didn't make any mistakes," she says. "I made the mistake. I fell in love with you." Now she doesn't "have the nerve to lie and make you love me again." She plans to leave before he returns for their dinner date. But she tears up the letter and decides to try to persuade him to love her as she is, with all her faults.

Ferguson takes Judy to dinner at Ernie's, but his glance wanders to another woman wearing a gray suit like the one Madeleine was wearing when she died. The next day, repeating his courtship of Madeleine, Ferguson asks Judy to quit her job and let him take care of her. They go wandering to the Palace of Fine Arts. But Ferguson is not impressed with Judy as she is. He repeatedly humiliates her with his sense of her inferiority to Madeleine. She puts up with his anger in the hope that he will finally accept the reality of her love and let the idealized Madeleine go.

But his thinking takes a surprising and peculiar course. He tries to make Judy over, Pygmalion-like, into another Madeleine. He takes her to buy the gray suit and then the entire outfit Madeleine wore on the day she died. Judy asks, in a panic, "If I let you change me, will that do it? Will you love me?" He sends her to a beauty shop for the final touch: Madeleine's blond hair and upswept hairdo.

Judy reluctantly goes along with everything except the hairdo. For the viewer, Ferguson's search for Madeleine becomes something more sinister than the foolish sentimentality it appeared to be at first. Is he really looking for the living Madeleine? If Madeleine is alive, Judy can't be Madeleine. Does he want the actual woman he lost, without the identity destroyed when "Madeleine" died, or does he want to preserve his idealization no matter who the woman is? How does he imagine he can do that? Or has he figured out Elster's plot, and is he preparing his revenge against the woman who betrayed him?

While Judy is away, Ferguson paces furiously at her hotel room, almost stalking her as she walks down the corridor from the elevator. Her hair is still down. He insists, angrily, that she redo it. She disappears into the bathroom. While Ferguson waits impatiently, Judy is transformed once again into Madeleine. She emerges into the hazy green light of the hotel sign shining through her window, now intensified so that it completely engulfs her.

Ferguson's resistance finally melts. He embraces her tenderly as the camera tracks around them very slowly in a complete circle. As the camera moves, the background changes imperceptibly from Judy's hotel room to the livery stable at San Juan Bautista, and then back again to the original point of view in the hotel room. As the livery stable appears, Ferguson looks up with an anxious and bewildered expression, then returns his gaze to Judy as if nothing had happened when it went by. The past is deeply embedded in this climactic moment.

Hitchcock's use of the circular tracking shot strikingly illustrates the power of film to draw the double imagery of the dream into a narrative sequence. Past and present are superimposed here without interruption of the surface action or loss of vividness in the emotional intensity of the scene. Ferguson embraces Judy in the present and Madeleine in the past. The embrace continues in the foreground while the situation in time alternates with the changes in the background. The linear sequence of the background settings is turned inward by the circular camera movement, so that it curls back to its starting point, coiling and closing on itself.

Ferguson's earlier attempt to interpret Madeleine's dream had been broken off in the livery stable. In the embrace it appears that their passion has been reignited. It flashes like a spark across the emotional gap between the kiss at the scene of Madeleine's death and the kiss now taking place. The discontinuity in Ferguson's self-image dating from that moment also appears to have been closed and healed by the circular embrace in Judy's hotel room.

Judy suggests they have dinner at Ernie's again. She dresses up in her new replica of the black dress she wore on the night Ferguson first saw her at the restaurant. She takes a necklace out of her jewel box. The viewer recognizes it as Carlotta's necklace, given to Madeleine by Elster.

Judy asks Ferguson to help her with the clasp. There is a moment before he notices the necklace. Does Judy believe that Ferguson has understood and forgiven her, or is this an unconscious slip? Will Ferguson be surprised to see the necklace? How will he react?

The answer comes quickly. Judy is in front of the mirror, with Ferguson looking over her shoulder. An expression of horror comes over his face. There is a brief flash of Carlotta's portrait, with the necklace prominently in place, just as in Ferguson's nightmare after the inquest. He has just realized (for the first time?) that Judy not only resembles Madeleine but *is* the woman he knew as Madeleine. Ferguson had managed to convince himself that he could find an exact replica of the dead Madeleine and, at the same time, that the replica would be someone new, different and alive. Judy's exposure of the necklace and herself has finally destroyed this fantasy.

With his illusion shattered, Ferguson sets out to restore what is left of his sanity. He resumes his effort to interpret Madeleine's dream, his own nightmare, but now with a difference. In the livery stable, he saw Madeleine as his ally and the beneficiary of his quest for the truth. Now Judy is his enemy, Elster's accomplice, Carlotta herself, as the nightmare had foretold.

Instead of driving Judy to dinner, he takes the road to San Juan Bautista. As night falls, Judy's anxiety mounts. She asks where they are going. Ferguson replies, "There's one final thing I have to do, and then I'll be free of the past." When they arrive she asks, "Why here?" He tells her, "Madeleine died here. I have to go back into the past once more, just once more, for the last time. . . . I need you to be Madeleine for a while. When it's done we'll both be free."

He points to the livery stable. "We stood there and I kissed her for the last time." As he pulls her toward the stairs of the church tower he says, "I said I wouldn't lose you, but I did. I couldn't get to the top. One doesn't often get a second chance. I want to stop being haunted. You're my second chance, my second chance. Go up the stairs and I'll follow."

They reach the window where Ferguson's climb ended on the day of Madeleine's death. He tells her, "This is as far as I could get, but you went on." When Judy's resistance escalates, Ferguson adopts the tone of the detective. "Remember the necklace. That's where you made your slip." He rehearses the murder scene with her, becoming enraged as he describes her compliance with Elster's plot. "You're just a copy, a counterfeit," he says with bitterness. "Elster made you over, just like I did, only better. Not just your clothes and your hair, but your looks and manners and words. . . . He told you exactly what to do and what to say. . . . Now we're going up to look at the scene of the crime."[14] He drags her, kicking and clawing, up the final stairs.

They reach the narrow platform from which the body of the real Madeleine was thrown. Ferguson continues his detective work, noting where Elster and Judy could have hidden after the crime, and describing how they escaped when he sneaked away. "You were his girl," he says, "and he ditched you. With all his wife's money and his freedom and power, he ditched you. Did he give you anything? Just some money and the necklace. You shouldn't keep souvenirs of a murder, that's where you made your mistake. You shouldn't have been so sentimental." Then, breaking into tears, "I loved you so, Madeleine."

Judy remembers that her mistake was to fall in love with Ferguson, but now she says it was no mistake. "I was safe when you found me. You couldn't prove anything. . . . I walked into danger and let you change me because I loved you." (Novak is splendid in this difficult scene.) Ferguson is moved for the moment by Judy's sincerity and devotion. He takes her in his arms, but draws back. "It's too late," he says (echoing Madeleine's final words before she entered the church). "It's too late. Nothing will bring her back." But then, as if taking back his words, he kisses Judy.

Judy's head is framed against the open arch through which the body of the real Madeleine had been thrown, the stormy twilit sky behind her. Suddenly a dark figure appears out of a gloomy corner of the tower. A look of terror comes over Judy's face. She breaks from Ferguson's embrace, takes a step backward, and falls screaming to her death. The dark figure is a nun. "I heard voices," she says. Ferguson steps through the arch to the edge of the platform and looks down, his arms outstretched as they were at the end of his nightmare, when *he* was falling from the tower. The camera regards him from outside the tower arch now. It tracks away abruptly, leaving Ferguson suspended at the top of the tower, frozen in his attitude of helpless affliction.[15]

The mythic resonance has shifted from the tale of Mélusine to that of Eurydice. Madeleine, like Mélusine, was a water-nymph, driven back to the spirit world by an excessively curious lover. Judy, like Eurydice, is a mortal woman, destroyed by Ferguson's morbid scrutiny of her tortured climb from the underworld.[16] The contrast between Ferguson's lifting of the fraudulently suicidal Madeleine out of the bay and his dragging of the protesting Judy up the stairs of the tower is the antithesis between a private daydream and a nightmare that grips his entire world.

In the end, Ferguson's oedipal conflicts converge with his anxiety about dependence on women. He is tormented with guilt over his triumph in winning Madeleine away from Elster. Nevertheless, he can feel himself equal to Elster's power of detachment from human life and need only by destroying his own creation, as Elster had done. We see him, finally, standing framed in the arch of the tower as if in the gaping mouth of hell, looking out over a world completely devoid of objects.

Conclusion

Freud's (*S.E.* 7:222) suggestion that "The finding of an object is in fact a refinding of it" was as much a statement about knowledge as about desire. We can't recognize what we haven't known earlier, and we can't desire what we don't recognize as desirable. It isn't possible to *experience* anything *for the first time*. In the double imagery of the dream we register the yet to be experienced, acquiring as we do so the ability to respond in kind. Art reflects our desire back to us as a special kind of knowledge, always, relative to the objective world, as a double image incorporating the past as well as the present.[17]

Art repeats, but not exactly. There is always the third term that emerges from the difference between the original and its facsimile. Montage in film is the means to mutation. In the film comedy of remarriage (Cavell 1981), the "second chance" allows the rejected lover to become a new person, clear of preconceptions—frailer, perhaps, but autonomous. For the lovers in *Vertigo,* the mutation is lethal. The opportunity is more than they can grasp; the dangers are equal to the opportunity. Unmitigated devastation is the consequence of their failure.

The "final thing" Ferguson is driven to do, the compulsion that vanquishes his newly rekindled desire for Judy, is to complete his interpretation of Madeleine's dream. He fulfills his mission by dragging Judy to the top of the tower and forcing her to acknowledge the actual events that gave rise to the fabricated dream that became his own nightmare. In the end he finally learns (or recognizes) the truth discovered by the viewer in Judy's flashback at the hotel room.

Since that moment the viewer has been immersed in a different dream from Ferguson's, a dream that contains Ferguson's and Madeleine's dreams within it, yet distances itself from them in a process that culminates as the camera tracks away from Ferguson in the final scene. Nevertheless, the viewer's dream experience is completed by the completion of Ferguson's interpretation. Unlike Madeleine, for whose enlightenment Ferguson saw himself laboring, or Ferguson, struggling desperately for the truth, the viewer is the true beneficiary of the completed dream experience.

How to describe the nature of this benefit is one of the great problems of criticism. To call it a catharsis is to ignore the intricate structure created by the application of montage at many levels of complexity and over a wide range of emotional experience. What is retained within the viewer at the completion of the film is surely more significant than what has passed through and out of him.

It is a kind of lesson, but not a schoolroom lesson. It is rather the kind of unconscious lesson we learn when our capacity for experience is enlarged by our own dreams. In the hands of a master like Hitchcock, the dream function is objectified on film, where it can serve as a stimulus not only to the conscious reflection of the viewer but to his nocturnal dreaming as well.

As it is, the viewer may need many viewings of *Vertigo* to comprehend its full effect. The superimpositions that form the structure of the film will need time to reach an equilibrium in the viewer's own unconscious; to be distributed, through many cycles of dreaming, to the appropriate intersections of the vast memory structure that summarizes his or her life history from its earliest moments. There the process of comparison by superimposition through which the film was created will be repeated in another way, at another level of complexity, so that some hitherto unrecognized discontinuity in the viewer's own view of himself may eventually be restored or secured.

Notes

1. In recent years, Kawin (1978), Petric (1981), and Eberwein (1984) have made major contributions to the study of film as psychological process. They describe the representation of dream and fantasy in film, giving special emphasis to the camera's ability to neutralize the conditions that normally allow us to distinguish between objective and subjective realities. Metz (1977) approaches this issue from a semiotic perspective, almost (but not quite) suggesting that *condensation* in dreams is the visual equivalent of metaphor in film.

2. For developments in the psychoanalytic theory of dreams, see Hawkins (1966), Breger (1967), Greenberg and Pearlman (1974), and Palombo (1977, 1978, 1984a, 1985).

3. See Chaplin's *The Kid* (1916) for a dream in which the magical flight from reality is tragicomically brought down to earth.

4. Quoted in Mast and Cohen (1985), p. 332.

5. After the First World War, German expressionist and French surrealist directors began to make their films more explicitly dreamlike in order to bring this intensification of reality into the foreground of film technique. However, it was not until the work of Bergman, Bunuel, Fellini, and others after the Second World War that the inherent affinities between film drama and dreaming were self-consciously explored in major works of film art.

6. Freud's (1900) method of dream interpretation, based on the serendipitous exploration of the dreamer's associations to the contents of the dream, has proven to be an invaluable clinical and analytic tool. It must be distinguished from his theory of dream construction, a set of speculative ideas that cannot be reconciled with the findings of the sleep laboratory.

7. How film resembles and extends the other arts in this respect is the subject for another essay. But I think film has a special capability for making visible the interplay of sequence and superimposition, of continuity and simultaneity, that underlies the power of the arts in general.

8. Rothman (1982) demonstrates in his discussions of five of Hitchcock's films how Hitchcock systematically exploited the camera's ability to move from the *world* as seen through the eyes of the character to the *character* as seen through the eyes of a remote and omniscient objective viewer, to control the viewer's expectations and identifications. Cavell (1984) develops similar ideas in recent essays, "*North by Northwest*" and "What Becomes of Things on Film?"

9. Johann Christian, the son of Johann Sebastian Bach, far outshone his father in public esteem during their lifetimes. No doubt it would be rash to suggest that Hitchcock had in mind the reversal by later critical opinion of the younger Bach's oedipal triumph. Nevertheless, it is this music that pierces Ferguson's composure in the scene with Midge. See Brown (1982) for a superb discussion of Bernard Hermann's musical contribution to the drama of *Vertigo*.

10. For a popularized version of Mélusine, see the sea-nymph Madison in Ron Howard's *Splash!* (1983).

11. It should be noted that this dramatic use of the dream is faithful to Freud's interpretive method rather than his dream theory, which puts little emphasis on the actual events incorporated into the dream imagery. The dream sequence in *Spellbound* illustrates the adaptive information-processing function of the dream. Like Shakespeare in *A Midsummer Night's Dream* (Palombo 1983), Hitchcock had an intuitive understanding of the important relationship between past and present events in the composite dream image.

12. William Kerrigan (personal communication) points out that the device of eliminating the heroine early in *Vertigo* was repeated with even greater dramatic emphasis in Hitchcock's *Psycho* (1960). A dead woman appears at the conclusion of that film, who, in the delusional view of the male protagonist, is a double for the dead heroine. In *Psycho* the psychological battle of the protagonist has already been lost when the film begins. The consequences of the lost struggle unfold as the film retrogresses from there.

13. In *The Year of Living Dangerously*, Billy is the creator of the fiction whose romantic protagonists are idealized projections of himself. Billy's angry withdrawal from the scene of the film is a dramatic representation of the creator's ambivalence about giving his characters lives that are really their own, beyond the limits defined by his self-projection. Hitchcock's master criminals generally take on this envious malevolence without the countervailing generativity, allowing the director to be identified with the just and benevolent fate that rescues the protagonists from their otherwise more powerful enemies. In *Vertigo*, Hitchcock declined the role of benevolent overseer, leaving Ferguson and Judy to fight the demoralizing effects of Elster's plot with their own limited emotional resources.

14. Hitchcock's attempts to "make over" his actresses, in the form of a tyrannical control of their personal as well as professional activities, usually accompanied by overt or covert sexual advances, is a constant theme in Donald Spoto's *The Dark Side of Genius: The Life of Alfred Hitchcock*. Spoto docu-

ments the devastating effects on Hitchcock's personal relationships with these women. He suggests that *Vertigo,* among other things, is a dramatization of this tendency of Hitchcock's and of its painful consequences for him. According to Spoto, the tendency went from bad to worse in his work with Vera Miles and Tippi Hedren in later films.

15. Cavell (1979) suggests that Ferguson is about to plunge from the tower to join Judy in death (p. 86). This is a highly plausible conjecture but not absolutely required by the film. Hitchcock allows for the possibility that Ferguson will react to Judy's death by reverting to the paranoid projection of his bad-mother imago (cf. *Psycho* and the final words of *Vertigo:* "I thought I heard voices.") rather than through identification with Judy.

Cavell's analysis of *Vertigo* apostrophizes the complicated interdependencies of fantasy and reality. He says, "Fantasy is precisely what reality can be confused with." But I believe his emphasis on the disfiguring power of Ferguson's fantasies must be balanced by attention to the insidious power of Elster's plot and of Judy's duplicity in undermining Ferguson's equilibrium. Hitchcock is telling us in *Vertigo* that Ferguson's fantasy is shaped not only by his infantile wish to revive and restore a lost or fallen mother but also by Judy's failure to reveal herself until *forced* to do so by Ferguson's reckless need to restore his shattered potency.

16. For a sympathetic analysis of Judy's psychopathology, see Spoto's (1976) fine essay on *Vertigo.*

17. Rothenberg (1978) studied the creative process in a large group of distinguished writers and artists. He recounts in great detail the critical importance of the double image in the formative stages of their work. Palombo (1984b) traces the role of a poet's dreams (reported by Rothenberg) in providing the crucial imagery that gave density and substance to the creation of an important poem.

References

Breger, Louis. "Functions of Dreams." *Journal of Abnormal Psychology Monographs* 72 (1967):1–27.

Brown, Royal. "Hermann, Hitchcock and the Music of the Irrational." *Cinema Journal* 22 (1982). Reprinted in Mast and Cohen (1985).

Cavell, Stanley. *The World Viewed.* Cambridge, Mass.: Harvard University Press, 1979.

———. *Pursuits of Happiness: The Hollywood Comedy of Remarriage.* Cambridge, Mass.: Harvard University Press, 1981.

———. *Themes out of School.* San Francisco: North Point Press, 1984.

Eberwein, Robert. *Film and the Dream Screen.* Princeton: Princeton University Press, 1984.

Eisenstein, Sergei. *Film Form* (1929). Edited by Jay Leyda. New York: Harcourt Brace, n.d. Excerpted in Mast and Cohen (1985).

———. "Montage in 1938" (1938). In *Notes of a Film Director.* New York: Dover Publications, 1970.

Freud, Sigmund. *The Standard Edition of the Complete Psychological Works of Sigmund Freud.* Edited and translated by James Strachey. 24 vols. London: Hogarth Press, 1953–74.
The Interpretation of Dreams (1900–1901), vols. 4, 5.
Three Essays on the Theory of Sexuality (1905), vol. 7.
Greenberg, Ramon, and Pearlman, Chester. "Cutting the REM Nerve." *Perspectives in Biology and Medicine* 17 (1974):513–21.
Hawkins, David. "A Review of Psychoanalytic Dream Theory in the Light of Recent Psycho-physiological Studies of Sleep and Dreaming." *British Journal of Medical Psychology* 39 (1966):85–104.
Kawin, Bruce. *Mindscreen.* Princeton: Princeton University Press, 1978.
Mast, Gerald, and Cohen, Marshall, eds. *Film Theory and Criticism.* 3rd ed. New York: Oxford University Press, 1985.
Metz, Christian. *The Imaginary Signifier: Psychoanalysis and the Cinema* (1977). Bloomington: Indiana University Press, 1982.
Münsterberg, Hugo. *The Film: A Psychological Study* (1916). New York: Dover Books, 1969.
Palombo, Stanley R. "Dreams, Memory and the Origin of Thought." In *Thought, Consciousness and Reality,* edited by Joseph H. Smith. Psychiatry and the Humanities, vol. 2. New Haven: Yale University Press, 1977.
———. *Dreaming and Memory: A New Information-Processing Model.* New York: Basic Books, 1978.
———. "The Cognitive Act in Dream Construction." *Journal of the American Academy of Psychoanalysis* 8 (1980):186–201.
———. "The Genius of the Dream." *American Journal of Psychoanalysis* 43 (1983):301–14.
———. "Deconstructing the Manifest Dream." *Journal of the American Psychoanalytic Association* 32 (1984a): 405–20.
———. "The Poet as Dreamer." *Journal of the American Academy of Psychoanalysis* 12 (1984b):59–74.
———. "The Primary Process: A Reconceptualization." *Psychoanalytic Inquiry* 5 (1985):405–36.
Petric, Vlada. *Film and Dreams: An Approach to Ingmar Bergman.* South Salem, N.Y.: Redgrave, 1981.
Rapaport, David. *Emotions and Memory* (1942). New York: Science Editions, 1961.
Rothenberg, Albert. *The Emerging Goddess: The Creative Process in Art, Science and Other Fields.* Chicago: University of Chicago Press, 1979.
Rothman, William. *Hitchcock: The Murderous Gaze.* Cambridge, Mass.: Harvard University Press, 1982.
Spoto, Donald. *The Art of Alfred Hitchcock.* New York: Hopkinson and Blake, 1976.
———. *Hitchcock: The Dark Side of Genius.* New York: Ballantine Books, 1983.

3 *Vertigo:* The Unknown Woman in Hitchcock

William Rothman

In a paper presented at the 1984 convention of the Society for Cinema Studies, Marian Keane contests the view—this view, inadequate on the face of it, dominates recent academic film criticism—that the camera in "classical" movies allies itself exclusively with the male position (Keane 1986).[1] She argues that *Vertigo,* like all of Hitchcock's films, concerns a search for identity and what Stanley Cavell has called "the identifying and inhabitation of a feminine region of the self" (1984, 179–80) and thus has a close affinity to "women's films." In October 1985, in the Edith Weigert Lecture published in the present volume, Cavell announced his discovery, within the body of "women's films," of a genre he terms "the melodrama of the unknown woman."

At the end of *Vertigo,* the James Stewart figure, like Louis Jourdan at the end of *Letter from an Unknown Woman,* awakens to the realization that he has failed to acknowledge a woman. In both films, this realization comes poetically too late. Then are we to count *Vertigo* as a member of Cavell's genre? If not, what does its exclusion from the genre, or rejection of the genre, reveal about the unknown woman melodramas, about the Hitchcock thriller, about the concepts of genre and authorship as instruments of film criticism, about the powers and limits of the camera, about the conditions of being human (Cavell's deepest concern and that of the films we both study)?

In the paper that follows, I address such questions obliquely, letting my thoughts emerge out of detailed "readings" of two sequences in the film. In contemplating *Vertigo*'s relationship to the melodrama of the unknown woman, a personal motivation was my wish to reflect on the relationship between Cavell's writing about film, guided by and to the discovery of film's major genres, and my own, drawn to meditate on film as a vehicle of authorship. Thus I follow the method of *Hitchcock: The Murderous Gaze,* in which I "read" five Hitchcock films from opening to closing (Rothman 1982).

The first sequence directly precedes the grueling passage in which Scottie (James Stewart), overcome by vertigo, fails to make it to the top of the bell tower and witnesses what he takes to be the death of Madeleine (Kim Novak).

The sequence opens on an extreme long shot of Scottie in his apartment, lost in thought, perhaps dozing, on the sofa. At the sound of a buzzer he looks up and goes to the door, the camera reframing with him. There is a cut to a shot in which Scottie, in shadow, is in the far left of a frame almost entirely occupied by the featureless expanse of the door. (This setup will be repeated, but reversed, when Scottie first visits Judy's hotel room in the second part of the film.) His hand below the frame line, Scottie opens the door, creating what I call Hitchcock's "curtain-raising" effect and opening a bracket that will be closed at the conclusion of this sequence. (*Vertigo*'s most celebrated curtain-raising effect occurs when Scottie, trailing Madeleine down a dark alley, opens the door through which she has disappeared—and a flower shop full of brilliant color fills the screen.)

As always in Hitchcock, when a curtain is raised, theater is invoked. Scottie is the audience—we are, too, of course—for this theatrical entrance. But whose entrance is it? We see only a silhouette, a shadow among shadows.

In *Psycho*'s famous shower murder sequence, Hitchcock films the murderer's entrance in this way. However, Marion Crane is turned away when the shower curtain is torn open—she does not open it herself—so that we alone see the knife-wielding killer framed in silhouette. Rhetorically, the *Psycho* sequence's identification of the shower curtain with the movie screen—that "safety curtain" we assume will separate us from the world of the film—presents this silhouetted figure not simply as a denizen of a world safely cut off from our own but as *real:* we are face to face with our own murderer.[2]

The filming of the woman at Scottie's door in silhouette, by contrast, intimates that she is not fully, or not exactly, real, as though we are seeing not a real woman but a ghost. Indeed, this silhouette prefigures the ghostly apparition that rises into Judy's view at the climax of the film, precipitating her death. Hitchcock understands that in the face of the camera, the future as well as the past may haunt the present. And it is one of his abiding insights that there is an aspect of the supernatural, a ghostliness, in all human beings on film, all subjects of the camera.

Scottie believes, or desperately wishes to believe, that human beings create their own destinies: if ghosts are real, human beings are not free, and he is condemned to his vertigo. Throughout the ensuing dialogue, Scottie is intent on proving that Madeleine's possession by Carlotta reveals no supernatural agency. Hence it is expressively appropriate that he immediately flips a light switch, causing the silhouette to be fleshed out: it's Madeleine (the eminently palpable Kim Novak).

For Scottie—at least, this is what he tells himself—Madeleine's mystery is only an enigma: how is Carlotta Valdes's hold over her to be explained and thereby overcome? In his role as investigator, but also as therapist, Scottie—Gavin Elster calls him "the hard-headed Scot" with veiled irony—undertakes to solve this riddle, to explain everything.

But Scottie makes a mistake: he falls in love. By a series of stages that Hitchcock precisely plots, Scottie's project in the first part of the film, which casts him at once as investigator/therapist and as romantic hero, becomes a calling—some would say an obsession—on which he stakes his entire being. By explaining everything, he will prove to Madeleine that she is free, will save and win this damsel in distress. But who is this woman to him? Scottie is intent on denying the Carlotta in Madeleine, but what if it is Madeleine's fatedness that really draws him, the doomed Carlotta with whom he has really fallen in love? Is Scottie, untutored in the ways of the heart, embracing her mystery, not denying it?

Scottie does not know, nor do we seeing *Vertigo* for the first time, that the woman at the door is not Madeleine, Gavin Elster's wife, but Judy Barton from Salina, Kansas, who is acting the role of Madeleine—more precisely, acting the role of Madeleine possessed by Carlotta Valdes—in a piece of theater authored by the diabolical Elster. What Scottie *cannot* know, but which Hitchcock calls upon us to acknowledge, is that Gavin Elster, despite his aspirations to authorship, is no less than Judy a creature of the *real* author, Hitchcock. Then, too, we know, as Scottie cannot, that Judy is Kim Novak acting the role of Judy. That is, Kim Novak is possessed by Judy, who is possessed by Madeleine, who is possessed by Carlotta Valdes, who is . . . Then who is this woman we know as Kim Novak? Who is she in the face of Hitchcock's camera? And who is Hitchcock, that he, like Scottie, has fallen in love with her? Who are we, that we, too, have fallen?

"Madeleine!" Scottie says, after switching on the light. "What's the matter?"

"The dream came back again."

Scottie reassures her, a trace of a smile playing on his lips. "It's going to be all right. . . . You're awake. . . ."

She stares at him as he concludes. "You're all right now."

His eyes narrow as he scrutinizes her closely, searching for a clue on which he might hang an explanation. "Now can you tell me?"

She turns away and walks across the room. The camera reframes with her as she begins to relate her dream of a tower in an old Spanish village. Then Hitchcock isolates Scottie and Madeleine in separate frames.

As Madeleine speaks, Scottie narrows his eyes, an explanation dawning. As she goes on, he moves left, the camera reframing with his gliding movement. Then he interrupts, gesturing in the inimitable James Stewart manner. "It's no dream. You've *been* there before. You've seen it."

She looks away and sits down. "No, never!" she says with all the petulance of disavowal.

"Madeleine, a hundred miles south of San Francisco there's an old Spanish mission. San Juan Bautista, it's called. It's been preserved exactly as it was a hundred years ago as a museum. Now think hard, darling. Think hard. You've been there before. You've *seen* it. . . . Now go on about your dream. What was it that frightened you so?"

To frame Madeleine telling the end of her dream, with its chilling anticipation of the nightmare that precipitates Scottie's breakdown, Hitchcock alternates a pair of close-ups, Scottie and Madeleine each framed in left profile, that are perfectly expressive of the intimacy and the separation of analyst and analysand. "I stood alone on the green, searching for something. And I started to the church. Then the darkness closed in. I was alone in the dark being pulled into the darkness. I fought to wake up."

The camera moves with Scottie as he goes to Madeleine's side. On his words, "You're going to be all right now, Madeleine," the lamp momentarily blocks our view of Scottie. Such expressive "eclipses," which appear in every Hitchcock film, constitute a quintessentially Hitchcockian effect.

Finally framed with Madeleine in a normal two-shot, Scottie takes charge. "I'm going to take you down there to that mission this afternoon and when you see it you'll remember when you saw it before and it'll finish your dream. It will destroy it. I *promise* you."

As Scottie speaks, Madeleine's eyes shift to the left, to the right, and then down. She looks incredibly beautiful.

Who is the figure of mystery on view in this frame? Are we viewing Judy acting in character as Madeleine—that is, playing Madeleine thinking about her dream, haunted by Carlotta's fate—or Judy stepping out of Madeleine's character to think about her own dream, her dream of happiness with Scottie, a dream that Scottie's plan, unwittingly crowning Gavin Elster's grand scheme, is indeed destined to "finish" and "destroy"?

Silently, Judy meets Scottie's gaze and then looks down, at which point Hitchcock cuts to a high angle shot (cutting to a high angle shot at the moment a human fate is sealed is another quintessential Hitchcock gesture). The camera glides with Scottie as he leads Madeleine to the door and announces, with an air of calm assurance, "You'll come back here around noon." (Scottie's manner brings to mind the penultimate sequence of *Notorious*. This is how Devlin [Cary Grant] leads Alicia [Ingrid Bergman] to safety.)[3]

The cut to the high angle shot is succeeded by yet another Hitchcockian declaration of the camera, actually a conjunction of Hitchcockian signature gestures. As Scottie opens the door and Madeleine passes through it, the door fills the frame, closing the bracket opened by Madeleine's entrance and creating a blinding white flash. (Another such white flash will occur within Hitchcock's presentation of Scottie's nightmare.)

There is a dissolve to an extreme long shot of Scottie's car moving along a mountain road, then to the two in the car, framed frontally. Scottie and Madeleine are looking at the road ahead, wrapped in their private thoughts. She turns to look out of the side window, which cues a shot from her point of view: trees hurtling by overhead, framed against the sky.

This is a significant moment. Hitchcock has presented us innumerable shots from Scottie's point of view, but except for the enigmatic view of flowers floating on the water that precedes her leap into San Francisco Bay, this is the first point-of-view shot granted to Madeleine, the camera's first direct acknowledgment that she possesses her own separate consciousness.

This shot, devoid of human countenances, represents Madeleine's view, what she literally sees, but it is also expressive and evocative, a *vision:* at once a terrifying vision of nothingness—Judy is hurtling blindly into the unknown—and a meditative vision of a higher, but inhuman, realm that "takes no notice" when human beings are born or die.

Scottie, *Vertigo*'s protagonist, intent on denying the mystery that also draws him, is an object of study to Hitchcock's camera: Scottie's thoughts are perfectly legible to us. The camera's relationship to Kim Novak / Judy / Madeleine / Carlotta is more intimate and ambiguous: she is an object of desire to the camera, but she and the camera are also *attuned*. This point-of-view shot and Madeleine's reaction to it do not allow us to read this woman's thoughts; they reveal only that she is meditating, as Scottie is not, on the mystery—the mystery of birth and death and freedom and love and entrapment—that lies at the heart of Hitchcock's films.

With a trace of a smile, Madeleine looks screen right toward Scottie, then left and down at the road going by, then *quickly* past the camera again, only then raising her eyes to look at Scottie. All this time she avoids, and *appears* to avoid, the camera's gaze. Sensing her eyes on him, Scottie looks with concern to Madeleine. When he sees the brave expression with which she meets his gaze, he turns his eyes back toward the road, a pleased smile coming over him (this is not a smile intended to be seen). We read Scottie—as does Madeleine—like an open book.

Looking away from Scottie, Madeleine breathes deeply and stares ahead. No longer avoiding the camera, she stares now directly into it, or through it, as if absorbed in a scene she is envisioning.

What follows is a series of hypnotically slow panning movements linked by equally slow dissolves that is uncannily expressive of this woman's entrancement. But their effect goes beyond this: coming in response to the shot of Madeleine staring into the camera, they affect us virtually as point-of-view shots, as if the views framed by the camera, our views, are projections of what she is imagining. As if what follows, perhaps all of *Vertigo,* represents Madeleine's meditation.[4]

The key shot in this series starts on a strikingly composed frame-within-a-frame. (Such compositions, which I take to be, at one level, invocations of the film frame, echo through *Vertigo* and, indeed, through all of Hitchcock's films.) Slowly, the camera pans to the right until stone wall finally gives way to archway and another curtain is raised, a curtain that will be lowered only in the final shot of the film.

The long duration of this movement combined with its elegiac slowness make this shot an *image* of the traversal of space and time, as if raising the question of how human beings ever get from there—from Madeleine staring into the camera as Scottie's car hurtles through the trees, for example—to here, and the question of where "here" is. How can human beings possibly exist in space and time? (This movement echoes the camera's exquisitely slow traversal of Scottie's apartment that prefaces his first conversation with Madeleine; and before that, its traversal of Ernie's preceding Madeleine's entrance into the film. The latter shot is itself repeated in the second part of the film when Scottie returns to Ernie's, this time with Judy. And at the end of the present sequence, this movement will be reprised, and then echoed in the beautiful slow pan across the San Francisco skyline that effects the transition to the second part of the film.)

Another slow dissolve takes us to the outside of the livery stable. The camera continues its movement until it frames the doorway in another perfect frame-within-a-frame. For a long moment, the camera holds this framing, through which the tiny, distant figures of Madeleine and Scottie are on view.

Finally, there is a cut to the interior of the livery stable, as Scottie asks,

"Madeleine—where are you now?" and Madeleine replies, with a smile, "Here with you." Then where has she been, and where have we been, while the camera was "away"? And what commits the camera—what commits Hitchcock, what commits us—to return to these human subjects?

"It's all real," Scottie says, as if convinced that Madeleine will now come to her senses. But as he speaks her eyes slowly turn toward the camera.

"*Think* of when you were here," he implores, taking her arm. As Madeleine begins, she stares into the camera, which moves in slowly toward her. "There were not so many carriages then. There were horses in the stalls. A bay, two black, and a gray. It was our favorite place, but we were forbidden to play here, and Sister Theresa would scold us." Her words come ever more haltingly, as if it is an effort to keep from being engulfed by her memory.

Realizing that Madeleine is slipping away, Scottie impatiently looks all around him until he discovers a wooden horse. "Here's your gray horse. He may have a little trouble getting in and out of the stall without being pushed [the story of Scottie's own life], but even so. . . . See, there's an answer for everything."

Scottie's claim occasions a memorable Hitchcock brilliancy, as the camera cuts to a shot that sums up everything that Scottie has no answer for. Framed with her back to the camera—in a charged frame-within-a-frame, within this world yet viewing it from the outside, attuned to the mystery Scottie cannot explain—Madeleine stares into the frame as if possessing it: she is the camera's subject yet also its stand-in within the frame, its embodiment.

Dropping his pretense of being the detached investigator/therapist committed only to finding rational explanations, Scottie pleads with her, revealing his desire. "Madeleine, *try.* Try for *me.*"

Yet her eyes remain fixed on the camera even as she lets him pull her into his arms and kiss her. Then suddenly she closes her eyes and joins with him in the passion of his romantic, heartfelt kiss. But she is allowed, or allows herself, only the briefest moment of ecstasy. Her eyes drawn to something offscreen, she pulls out of the kiss just as Scottie at last declares himself. "I love you, Madeleine!"

Still looking off, she says, "Too late. Too late. . . . There's something I must do."

"No, there's nothing you must do," he says, trying to kiss her again. "No one possesses you. You're safe with me." But she pulls away and leaves the frame.

He runs after her, catching her on the green. Looking into his eyes, she says, "You *believe* that I love you?"

"Yes."

"And if you lose me then you'll know I . . . I loved you and wanted to go on living with you?"

"No, I won't lose you."

"Let me go into the church. Alone."

She kisses him and he lets her leave. When she pauses to look up at the tower, Hitchcock cuts to Scottie's view as he follows her gaze. Alarmed, he cries out "Madeleine!" and a chase begins. It is, of course, Scottie's vertigo that prevents him from making it to the top of the tower before Madeleine disappears behind a trap door and a body plummets to the roof of the church far below.

There is no denying the violence in Scottie's entire project in the second part of the film, the project of making Judy over into the semblance of Madeleine. Yet before condemning Scottie it is best to keep a number of points in mind.

First, Judy *is* Madeleine. While Scottie can't bring himself to touch Judy until she acknowledges the Madeleine in her, from the outset he glimpses the woman he loves in Judy ("No, Judy, there's something in *you*"). When Judy writes the note she never sends to Scottie—and what a remarkable gesture it is for Hitchcock to let us in on Judy's secret, apparently breaking all the rules of the Hitchcock thriller—she contemplates staying and lying and making him love her "for herself" and thus making him "forget the other, forget the past." She may think that the Judy persona—Judy's way of dressing, making herself up, carrying herself, speaking—*is* her self, at least is her own creation (but whose creation would she then be?). Yet "Judy" is unfinished, uncreated: surely, it was her longing for creation that drew her into the role Elster created for her. Once she was transfigured into Madeleine there was no bringing Judy back. She might act the part of Judy but only by repressing the Madeleine within her, only by theatricalizing herself. In any case, who now is "she"? Who is the agent of this repression? Who is acting? This line of thinking leads to the understanding that no matter how violently Scottie treats Judy and however little self-awareness he may possess, his goal is to liberate this woman's self, not suppress it. Furthermore, he is acting out of love for *this* woman. If Judy were some other woman who simply looked like Madeleine, would he treat her—and would she let him treat her—like this? I take it that Scottie knows in his heart—and in her heart Judy knows that he knows—that Judy and Madeleine are the same woman.

Second, Scottie promised Madeleine that he wouldn't lose her, which means, in part, that he wouldn't let her be lost, that he would keep her safe. His desperate project is undertaken not only for himself but for Madeleine's, hence Judy's, sake as well. Again, were Judy any other woman, it would be wrong—although psychologically understandable and in principle forgivable—for him to treat her only as a means of keeping a promise to Madeleine. But Judy is not another woman, she is who Madeleine is. *Vertigo* is the story not of the creation but the re-creation of a woman.

Third, while we tend to think of Judy as an innocent victim, like Carlotta Valdes, of "the power and the freedom" of men, Judy was party to a murder (even if she tried to prevent it when it was too late) and to a diabolically cruel plot against Scottie. How can Judy make Scottie love her "for herself" if, even now, she lies to him, denying who she is? The deepest interpretation of Judy's motivation for "staying and lying" is that she *wishes* for Scottie to bring Madeleine back (which means that it is no accident when she puts on the incriminating necklace). Judy wishes for Scottie to lead her to the point at which she can reveal who she is—but without losing his love. As cruel as Scottie is in "changing" Judy, he would be crueler if he failed to fulfill the role Judy calls on him to play. Scottie himself desperately needs healing, yet he heeds Judy's plea and becomes her therapist.

Fourth, Scottie promises to love Judy if she lets him change her. And he keeps his promise, as James Stewart always does in his truest movie incarnations. This is a point at which Marian Keane's reading and my own diverge. Hitchcock indicts many of his ostensible heroes, such as Sir John in *Murder!,* but I do not believe that he indicts Scottie's project, although *Vertigo* insists on its monstrous, inhuman aspect and also insists that it cannot succeed. For what gives rise to Scottie's monstrousness is his heroic refusal to let his love be lost and his equally heroic willingness to plunge into the unknown. His failure is a tragedy.

The second sequence I would like to examine is the film's ending, starting with the completion of Judy's "change."

Within the frame of Scottie's point of view, Judy / Madeleine steps out of the bathroom, suffused in a green haze (ostensibly from the neon sign outside the window). Then she steps forward, desire in her eyes, and becomes "real."

Their kiss is rendered in a glorious 360-degree camera movement in the course of which, famously, the background changes to the livery stable. Scottie notices this and, like Buster Keaton in *Sherlock Jr.,* is momentarily bewildered—this is a great touch—yet he lets himself be absorbed again by the kiss. There is a fade-out: presumably, they make love for the first time.

When the view again fades in, *Scottie* has undergone a transformation: this is a man blissfully in love. And the "real" James Stewart, boyish and chipper, has come to life. (This is like the moment in *Notorious* when, in peril down in the wine cellar, Devlin finally stops sulking and becomes the "real" Cary Grant.) But then Judy puts on Carlotta's necklace.

This occurs within a conversation about where they'll go for dinner ("Ernie's?" "You have a thing about Ernie's, don't you?" "After all, it's our place") that is interrupted for a digression that is studded with ironies ("C'mere." "Oh, no, you'll muss me." "That's what I had in mind, now *c'mere*." "Too late, I've got my face on"). Judy says, "I'm suddenly hungry." "Would you rather go somewhere else?" "No, no, Ernie's is fine. I'm gonna have—I'm gonna have one of those big beautiful steaks. Let me see, to start, I think I'll . . ."

At this comical revelation of Judy's enormous appetite, she turns to him for help with her necklace.

"How do you work this thing?"

"Can't you see?"

Finally he *does* see, and we cut to his view, the camera moving in on the necklace reflected in the mirror. This provides an occasion for another of Hitchcock's virtuoso declarations of the camera. There is an "invisible" cut to the portrait of Carlotta, the camera continuing its movement in, then pulling out until it frames Madeleine in the museum, spellbound in front of the painting. As the image slowly dissolves back to the present, for a lingering moment the portrait's frame perfectly frames Scottie's eyes.

Knowing now—but what does he know?—and without Judy's knowing he knows, Scottie's manner changes ominously. Saying "First muss me a little," she puts her arms around him, but his lips will not meet hers. Less claiming possession than seeking reassurance, she asks, "Oh, Scottie, I do have you now, don't I?" but he suggests they drive out of town for dinner, withholding his answer.

There is a dissolve to the car on the road. In this passage, Hitchcock repeats shots from the earlier drive to the mission, crucially including the shot of trees and sky from Madeleine's point of view, making us conscious of Judy's consciousness that what is happening is a repetition and renewing our sense of her attunement to the camera.

Finally Judy asks, "Where are you going?" Scottie replies mockingly, "One final thing I have to do" and Hitchcock cuts to Judy's point of view: Scottie's face chillingly turned away in profile. (Using such a profile shot to signify withdrawal or withholding is yet another Hitchcockian signature.) "And then I'll be free of the past."

There is a dissolve from Judy's troubled face to the car pulling onto the mission grounds. When she asks Scottie why they are here, he replies that he has "to go back into the past . . . for the last time. Madeleine died here, Judy. I need you to be Madeleine for a while. And when it's done we'll both be free."

Judy is reluctant, to say the least, and makes several attempts to break away, but Scottie makes her go with him to the church, all the while relating what happened on the fatal day Madeleine ran into the tower. (Throughout this passage, and in the grueling ascent of the tower, Hitchcock repeats shots from the earlier sequence.)

At the base of the tower, Scottie says, "One doesn't often get a second chance. I want to stop being haunted. You're my second chance, Judy. You're my second chance. You look like Madeleine now. Go up the stairs!"

"No!"

He pushes her. "Go up the stairs!"

As Scottie follows Judy up the stairs, waves of vertigo assault him. Hitchcock again reprises shots from the earlier sequence, including Scottie's famous views down the stairwell that vertiginously combine zoom and pan, creating the illusion of a space at once receding and unmoving. *What* recedes in Scottie's vision is the bottom of the stairwell, which forms another emblematic frame-within-a-frame, another invocation of the film frame. The shots that express Scottie's vertigo are also Hitchcockian declarations of the camera. Scottie's vertigo is his intimation that he is condemned to the gaze of Hitchcock's camera.

Finally Scottie reaches the point at which, the first time, his vertigo made him stop. "This was as far as I could get." He looks at her. "But you went on."

She stares at him in alarm.

"The necklace, Madeleine. . . . I remembered the necklace."

"Let me go!"

"No, we're going up the tower, Madeleine!"

"You can't, you're afraid!"

"Now we'll see. We'll see. This is my second chance."

"No, please!"

"But you knew that day that I wouldn't be able to follow you, didn't you? Who was up there when you got there? Elster and his wife?"

"Yes."

"Yes, and she was the one who died. The real one, not you. You were the copy, you were the counterfeit, weren't you?"

Scottie's hands are on Judy's throat; he is in a terrifying fury. "Was she dead or alive?"

"Dead. He had broken her neck."

"He had broken her neck. He wasn't taking any chances, was he?"

He drags her bodily up the stairs.

The power of *Vertigo*'s climax turns on our conviction that Scottie really has it within him to strangle Judy, to break her neck, to throw her off the tower. And James Stewart's enactment of rage and Kim Novak's of terror are so compelling that I've found myself fantasizing that at this point in the filming, Stewart lost control, that what the camera then recorded was no longer acting. Hence that Hitchcock, himself carried away, continued shooting anyway—or had he anticipated Stewart's breakdown, was this the cream of Hitchcock's diabolical jest? This fantasy brings out a crucial feature of *Vertigo*'s climax: once Scottie drags Judy to the top of the tower, no human being on earth can know what he will do. (Frank Capra's *It's a Wonderful Life* first plumbed Stewart's capacity for rage, the dark side of his unequaled willingness to stake his entire being on a wish.)

"So when you got up there he pushed her off the tower. But it was you that screamed. Why did you scream?"

"I wanted to stop it, Scottie. I ran up to stop it. I. . . . "

"You wanted to stop it. Why did you scream? Since you'd tricked me so well up to then? You played the wife very well, Judy. He made you over, didn't he?"

"Yes."

"He made you over just like *I* made you over. Only better. . . . And you *jumped* into the bay, didn't you? I'll bet you're a wonderful swimmer, aren't you? Aren't you?"

Her "Yes" is barely audible.

"*Aren't* you?"

"Yes."

"And *then* what did he do? Did he train you? Did he rehearse you? Did he tell you exactly what to do, what to say?"

She nods.

"You were a very apt pupil, too, weren't you? You were a very apt pupil. Well, why did you pick on *me? Why me?!* I was the setup, wasn't I? I was the setup. I was the made-to-order witness. I was. . . . "

Suddenly realizing that he has reached the trapdoor to the top, Scottie becomes strangely calm. "I made it. I made it."

"What are you going to do?"

"We're going up and look at the scene of the crime. C'mon, Judy."

When finally Scottie pulls Judy to the platform on top of the tower, he flings her to the far end. (They are framed in a charged setup that repeats the key shot of the flashback sequence.) "So this is where it happened. And the two of you hid back there and waited for it to clear and then you sneaked down and drove into town, is that it? And then— you were his girl, huh? Well, what happened to you? What happened to you? Did he ditch you? Aw, Judy, with all of his wife's money and all that freedom and that power. . . ."

Scottie moves toward Judy, the camera following him to the left. Recoiling from him, she desperately presses herself against the wall.

"And he ditched you. What a shame. But he knew he was safe. He knew you couldn't talk. Did he give you anything?"

"Some money."

"And the necklace. Carlotta's necklace. There was where you made your mistake, Judy. You shouldn't keep souvenirs of a killing. You shouldn't have been. . . ." Almost overcome with the memory of his love, Scottie takes a deep breath, choking back sobs. "You shouldn't have been that *sentimental*." He rears his head back, rolls his eyes, takes another deep breath, and pours all of James Stewart's longing into his next words, "I loved you so, Madeleine!"

"Scottie—I was safe when you found me. There was nothing that you could prove. When I saw you again, I, I couldn't run away, I loved you so. I *walked* into danger and let you change me because I *loved* you and I wanted you." She inches forward. "Oh, Scottie. . . . Oh, Scottie, please. . . . You love me now. Love me."

Hitchcock has filmed this part of the dialogue as an alternation of shots that isolate Judy and Scottie in separate frames. Still coming forward, she enters the frame of "his" shot and throws her arms around him. "Keep me safe!"

"Too late, it's too late," Scottie says, echoing Madeleine's words. "There's no bringing her back."

"Please!"

Scottie looks at Judy, stares at her, and then—*kisses* her passionately as he had in the hotel room and before that the livery stable. He does not ask for proof of Judy's love; he *believes* her, as he had the first time. Whatever the woman in his arms has done and whoever she is, he loves and forgives her. As far as *he* is concerned, their kiss is forever. He has overcome his vertigo and fulfilled his quest. But Scottie, worthy romantic hero though he may be, exists within the frame of a Hitchcock film. He does not have the power or the freedom to keep Judy safe.

As at the stable, Judy pulls out of the kiss, her eyes drawn to something offscreen. This time Hitchcock cuts to her point of view. Judy sees a frame devoid of human figures, like the repeated point-of-view shot of trees and sky. Then, within this haunting vision of nothingness, a silhouette appears, barely discernible in the shadows.

Judy's eyes widen in horror, but Scottie, not granted her vision, is unaware that anything is wrong until, crying "Oh, no, no!" she slips screen left out of the frame. Then Scottie turns and, moving toward the camera so that his face is magnified in the frame, looks screen right as a woman's offscreen voice speaks the words, "I heard voices." There is a chilling scream, and Scottie wheels around with a look of horror and dread.

The scream still reverberating, the silhouetted figure steps into the light. It is a nun. And she is looking straight into the camera. Crossing herself, the nun intones "God have mercy" and begins tugging on the bell rope.

As the great bell tolls, the camera pulls out and twists counterclockwise so that the white wall of the tower fills the frame, creating yet another of Hitchcock's blinding white flashes and at the same time imaging the *lowering* of a curtain. The nun, pulling on the rope, rings down the final curtain, signifying the end of the performance. Yet Hitchcock's final virtuoso turn remains to be completed.

The movement continues, now revealing the camera to be—all along to have been—outside the tower chamber, occupying a position inaccessible to any human being on earth. The camera keeps pulling out until it frames Scottie, looking down, his hands at his sides in mute anguish and supplication, as the bell continues to toll. And it is with this declaration of the camera that Hitchcock ends his film.

What vision impels Judy to plunge to her death? Who or what gives rise to this vision that Scottie does not, and perhaps cannot, share? And whose vision is it?

Surely, Judy thinks she sees a ghost. But whose ghost will not rest until Judy takes her own life? And why would any ghostly apparition have such power over her? Is it the ghost of the real Madeleine, Gavin Elster's wife, seeking to avenge her murder? The ghost of Carlotta Valdes, passing on her curse to Judy, calling upon her to take her life? Or is this Judy's own ghost, her vision of herself as already dead? (Here in Scottie's arms, Marian Keane suggests, the arms of the man she loves, Judy is forever condemned to be the ghost he loves.)

This ghostly apparition is "really" a nun. Perhaps Judy also sees this figure as exactly who she is, an agent of God's law and a representative of the world of women. In the nun's religion, Judy is a sinner who has not earned the happiness that seems within her grasp. But if Scottie can forgive Judy, why can't she forgive herself? Why should the nun's religion have such a hold over her? Or is it to the mad Carlotta Valdes's eyes that this vision is given? Is it Carlotta, possessing Judy, who sees the shadow of the feared Sister Theresa and jumps to her death?

Or is it the specter of Gavin Elster that Judy sees?

To this characteristically Hitchcockian thicket of ambiguities and paradoxes another complication must be added: the framing of this apparition is also a Hitchcockian declaration of the camera. In Judy's vision, the author also steps forward: *Hitchcock* is the ghost, *Hitchcock* the God whose law has been transgressed, *Hitchcock* the mother superior, *Hitchcock* the diabolical Elster.

In plunging to her death, Judy acknowledges the conditions of her existence, the conditions of any being condemned to the gaze of Hitchcock's camera. Scottie has banished his vertigo, shaken off his intimations of the truth that stares Judy in the face. Kissing Judy, he genuinely believes that happiness is within their grasp—and Judy loves him for his innocence. But Scottie has no access to Judy's vision, no idea of what haunts and ultimately claims her. *Vertigo*'s author is as diabolical, as murderous, as Gavin Elster and as much a victim, as much unacknowledged, as much a woman, as Judy.

Vertigo is not a melodrama of the unknown woman, although an unknown woman in precisely Cavell's sense—a woman who apprehends her condition more deeply than do the men in her world, who possesses a deeper vision, intelligence, and depth of feeling—plays an essential role in the film and in the Hitchcock thriller generally.

Judy's and Carlotta's stories are the very stuff of the unknown woman melodramas, yet they can seem to lack connection: why should Judy be haunted by Carlotta's tragedy? It helps to think of Judy's bond as being not only with Carlotta Valdes, the mother whose daughter was taken from her, but also with Carlotta's daughter, the little girl whose mother failed to keep her from becoming lost.[5] This provides a key to Judy's psychology—she keeps a photograph of herself with her mother, who, after her first husband's death, married a man her daughter didn't like, precipitating Judy's move to the big city in search of a man who would love her for herself, and her ensnarement by Elster. (Much critical attention has been given to the relationship of mothers and sons in Hitchcock's films but none to the tragedy that befalls women when the love between mother and daughter is thwarted, although this is a central theme in *The Birds* and *Marnie,* Hitchcock's last masterpieces, and is a thread that runs through the films that precede them. I am thinking, for example, of an extraordinarily suggestive line in *Stage Fright.* After her guilt is exposed, Charlotte [Marlene Dietrich] tries to tell the respectful Detective Mellish how it is with her, to evoke the feeling that gives rise to murder. "When you give all your love and get nothing but betrayal in return, it's as if your mother had slapped you in the face.")

At one level, it is the figure of Gavin Elster—the man who gets to Judy first and, with her participation, first changes her into Madeleine— that separates *Vertigo* from the unknown woman melodramas. Of course, Judy's past with Elster, which haunts her, is also her guilty secret.

The woman's guilt is another aspect of what separates *Vertigo* from Cavell's genre. If it weren't for Judy's guilty past with Elster, *Vertigo* would be very much like *Letter from an Unknown Woman* or *Random Harvest*: a melodrama about a woman in love with a man who fails to recognize her. Then nothing would keep the film from ending with the kiss on the tower.

But without Elster and Judy's attendant guilt, *Vertigo* would not be a Hitchcock thriller. Part of what this means is that the film would not call for the declarations of the camera through which, as we have seen Hitchcock claims his authorship. For in a sense it is the Gavin Elster in Hitchcock who declares himself in these signature gestures.

In genres Cavell studies, the camera is a machine that transfigures human subjects independently of human intentions. In the Hitchcock thriller, as *Psycho* explicitly declares, the camera is an instrument of taxidermy, not transfiguration: the camera does violence to its subjects, fixes them, and breathes back only the illusion of life into these ghosts. (The camera is an instrument of enlightenment as well as for Hitchcock, although its truths are also blinding.) It is this murderous camera, mysteriously attuned to the unknownness of women, that is the instrument of authorship in the Hitchcock thriller, the truest expression of who Hitchcock is.

Thus it is also the whole panoply of Hitchcockian signatures the curtain raisings, eclipses, white flashes, frames-within-frames, profile shots, symbolically charged objects, and so on that mark every Hitchcock sequence—that excludes *Vertigo,* or by which *Vertigo* excludes itself, from the melodrama of the unknown woman. For Hitchcock's signatures are expressions of his unwillingness or inability ever to forsake his mark, ever to absorb himself unconditionally in the destinies of his characters, ever to leave his own story untold.

Yet these gestures, as we have also seen, at the same time reveal Hitchcock's affinity, his *identification,* with the unknown woman desperately longing for existence. Hitchcock never gets beyond his own case, his own longing for acknowledgment. Hitchcock *is* the unknown woman, and this, too, separates *Vertigo* from Cavell's genre.

To be sure, as Cavell argues, *Letter from an Unknown Woman* metaphorically identifies itself with the letter that brings about the man's awakening, hence identifies its author with the unknown woman who wrote the letter. But *Letter* is such a dazzling spectacle that Ophuls's gesture of identifying himself with the woman who wrote the letter may well appear only rhetorical, only ironic, as if he had nothing on his mind but the creation of a perfect aesthetic object. (To be sure, Ophuls's ironic, distanced stance may itself be a mask for the unfathomable depth of his identification with—perhaps his indifference to—the unknown woman in the film.) By contrast, *Vertigo,* for all its irony, nakedly opens Hitchcock to be read.

Cavell, in his readings of melodramas of the unknown woman and remarriage comedies alike, aspires to put into his own words what these films say to their audience. Speaking in his own philosophical voice and out of his own experience of these films, he declares himself to be, despite everything, a representative member of that audience. The films' Emersonian aspiration of creating a more perfect human community, shared by their audience, is his as well. I find that reading a Hitchcock thriller, reading *Hitchcock,* with his ambiguous relationship to America, is a very different proposition. I find myself continually called on to make discoveries, to see things that viewers don't ordinarily see, or to see familiar things in an unfamiliar light, discovering unsuspected connections. The *Vertigo* that emerges, at least in fragments, in this essay is not the film as viewers ordinarily view it (although my reading is meant to account for the ordinary experience, which it interprets as the experience that fails to acknowledge Hitchcock and hence misses his meaning).

To read a Hitchcock film is to understand that Hitchcock is the most unknown as well as the most popular of filmmakers. His films are meditations on unknownness, emerging from and addressed to a condition of unknownness. In its tragedy, *Vertigo* envisions no transcendence, no ideal community or marriage or fulfilled human existence on earth; within every salvation there is a damnation; Hitchcock himself is damned, not saved. Hitchcock's films are also demonstrations that human beings *can* be known. Yet to receive Hitchcock's instruction, to know Hitchcock through his films, is to be condemned to unknownness, not to transcend it.

To investigate the relationship of a film such as *Vertigo* to the melodrama of the unknown woman and the remarriage comedy, it is necessary to articulate the central role played by the figure of the author in the Hitchcock thriller. Do films such as Hitchcock's that tell an author's story constitute a genre adjacent to those Cavell studies, or perhaps a constellation of genres (perhaps every authentic authorship discovers its own story)? Or are they inaccessible by the concept of genre, beyond its reach as a critical tool?

Notes

1. Although there are significant points at which they diverge, my understanding of *Vertigo* and Keane's exemplary essay are in such close sympathy that I will not attempt to note all the places where our readings are congruent. For

me, this sympathy is one of the richest rewards of the years we both spent at Harvard, with Stanley Cavell's unflagging support, aspiring to develop ways of teaching what is fundamental, and perhaps unteachable, about the art of film.

2. For an extended analysis of this sequence, see Rothman 1982, pp. 288–312.

3. See Rothman 1975 for a reading of *Notorious*.

4. For pointing out the strangeness of this passage, I am indebted to James Shapiro, whose doctoral dissertation on the role of the artist in the films of Hitchcock (among other matters) promises to be studded with such discoveries.

5. Charles Warren helped me to appreciate the significance of this point.

References

Cavell, Stanley. "What Becomes of Things on Film?" In *Themes out of School*. San Francisco: North Point Press, 1984.

Keane, Marian. "A Closer Look at Scopophilia: Mulvey, Hitchcock and Vertigo." In *A Hitchcock Reader*, edited by Leland Poague and Marshall Deutelbaum. Ames: Iowa State University Press, 1986.

Rothman, William. "Alfred Hitchcock's *Notorious*." *Georgia Review* 29 (Summer 1975):95–120.

———. *Hitchcock: The Murderous Gaze*. Cambridge, Mass.: Harvard University Press, 1982.

4   Witnessing and Bearing Witness:
      The Ontogeny of Encounter in the
      Films of Peter Weir

Robert Winer

During the opening credits of the film *Witness* the community declares itself as its members rise amid waves of grain, and we recognize them as Amish. The image is paradoxically accompanied by the Oriental music of wind chimes, and we are reminded of the gamelan orchestra that accompanied the Javanese silhouette puppets as they welcomed us to *The Year of Living Dangerously*. Some of us are drawn to the cinema this evening by precisely this prospect of witnessing the new Peter Weir film. While from the twenties to the sixties the public's response to English-language cinema was dominated by genre and star considerations, in the past two decades we have become more responsive to the auteur. Sectors of the film audience are eager to engage the specific concerns of the director.

I take Weir's five major feature films to elaborate a developmental sequence of modes of participation and encounter that correspond to critical tasks from early adolescence to mature adulthood. These are the years past childhood in which we progressively define our relation to the world beyond the family, mapping out the terms of our exchange with our society and culture. Over this period Weir demonstrates a crucial shift from witnessing to bearing witness. While the sequence of modes of encounter corresponds to specific developmental contexts, each mode, once established, remains available for future use. (This schema is analogous in this regard to Erik Erikson's epigenetic construction of psychosocial development [1959].)

That Weir's films fall into such a sequence may reflect progressive developments in his own psychology over that decade of his life. With more direct evidence, we can locate a developmental progression in his filmmaking by examining the films and his published comments about them.

John Book (Harrison Ford) dancing with Rachel Lapp (Kelly McGillis) in Peter Weir's *Witness* (1985).

Weir's growth as a filmmaker has paralleled and reflected the growth of the Australian film industry. After a period of brisk contribution to world silent cinema in the first two decades of the century, Australian cinema was forced into total eclipse by Hollywood's aggressive merchandising of its product overseas and by the overwhelming technical requirements of the "talkies." In 1970 Prime Minister John Gorton reestablished a national film industry by offering government support to independent film productions. Films were funded on their individual merits, an arts council was created, a film school was established, and by 1980 two hundred feature films had been produced. It was during this time of discovery and invention, driven by a spirit of adventure, community, and earnest naïveté, that Weir developed as a filmmaker. Without the apprenticeship the Hollywood studios offered young American directors, Weir and his colleagues had to work it out for themselves. The development of Weir's attitudes about filmmaking—both from the internal viewpoint of film construction and the external referent of film's role in culture—can be traced by examining his films. A pattern of approaches emerges that parallels the developmental sequence in the five films.

The proposed sequence of modes of encounter constitutes a paradigm that underlies not only human development and filmmaking but also film viewing. I will also suggest that this sequence has a bearing on our understanding of modes of film viewing. Filmmaking and film viewing, by their very nature, have a great deal to do with ideas about witnessing and bearing witness.

The relation between witnessing and bearing witness is the same as that between taking in and giving forth, between passive registration and active testifying, between the present moment (to be held for the future) and the recollected past (to be disclosed in the present), between discovery and revelation. While witnessing requires an openness to new experience, bearing witness calls for bringing forth acquired knowledge. To be a witness is to observe; to bear witness is to be evidence or give evidence, to stand as a sign or to give proof. Development requires both the capacity to witness and to bear witness, as do the making and viewing of film, and I will now trace the interplay of these activities through Weir's films.

Picnic at Hanging Rock tells the story of the disappearance, on St. Valentine's Day in 1900, of three girls and their mathematics teacher during a school outing to Hanging Rock, a volcanic formation on the slopes of Mount Macedon, which was sacred aboriginal ground. The last person to see them as they set off is a young Englishman, Michael, who is also picnicking at the rock with his aunt and uncle. Enchanted, he watches the hauntingly beautiful Miranda as she gracefully picks her way across a stream leading to the path up the rock. The police are notified when it is discovered that the four are missing, and they conduct a fruitless search. Michael, obsessed with his vision of Miranda, returns to the rock to look for her and also disappears. His coachman, Albert, finds him unconscious, clutching a fragment of a white lace dress in his hand. Albert also finds one of the girls, Irma, bruised and unconscious. When they recover, Michael and Irma are unable to explain what has happened; the tone is similar to the episode in E. M. Forster's *A Passage to India* in which a woman is overwhelmed by her experience in an Indian cave. The mystery is never solved. Parents withdraw their children from the school. An orphan classmate, Sara, who had lived to be in Miranda's shadow, is devastated both by that loss and by the news that her guardian's failure to pay her fees necessitates her dismissal, and she commits suicide. Michael's relationship with Albert deepens as Michael crosses class lines. During a private boat ride, Michael challenges Irma about the happenings on the rock; we do not know her response, but Michael subsequently decides to leave. The dour headmistress is destroyed by the collapse of her school and the loss of her teacher (a special attachment is implied) and dies under mysterious circumstances at the rock.

Picnic is about an outing at the edge between innocence and experience, where the starched white linens end, the earth begins, and romance encounters passion. During the carriage ride there, Irma, upon hearing of the rock's geological history, radiantly exclaims, "Waiting a million years, just for us!" and they seem worth the wait. We watch them climb; we are hypnotized as we watch Miranda slip out of her shoes and stockings, preparing to surrender herself to the ancient mysteries of the rock. Her last words are "Everything begins and ends at exactly the right time and place." The girls are the point of fascination for the audience; our point of view initially is Michael's. His experience—and theirs—is the encounter at the heart of early and middle adolescence: fascination with the material world as a projection of changing body and awakening desire, desire caught between idealization and carnality. Michael objects to Albert's explicitness, but meets the reply: "I say the crude things, you just think them." The girls' bonds of loyalty, the valentines exchanged and promised, serve to conceal the disruptive tensions of same-sex yearning and other-sex rivalry. The self-absorption of early and middle adolescence is an adaptive response that aids the mastering of somatic and drive developments. Thus this form of encounter, structured in accordance with narcissistic developmental needs, locates (and re-creates) the world as a projection of sexual tensions.

The film's structure follows this mode of encounter. Weir begins by enchanting us—first with the girls, later with the rock. This is Weir's most visually appealing film; the British Film Academy gave Russell Boyd its 1977 award for best photography. The girls' evocative charm is not happenstance. Weir screened five hundred teenagers from various areas of Australia before finding the particular pre-Raphaelite look he was searching for. This attention to appearance is consonant with the early adolescent preoccupation with perfection. As audience, we are drawn in by the idealization, the promise of dark secrets revealed, the answer to Freud's question: What does Miranda want? Awaiting the resolution of the disappearance, we reexperience our own adolescent tensions, in themselves reawakenings of even earlier passionate curiosities (What do my parents do?). Michael's amnesia echoes our repression.

At this point the film's structure takes a turn. The disappearance is not going to be explained. The second half of the movie explores the effects of the disappearance on the characters in the story, culminating in Sara's suicide, the headmistress's death, and Michael's coming of age. Weir felt that constructing a film of an unexplained disappearance was risky business, given the audience's conventional expectations. He must have felt personally caught between two opposing motives. On the one hand, filmmaking was storytelling for him—his father was a great bedtime storyteller—and storytelling requires narrative closure. Yet a story haunting him from childhood was about an ocean liner that was found completely deserted, but with food on the plates, the ship's cat sitting on a chair, a filled pipe on the table. He'd imagined that when he died and went to heaven he'd first ask God, "Whatever happened to those people on the *Marie Celeste?*" (Stratton 1980, 75). His opposing motive was to express the notion central to his experience (and filmmaking) that "the great black joke is that we agree on a certain reality that's to me plainly full of holes, with great gaps of reason" (McFarlane and Ryan 1981, 325). Thus he opens the film with Miranda quoting Edgar Allen Poe: "What we are and what we seem are but a dream, a dream within a dream." Weir distrusts appearances, analytic thinking (I can imagine his response to this essay), and solutions. He has said that he's usually disappointed by endings, and he keeps a cartoon on his office wall of an elderly lady at a ticket window saying "I want my sense of wonder back!" Reality is unstable for Weir, rationality seems an illusory and misleading crust, and his early films especially focus on the uncanny in the everyday (Hitchcock's genre). I will explore the consequences of this position further in my comments on *The Last Wave,* but for the moment I would like to suggest that Weir, in fact, mistrusts irrationality and needs to locate it projectively in the material world.

Weir has said that in the condition of ambiguity he finds danger and potential interlocked (Mathews 1984, 107). The potential for the protagonists and the audience is the opportunity to wrestle with a developmental challenge. Withholding answers, Weir offers us process. Michael's response is to reach across a social barrier, so that he can use Albert, with his lower class ways, as a point of entry for his own darker passions. Weir's instruction for us here is crucial, because it points to the escape from the narcissistic immersion. The necessity for projective recruitment of the world outside the family (the world within the family being too incestuously proximate now) propels the adolescent into involvement with society, culture, and the natural world; this experience transforms him. The encounter with Albert enables Michael to acknowledge his longings for Miranda and risk his life to search for her on the rock, to confront Irma and risk having his idealization shattered should he hear that Miranda is not what he would have had her be. The implication follows that he might now be free to face his own passions.

The opening up of these possibilities in adolescence requires relinquishing the certainty of earlier childhood where rules are rules and virtue is rewarded. Much is not right with the world: Albert and Sara are brother and sister, separated after the orphanage and unable to find each other except in a dream, and Michael's desperate, fruitless search for Miranda symbolizes their fate; Irma cannot reach Michael because he cannot let go of Miranda; Albert cannot imagine himself worthy of Irma's gratitude; the headmistress can neither deserve her ancestors' admiration nor reach out to the teacher she has taken to replace her husband, and in her lonely impotence bullies her assistant. It is as though Weir is holding out against an acceptance of the irrational nature of existence (Albert and Sara neither chose nor deserved to be orphans) by invoking a superordinate coherence in nature that is expressed in Miranda's notion that everything begins and ends at exactly the right time and place. This is a quintessential adolescent search for structures of meaning and unification that can compensate for the loss of a certain and just world.

The film contains a mystery within a mystery: it is uncertain whether the disappearance is a historical reality. The original book was written in 1967 by Joan Lindsay. It was her only novel, written in just ten days when she was in her sixties. Lindsay chose to keep the issue ambiguous, but Weir assumes that the events are real and that the characters lived. The movie, an enormous commercial success at home, provoked a flurry of journalistic research, which came up empty-handed. Finally, under substantial pressure, Lady Lindsay asked Weir whether she should reveal what had happened, and he advised her to let the secret go with her (Dempsey 1980, 9). While this ambiguity suited Weir for a number of reasons (including, presumably, the film's reception), it is consistent with the blurring of the distinction between inner and outer reality in adolescence, a consequence of the distortion created by the projective mode. It has been observed that white Australia is an ahistorical society, that the Aussie thinks himself British and knows British history better than his own. The protagonist's wife in *The Last Wave* comments that she is fourth-generation Australian (as is Weir) and has never met an aborigine. The aborigine seems to stand as a mystical or sexual symbol, not as a real person one might get to know, and that seems implied in *Picnic* as a meaning of the rock. It therefore occurs to me that the public's interest in the historical factuality of the film may be part of a larger wish to create a history: the explication here would be of the primordial encounter between the Briton and the aborigine, culture and nature, a revealed primal scene.

Weir remarked that the film wanders through the ruins of the British class system (McFarlane and Ryan 1981, 326). The particular ruins are Queen Victoria's, and the headmistress is her curator. If the Victorian sexual repression is taken to symbolize what the girls are struggling against, we must be witness to its toll on the headmistress, who seems most out of touch with herself, trying to manage her own inner tensions through her autocratic control of her school. Her participation through projective recruitment has reached the dead end of creating a claustrophobic closed society in which the illusion is maintained that the unconscious can be denied. Such a society, Weir tells us, becomes a ghost ship.

Participation by projection is the popular mode of cinema viewing. This is at the heart of cinema as escape: we escape to that which we wish to experience vicariously while denying our own intentions in the matter, or at least their consequences. In this context, we expect cinema to be faithful to our expectations, and film genres keep their promises (notwithstanding that at their best they deliver more than we asked of them). Weir eludes genre. *Picnic* begins as a Gothic horror film and then shifts gears, inviting us to follow at a different pace. The relation of film to dream as wish fulfillment is relevant here. (The broader relations of film and dream are discussed in this volume in Stanley Palombo's essay on *Vertigo*.) Some things are merely seen, while others are witnessed: we witness a spectacle, a catastrophe, a primal scene. Witnessing implies awe, a stance separate from the happening. When we apply the term "witnessing" to primal scene experience, we are attempting to emphasize the role of the child as a passive, victimized observer—to deny the possibility that the child's search for the primal scene expresses the need to find a projective screen for disturbing fantasies and nightmares. The child knows not one iota more after witnessing the event than before—the primal scene is still the child's projective creation, serving to concretize his fantasies. This does not exclude the possibility that the child gets more than he bargained for, creating a traumatic situation. These first exposures may be sufficient to drive the issues back into hiding for years to come. The opportunity to work them through awaits their resurgence in adolescence, with its possibilities for nonincestuous realization and sublimation. These structures are at work when we witness cinema in a projective mode.

Weir's next film, *The Last Wave,* begins in an outback township with hail falling from a cloudless sky, terrifying a group of schoolchildren, one of whom is bloodied by a smashed windowpane. In Sydney, David Burton is troubled by a recurring dream in which an aborigine appears, holding out a sacred stone to him. Although a corporation lawyer, he is asked to defend a group of aborigines accused of murdering another aborigine, Billy Corman. David recognizes one of the group, Chris Lee, as the person in his dreams and discovers that the members of the group are tribal aborigines, thought not to exist in urban areas. Billy had tried to steal tribal artifacts and was killed by death bone sorcery, practiced by Charlie, a tribal elder. Chris and Charlie reveal to David that they believe that his dreams are evidence that he is an instrumentality of a prehistoric race of spirits from South America that established an aboriginal tribe in prehistoric times in what is now Sydney, and that his dreams are the foreshadowing of an apocalypse. The film is awash with rain, constant storms, a downpour of frogs and of black oil; a bathtub overflows and pools down David's carpeted stairs, his car radio gushes water, the rains increase in savagery. At the trial, David tries to reveal the tribal meaning of the death, but Chris, after initially responding, refuses to cooperate for fear of betraying his tribe. They are convicted. David's stepfather tells him that as a child his dreams had foretold his mother's early death. Chris takes David into grottoes near Sydney's sewage tunnels where painted hieroglyphics tell the tribal history, leading to a huge tidal wave that will drown the earth, preparing for a cycle of renewal. Among the artifacts, David finds his own mask. Charlie appears and is apparently enraged by David's intrusion on the sacred space; David kills him in self-defense. Working his way back to the surface through the sewers, he arrives at a beach where he encounters or envisions an enormous wave.

The Last Wave is Weir's most personal and most difficult film. It is the one of these five films in which he was the principal author; he was dissatisfied with the script and called in two collaborators, and he still rewrote it during the shooting. After trying various endings he decided that he had painted himself into a corner. He commented recently that he hasn't been able to look at the film for years (Mathews 1984, 99). Together with his following project, *The Plumber,* a movie made for television, it concluded a cycle of five films that centered on uncanny, irrational experience.[1] *The Last Wave* is intellectually Weir's most ambitious film, but the ideas in it are not coherently worked through. Pauline Kael thought the film a victim of Weir's penchant for the Major Arcana.

Both in construction and content, the film evokes late adolescence, which is the psychological birthplace of the Major Arcana. The developmental tasks of this epoch are separation from the family, personality consolidation, and the achievement of ego continuity—the adolescent's construction of himself as a historical being with a past, present, and future. Developmental failure here is manifest as identity diffusion. The late adolescent's turning to the Great Questions (for which various Great Answers will be tried) reflects an attempt to master through intellectualization the anxiety generated by the psychological cutting loose from the family moorings. "What is the meaning of life?" is a defensive and adaptive turning outward to answer the internal question, "Who, after all, am I?" (since it is no longer sufficient to say "My parents' child"). This externalization brings the late adolescent into an engagement with his society and culture as a projective solution to the problem of separation, in a manner analogous to the engagement through projection of sexual tensions typical earlier in adolescence. The sexual aborigine of *Picnic* becomes the mystical aborigine in *The Last Wave,* and Weir explicitly links the two by beginning the latter film with a shot of the tribal elder painting hieroglyphic symbols on an overhanging rock.

It is only in late adolescence that it becomes possible to appreciate the painful meanings of mortality, and this spurs the search for historical continuities. This is one meaning, in the film, of the linking of white man and aborigine, although the linkage is not through a historical rendering that would bring the European to account for his relation to the aborigine, but through a mystical connection that leans toward denying mortality. These are personal issues for Weir. He has often told the story of walking in Tunisia in 1971 on a trip to the Roman ruins, having a premonition that he would find an artifact, and then discovering a carved child's head on the ground. It was considering how a very rational person—a lawyer, perhaps—might experience this discovery that gave him the idea for *The Last Wave.* He has made his own stone sarcophagus. When his grandfather died salesmen came around with brochures for various coffins, and he vowed that they'd never get him (Stratton 1980, 75). In the film he has an ambivalent relation to the idea that you cannot steal the tribal artifacts as a means of appropriating sacred powers—Billy dies, but David's entitlement and fate are ambiguous. Weir seems to be trying to define the limits of his wish to control his fate after death.

Weir has commented that the ideas in a film often come into play on the set. That was nowhere more true than with this film; it is both the strength of the film and part of the reason for its ultimate lack of artistic cohesion. A meeting years earlier with the aboriginal actor Gulpilil, who plays Chris Lee in the film, led Weir to thinking about different modes of perception. The tribal elder, Charlie, was played by Nandjiwara, who is actually an esteemed tribal elder on Groote Island. Weir courted Nandjiwara, was fascinated by his ideas and quite in awe of him, discussed his own Celtic mythology with him, and let Nandjiwara revise the dialogue. When each scene's shooting ended, the conversations continued (Mathews 1984, 97). Militant aborigines picketed the set, sending the film over budget. It seems that Weir was working through personal issues about the nature of existence in the act of making this film, in the mode of encounter described above, and in the process bringing himself into a deeper relation to his own origins and to aboriginal culture. Again, historical relatedness is a particular issue for Australians, and Weir says here that urban Sydney was built atop tribal caves with no awareness of their existence. When the aborigines find Billy Corman in a bar, the entertainers there are playing a spirited Irish jig. White Sydney considers the aborigine its sewage.

Thus far I have neglected the most immediate quality of this film: it is very spooky. Weir's strong suit is his capacity to dislocate time and space; dream and reality merge, evoking a sense of the uncanny. Viewers of this film hold vivid images from it for years, much as one might with *Gaslight* or *Vertigo*. It plays on ancient fears, the way a horror movie does, but without explicit violence. Weir has said that he's very easily frightened and doesn't know why, and these early films suggest something about an anxious childhood being reworked. Unlike horror films, *The Last Wave* is scarier for adults than children, because it represents the adult transformation of these anxieties. The protagonist in the film had dreams as a child that when he slept people came and stole his body, taking it for a long ride and returning it in the morning. This seems echoed in Weir's reaction to his grandfather's casket and his building of a sarcophagus. Themes of intrusion run through the film, and the viewers frequently observe private scenes through doorways or passages. A door they pass through in the sewer tunnels has a sign reading "Gas, Water & Manproof—To be kept closed at all times." We hear of a woman's throat being cut for overhearing tribal secrets; before that, David's daughter was sleepwalking.

The sense I mean to convey here is of childhood anxieties unmastered and alive in the filmmaker. The aborigine's idea of dreams is that they are real and prophetic, and this is also the child's idea, but both recognize the dreams as dreams. The adult, cut off from knowing his dreams, is possessed by them. Weir has said that he believes that his capacity for creativity requires maintaining a child's openness, that craft threatens to extinguish art, that intuition is the keystone of his approach. When David's daughters dress in costume they are magical; when the adults put on masks for a party they look foolish. The unresolved trauma of childhood is an organizing focus for the personality consolidation of late adolescence, which is reflected in, among other things, vocational choice. Becoming a maker of spooky films is a way of mastering childhood fears (as it was for Hitchcock); becoming a filmmaker may be a way of mastering anxieties about the primal scene (by projection). Growing up becomes clamping down only when the unresolved infantile conflict cannot be contained in an adaptive adult personality structure, and excessive repression, manifest as constriction, is the result. It is this outcome that Weir fears; this conflict motivates the making of this film. To the extent that the film fails, it does so because the late adolescent modality of filmmaking here leads to an overly intellectualized grandiose resolution.

Peter Blos (1977) has observed that resolution of the negative Oedipus complex is crucial for late adolescent identity formation. David challenges his stepfather: "Why didn't you tell me there were mysteries? . . . You stood in that church and explained them away!" The mystery is how one becomes one's own father, how one moves past identification to become oneself. Weir's turning the film over to Nandjiwara and then struggling to reclaim it seems an expression of this conflict. Weir said that the heart of the film is this idea, expressed by Nandjiwara: we are nothing but the law we learned from our forefathers, the law is more important than the man (Mathews 1984, 97). The resolution to the developmental crisis lies in transforming identifications and the creative outpouring consequent to their relinquishment into guiding principles for leading a life, transforming the Major Arcana into common wisdom. After discovering the shrine and committing parricide, David discovers that he cannot return though the manproof door he was led in by; he breaks down sobbing, now realizing that he must find his own way out. The law is not simply inherited, it is created anew as an abstraction that draws upon past precepts and their constructive elaboration. The child is a lawyer, interpreting received law; the adult becomes a legislator, proposing law, thus participating in the evolution of society and culture. The film viewer in this mode takes the film's ideas as a source for his own construction; he might even choose to take the film's point of view as material for an essay on psychoanalysis and the cinema.

The title of Weir's next feature film, *Gallipoli,* refers to a Turkish battlefield in the First World War where forces from Australia and New Zealand fought a diversionary battle allowing the British to land their troops elsewhere on the peninsula. The movie is told through the experience of two Western Australian boys, sprinters who first meet on a racetrack. Archy, a blond eighteen-year-old rancher's son, is the disciple of his uncle, Jack, who is honing him to run as fast as a leopard. Archy leaves home for the race, intending to enlist after it in a patriotic gesture, without his parents' knowledge and against his uncle's better judgment. Frank, a few years older, darker, less idealistic, and more engaging, parts ways with his railroad worker compatriots who are joining the infantry in the spirit of wanting to improve their lives. Archy wins the footrace and tries to enlist in the Light Horse, an elite cavalry, but is exposed as underage.

The two young men become mates, and Frank persuades Archy to join him in traveling to Perth, where Archy might try to enlist again. A detached railroad car leaves them stranded fifty miles from their destination. Foolhardy, they set out across the desert in a rite of passage and miraculously survive. Archy's efforts to shame Frank into enlisting fail, but the esteem in which Archy is held in the eyes of a family they spend the night with (especially the daughter's eyes) changes Frank's mind. He tells his father that he'll come back an officer and not be pushed around the rest of his bloody life. Frank helps Archy con his way around the age barrier, but Archy is less successful in teaching Frank to ride a horse, and Frank settles for the infantry, rejoining his old friends. To cheering crowds and martial bands, they ship off to Cairo for training. With indomitable spirit the boys mock their British superiors, haggle with merchants, listen to a VD lecture and take on a prostitute, crash an officers' ball, race to a pyramid and etch their names on its top, and learn a little warfare. Archy persuades his White Horse major to take Frank on. An elegiac boat crossing brings the film to Gallipoli. We are witness to the hopelessness of their situation, their shoddy equipment and inadequate preparation, their wretched position relative to the Turks, their growing despair. Feeling responsible for Frank's presence in the war, Archy turns over to him the safer position of being a runner. As a consequence of this situation, compounded by senior British arrogance and a technical error in timing, the assault on the fortified Turk trenches becomes a suicidal massacre, and the final freeze frame holds Archy, racing forward, arms flung out, meeting death.

The participatory mode in *Gallipoli* is located at the transition into adulthood, the coming of age. Whereas the previous two modes involved working out tensions about sexuality and separation intrapsychically and then recruiting the world projectively, the encounter here is giving oneself over to new experience in the spirit of beginning to fashion one's adult life. The film's mood is openness and enthusiasm, a sparky challenge to the deserts of Western Australia, Egypt, and Turkey, boys measuring themselves against the world in rites of passage. When Archy, challenging, reminds his uncle that he himself had been an adventurer as a youth, Jack replies, "I judged the risks and took my chances. War's different! It's just different!" After landing at Gallipoli the boys strip down and dive into the water. This otherworldly space of Weir's is shattered when a shell breaks through and tears a boy's arm. These scenes and the fateful ending are confirmation that the world is not just a recipient of their adventurous spirit—it has an existence of its own, bearing consequences beyond their prediction. Whereas in child-hood adversity is essentially traumatic, in adulthood, where choices are made, we discover the tragic.

Gallipoli represented a coming of age for Weir: he calls it his gradua-tion film (Mathews 1984, 69). In his earlier filmmaking he felt he'd been charging on and letting technique follow, then often being unable to account for his success or failure. At this point he felt an approach had come together, the essence of which was a working toward simplification and abstraction. Weir's capacity for making eerie films had been instinc-tive, but now he was capable of wittingly broadening his evocative range. In the scenes at Gallipoli he follows a less linear approach, allowing the juxtaposition of fragments to articulate dimensions of loss. This shift from a narrative to an implicative method is taken further in his next film, *The Year of Living Dangerously.* Weir is no longer in an adolescent mode, turning his film over to others; despite his misgivings about developing craft, he now acknowledges himself as an auteur. His choice of topic here is significant: in the mode of this developmental epoch, he takes on a real historical event and explores its meaning for Australians.

Weir argues that Gallipoli, for white Australia, was the birth of a nation (Fonda-Bonardi and Fonda-Bonardi 1982, 42). Participation in the war in 1915 was voluntary, and Australians went off as Britishers to help Mother England. In the battle of the Nek in August (depicted in the film's final scenes) they came to realize that they were going to be used, and out of this they developed a sense of themselves as an entity capable of being used. This forming entity became a sense of separate nationhood (analogous to the selfhood of this developmental epoch), achieved through an encounter in the world of nations. An establishment-sponsored referendum on conscription in 1916 met a re-sounding no vote. They were no longer an extension of Britain, but neither was their self-definition simply an anticolonial reaction. Gallipoli is an Australian national holiday, celebrated every year, a creation of history for this ahistorical country. But for all its importance, Gallipoli had not been celebrated in film, literature, or verse; it was not remem-bered when the question of participation in Vietnam heated up. Making this film was not an attempt to make a fair reckoning or documentary. Rather, Weir saw himself in the role of balladeer, contributing to the creation of an Australian mythology, specifically the myth of the frontier days. As a mode of filmmaking, this is a marked shift from using aboriginal myth as a projection of the unconscious; here Weir is self-consciously expanding his native culture.

A further resonance of this developmental theme is Weir's manner of entry into filmmaking. After a dismal year at a university, he spent a couple of years working in real estate, his father's field. When he had earned enough money, he followed the course typical for Australian young men and shipped off to Europe. During the voyage he got together with new chums and organized a satirical ship's review, using closed-circuit TV. When he returned in 1967, he took a job at a television station and made his first short film for the social club's Christmas show. Two years later he joined the Commonwealth Film Unit, then making only documentaries, and in 1970 (the year the cinema revived) he had his first serious shot at filmmaking. It was by leaving family aspirations behind and setting off for a new experience in an expanded world that he was able to discover his metier.

For Weir, as for the boys in *Gallipoli,* growth was linked with the experience of mateship. Every film of his centers on a closed society—the girls in *Picnic,* the aborigines in *The Last Wave,* the Western Australian youths in *Gallipoli,* the journalist community in *Year of Living Dangerously,* and both the Amish and the Philadelphia police in *Witness*—and elaborates the functions that society serves for its membership. (Perhaps living in an island nation makes one more interested in such an issue.) The mateship society in *Gallipoli* is the least restrictive, least ritualized of the group. It offers its members a relatedness, a form of support, and a basis for loyalty intermediate between family and more complete autonomy. Women are not present to complicate the mateship society, except as prostitutes to be shared in a communal rite of passage. Weir is proposing that the sublimated homosexual bond creates a ground particularly fertile for this transitional developmental phase. In mateship we find an affective reaching out that offers potentials not found in the relatively narcissistic object choices of adolescence. These young men care for each other, and that caring enables them to offer themselves to each other as identificatory models. Frank has decided that he's learned all there is to learn from his dad, but he is open to influence from Archy. It is through mateship, not through heterosexual conquest, that they can develop their affective (feminine) sides, and only in an affectively informed life can instrumental choices be wisely made. In Kipling's story of Mowgli, read by Uncle Jack to the children, it is only when Mowgli cries that he is recognized to be human; Bagheera tells him that tears are what men use.

Weir wishes to bring us to tears in this film. In *Gallipoli* he moves from witnessing to bearing witness, from viewing (naively) to testifying, honoring the original meaning of witness, now obsolete: knowledge, industry, wisdom. As conveyed by its Greek root, martyrdom is the ultimate form of borne witness. Bearing witness reflects both a commitment to oneself and loyalty to one's community (which gives one the authority to bear witness). Its antithesis is alienation. The spirit of this film is not that war is hell; it is a celebration of the spirit, of life to be lived, even in the face of death. The corresponding mode of film viewing is attending not to escape, but to be informed, expecting to encounter a facet of life previously unknown, prepared to witness a filmmaker willing to bear witness.

Indonesia's President Sukarno entitled 1965 "The Year of Living Dangerously" in his annual Independence Day speech. What he had in mind was ending dependence on the West, tricky business indeed since he had spent the past twenty years maintaining the peace precisely by a complex balancing of the military, the Moslems, the Communists, the West, and the poor. Peter Weir's film of that name takes that as a backdrop against which he views competing sensibilities of faith and morality.

Mel Gibson, who played Frank in *Gallipoli,* is now a few years older and not much wiser as Guy Hamilton, an Australian journalist on his first overseas assignment. In Jakarta he is quickly befriended by the goblinlike Billy Kwan, a dwarf cameraman of mixed Chinese and Australian parentage (played, as a male, by the diminutive actress Linda Hunt). Billy takes Guy into the Asian slums and challenges him with the words of Tolstoy and St. Luke: "What then must we do?" Guy demurs that journalists can't afford to get involved. Billy replies that you must do what you can about the misery in front of you, and we later learn that Billy has taken on the care of a young woman, Ibo, and her sickly infant. We also discover another persona of Billy's: the great Javanese wayang silhouette puppet master, who contemplates the meanings of his associates' lives through laboriously assembling dossiers of print and film. As he types he muses, "Here on the quiet page I am master, just as I'm master in the darkroom. . . . I shuffle like cards the lives I deal with, people who will become other people, people who will become old, become ghosts, betray their dreams." Billy is identified with Sukarno as the great balancer of forces and keeps on his wall a photograph of himself posed as Sukarno. Billy wants to find in Guy the "unmet friend" with whom he can form a partnership—"I can be your eyes." He has the power and contacts to arrange a meeting for Guy with the head of the Communist party, who reveals that he has worked out an agreement with Sukarno under which the peasants will be armed as a fifth force. This story gives Guy a reputation.

Billy brings Guy together with Jill Bryant, the assistant military attaché at the British Embassy. Although the same age as Guy, Jill seems wiser, more self-assured. While attracted to Guy, she is determined to keep at a safe distance since she will shortly be returning to London. Billy is enormously invested in promoting their relationship—it is the creation of a fairy tale for him, a bringing to life of the prince and princess of the wayang puppets. Other threads parallel the love story—the growing political unrest, with Communists rioting at the American Embassy, and the macho byplay of the international journalist community, its most exploitive manifestation being the conversion of the streets of Jakarta into a sybaritic funfair for the press.

The manic romance is interrupted when Jill decodes an embassy message revealing that a ship has left Shanghai bringing in arms for the Communists. About to depart herself, and fearing that the ensuing revolution will mean death for all Westerners, she decides to share the story with Guy. Guy violates her trust by choosing to pursue the story investigatively, even though she will surely be exposed as having leaked it. Billy is shattered by Guy's betrayal of Jill. Ibo's baby dies, hopelessly infected by the canal's pollution, and Billy's reaction is to be enraged with Sukarno. In a suicidal action, Billy hangs a banner, which reads "Sukarno—Feed Your People," out a hotel window in anticipation of the passage of Sukarno's caravan. He is discovered by police and pushed out the window to his death; the banner is removed, and Sukarno does not see it. There appears to be a Communist coup in the works, and Guy learns that he is on their death list. He decides to leave with Jill but first goes to the presidential palace. Defying the guards there, he is smashed on the face with a rifle, causing a detached retina. Invalided, he learns that the coup has failed, the right is back in power, and that he could thus stay and cover the story, but he chooses instead to join Jill on the plane, even at the price of loss of vision in his left eye.

The Year of Living Dangerously picks up the developmental progression at the juncture beyond leaving home, when the question becomes: What then must I be? This moves beyond the door opening of adolescence, in which *being* is first registered as a question at all. The issue now is the making of choices, of commitments to others, to a vocation, to a morality. The self is not formed in a leap of affirmation or commitment, Hollywood notwithstanding. It is constructed in the dialectic of bringing oneself, as now formed, to encounter the world and allowing the world to penetrate one's selfhood. The equipment that one brings to adulthood needs both testing and revision through experience. The rhythm must be between declaring oneself and listening (listening both to the response and to the surround). Development comes to a standstill when the present self must be maintained at all costs, or when the self is infinitely permeable to experience.

This developmental step, accordingly, is at the interface between witnessing and bearing witness, between listening and testifying. Weir found the role of journalist a natural vehicle for exploring these issues, since the journalist must operate at the edge between registering experience and taking a point of view. By telling the story from the vantage point of the reporters' community, he contributed to a new genre of films about the third world in which journalists are the protagonists (e.g., *Under Fire, The Killing Fields,* and *Salvador*—stories of Nicaragua, Cambodia, and El Salvador). The problem for the journalists in these films is, in part, their relation to the events they are covering. The genre's convention is their conversion to activism, spurred by immersion in the unbearable political realities of the country they are covering.

For Weir, however, the problems are more complex. Guy Hamilton has left the security of home (Australia) and finds himself adrift in Asia. The film explores both his struggles with his identity as a journalist and his conflicts over desire. Regarding the former, for Guy the crucial issue lies anterior to journalist ethics: it is whether he is to become a journalist at all. He arrives in Jakarta with only the vaguest notion of what it means to be a foreign correspondent (his first broadcast could be viewed as a parody of such scenes in the war films one presumes he grew up watching). He's late for his first press conference and he seems content, in a naive way, just to want to be in on the action. Billy Kwan's contribution is most fundamentally to teach Guy journalism, although Billy's motive is to create a social commitment. At the same time, Guy is falling head over heels for Jill Bryant, awash with desire but unable to pursue her effectively. The crisis comes when she tells him about the arms shipment. We sense that she is motivated by her wish to be able to care for someone, and Guy is incapable of accepting this offering. His decision to pursue the story is as much a flight from her as it is an attempt to realize his vocation. He then tries to reconcile the two by seeking independent confirmation of the story and wanders off into the hills with his Indonesian assistant, Kumar. Through a dream he recognizes that Kumar and his wife are members of the Indonesian Communist Party and that he has put himself in jeopardy by not realizing this earlier: conflicted desire had clouded his judgment.

The second crisis comes when he decides to go to the palace, having heard that the Communists' coup is succeeding. This action seems bizarre since he has already decided to flee the country on the afternoon

flight, knowing that he is on the Communists' death list. Acting provoc-
atively at the palace, he gets his head smashed by a guard's rifle butt.
While this could be understood as motivated by guilt over Billy's death
and guilt about leaving with Jill, it could also be taken as a conflicted
identification with Billy's ambition for him, that he become a journalist.
Weir understood Guy's decision to leave with Jill as expressing his desire
to rejoin his own personality: "He is like a man who has lost his shadow
towards the end; the only way he can ever continue to be a good journalist and a complete human being is to take that plane" (Mathews 1984,
106). For Weir, contrary to genre conventions, realizing a vocation might
require giving up an opportunity because, within the constraints of one's
own personality as one has come to know it, the opportunity is unrealizable. This is the nature of the encounter required in young adulthood.

The making of this film required a similar developmental step for
Weir—a broadening both of the scope of his concerns and of his technique. Weir has consistently maintained that both his scope and technique are defined and circumscribed by his ambition to be a storyteller.
When interviewers have commented on his addressing such issues as
Victorian sexuality in *Picnic* or racism in *Last Wave* or Empire exploitation in *Gallipoli*, he has insisted that his intent is only to find contexts
for narrative and that social meanings of the contexts are incidental.
Nonetheless, his feature films follow an oblique progression toward contemporary concerns. *Picnic* was about an event of no special importance
that may or may not have happened; although *The Last Wave* was about
a mythological event, it was set against a backdrop of real racial tensions;
Gallipoli moved on to concern with an actual chapter of history and an
outdated context; with *Year*, Weir turned to the contemporary problem
of third-world politics. Relinquishing the safety of confining his work to
Australian concerns, he moved onto the world's stage. (Therewith encountering in the audience Bernard Kalb, the Indonesian correspondent
for *The New York Times* in the late 1950s, who wrote a piece for the
Times's cinema section taking sharp issue with Weir's political account-
ing.)

What is most interesting in *Year* is not the narrative—in fact, the plot
construction is erratic—but the renderings of Jakarta. And these renderings are achieved through a broadening of Weir's technique. The need to
represent the world he was now encountering in all its complexity led
Weir to develop a nonlinear mode of expression in dynamic opposition to
the linear structure of narrative storytelling. This style characterized the
last section of *Gallipoli* and makes *Year* a richer film than his earlier
efforts. The integration of linear and nonlinear elements also represents a
synthesis of Western and Eastern modes of experience. Weir has charac-

terized Australia as a European fortress in Asia, and this film thus reflects his moving beyond those borders in bringing together Occident and Orient experientially.

Throughout the film we are simultaneously exposed to many Jakartas and Indonesias. We have the journalist community's Indonesia, a country to be exploited in the macho competition for front page linage, a way station to the big time—Vietnam, a land of exotic drinks and inexpensive girls available for journalists' consumption. We also have Billy Kwan's Indonesia, a many-layered structure itself—a mystical land in which the wayang puppet shadow drama expresses the play of forces, with the end to be found not in final conclusions but in the achieving of balance, this made manifest by Sukarno, the great puppet master (who is in turn a fantasy figure taken to represent projectively Billy's grandiosity, that being his way of managing his feelings of being profoundly incomplete). For Billy, Jakarta is both a fantasy land where he can create an illusion of omnipotent control, where he can imagine himself puppet master, and a land in which, so fortified, he can make a personal commitment to care for another. We see the political Indonesia, a formidable third-world nation, the country with the fifth largest population in the world, wooed by both the West and by the communists. We have the British Embassy's Indonesia, a land to be viewed as an obstreperous colonial outpost. And we have the Indonesians' Jakarta, a city of people who are proud and defeated, belligerent and passive, poor but not emaciated, filled with hatred for the white man, desperate and resigned, pandering and defiant—a city of carnal nakedness and threadbare nakedness.

The task in the filmmaking is to keep those elements in balance, through juxtaposition, montage, symbolization, and implication. Weir does a remarkable job of evoking those· representations through the sound track. As one writer expressed it, "noise itself is a constant murmur, fragmented and mysterious, bamboo creaks ominously, the night wind carries a snatch of laughter, the sound of weeping, a cry of alarm, the echo of a sigh" (Bennetts 1983, 23). Weir is using these devices to establish more than a mood—his interest in earlier films—he is evoking an experience of the actual world. (The mysterious hailstones that came from a cloudless sky and smashed the classroom windows in *Last Wave* are replaced here by stones that are thrown by children and which shatter windows at the Embassy while the guards look on helplessly, afraid to provoke more violent rioting.)

Weir is exploring in this stage of his filmmaking the relation of art to the affairs of man, and bears witness to this struggle in the shaping of the film. It seems no longer sufficient to make broad allegorical statements: preoccupation with one's allegories can leave one ill equipped to survive the world's traumas (this being Billy Kwan's fate when Ibo's child dies). Weir is less precious and self-protective here, less encapsulating of his art, more confident in his expression. In both the making and the content of the film he is able to explore the complex relationship of a developmental imperative (becoming an adult) to a social imperative (being accountable as a citizen of the world). These issues again appeared on the set. The movie was filmed in the Philippines—it was felt to be impossibly risky to film it in Indonesia. Nonetheless, by the fourth week the cast and crew were receiving death threats from Moslem extremist groups who feared the film was anti-Moslem. Out on a little barge on a canal one night, Weir heard the unmistakable sound of the cocking of an automatic weapon. Deciding he could not justify such a risk, Weir pulled up stakes and completed the film back in Australia, respecting limitations as Guy had. For Sukarno, the slogan "The Year of Living Dangerously" expressed an intent to go it alone; for Weir it speaks to his risk-taking movement toward a more mature autonomy.

Weir's next film, *Witness,* is structured around two genres, the crooked cop and the doomed romance. Its third organizing element is the familiar Weir motif of clash of cultures, here the inner city (Philadelphia) police and the Lancaster, Pennsylvania, Amish. The film opens with the Amish community gathering to bear witness to the passing of the husband of Rachel Lapp. Soon after, equipped with advice to be careful among the "English," Rachel sets off with her eight-year-old son, Samuel, to visit relatives in Baltimore. The Amish value humility, plainness, and pacifism; they live without electricity, thus without television. Waiting in a train station in Philadelphia, Samuel encounters this strange new world, and in the men's room he witnesses a violent murder of a plainclothes cop. John Book, the police captain assigned to the case, appropriates Samuel as his eyewitness and takes him into the Philadelphia underworld over Rachel's vigorous protest. At the police station, Samuel recognizes an honored narcotics detective in a posted newspaper photograph as the murderer. John notifies his superior, Schaeffer, that the murder was committed by two members of the force who had maneuvered a huge theft of confiscated narcotics. When John is subsequently attacked by the murderer, he realizes that Schaeffer was in on the theft. Wounded, Book gathers up Rachel and Samuel from his sister's house, where he had stashed them, and flees to Rachel's farm.

The Amish take Book in, to protect Samuel from discovery, and treat his gunshot wound with herbal medicine. Over the ensuing days John and Rachel negotiate a crosscultural relationship (she objects to his "whacking" people, he to her piety) and fall in love. John discovers that he has an Amish rival, Daniel; he learns the ways of the farm and participates in a barn raising (he's an experienced carpenter, better than Daniel); and his romance with Rachel offends her father-in-law, Eli, and the Amish community. Meanwhile, Schaeffer is having great difficulty tracking Book down among the Amish; when threats to Book's black sidekick fail, he is murdered. Book, upon discovering this, is moved to rage and finds a target in town bullies who are taunting his Amish friends. The event leads to his loss of anonymity, and Schaeffer and his two henchmen come to the farm to get him. In the climactic scene, aided by Samuel's and Eli's bravery, and by his own knowledge of the farm, Book takes on the enemy, asphyxiating one in a grain silo and shooting a second. Schaeffer captures Book by using Rachel as a hostage, but by this time Samuel has rung the farm bell, bringing the male Amish community on the run to the Lapp barn. Facing this unarmed multitude, Schaeffer yields. It had become clear to Rachel and John that their romance was impossible, given the opposition of their cultures. They had thus only been free to make love after John had committed himself to leaving. The film ends on a bittersweet note, Book driving away as Daniel strides toward the farm.

Developmental progression brings us here to mature adulthood. John Book and Rachel Lapp are fully formed adults, each living a life that integrates cultural values and personal values that they bear witness to in their daily lives. It is not their capacity to bear witness that is at issue; instead it is whether they can be open to new experience. In contrast to all Weir's earlier wide-eyed protagonists, we have no doubt about this couple's capacity for stubbornness. And so we come back, in adult life, to the need for listening. (This is the theme of interest in the remarriage comedies Stanley Cavell studied [1982].)

In relation to this issue, Weir explores in this film the relation of witnessing to learning, and he begins by describing each culture's attitudes toward the visible. The Amish give great weight to what is seen, in the belief that witnessing creates character. Thus, television and movies are forbidden, in part out of the conviction that viewing them will be corrupting. Eli, upset by Samuel's interest in Book's gun, challenges Samuel's idea that he would only kill a bad man: "You know these bad men by sight? You are able to look into their hearts and see this badness?" "I can see what they do," Samuel replies, remembering the killing, "I have seen it." "And having *seen,* you become one of them," Eli answers, "What you take into your hands, you take into your heart." This ominous view of knowledge is reflected in the Amish concern with the weight of appearance, from clothing to behavior. In the face of Rachel's growing infatuation with Book, Eli is worried that the community will take offense and shun her. When she argues that she hasn't been unfaithful, Eli replies, "It does not *look!*" Behind his scolding, he is afraid that he will lose her, for shunning requires that he exclude her from his life, but he cannot acknowledge that. Amish family and community life is regulated by the threat of shame, which speaks to the centrality of appearance.

In the dark city, it is taken for granted that appearances are misleading. As Samuel quickly learns, *Hasidim* only look like Amish, a bum is an undercover cop, and the police are murderers. Survival requires skepticism, not belief, and the tempo is to shoot first and ask questions later. The stairs of Book's sister's house are lined with needlepointed owls, but she is unmistakably savvy. Shame has little leverage in the city—the threat of retaliation is the guidepost. The dialectic in the couple, reflecting these contrasts, matches Book's irreverent irony against Rachel's sanctimonious earnestness. Both her mistrust and his cynicism as attitudes toward learning ultimately lead to dead ends, and the movement in the film is toward letting John and Rachel influence each other.

The learning that is possible, Weir tells us, requires more than passive viewing; witnessing must come through the heart. His protagonists in earlier films are typcially alienated or frozen (the most telling criticism of his work was that is was only cerebral) or, when impassioned, like Guy Hamilton, are out of control. While the quality of excessive control again troubles this film, especially when we're watching the Amish (and we feel a wave of relief when Book finally explodes against the town toughs), both Rachel and John have a capacity for passion not previously found in Weir's films, a passion realized through a relationship, and it is this capacity for passion that critically shapes their new experience. The steps in the process are worth detailing.

During the Philadelphia scenes they both demand respect from each other and earn it: she accepts his claim for an investigation and he honors the limits of her acceptance. Given the profound gender divisions in both societies, this accomplishment speaks to something remarkable in their natures. While his injury brings them closer together, as nurse-mother and victim-child, their adult romance begins when, after a trip to town, he returns his bullets to her care. He affectionately closes her hand on them and teases her that she shouldn't store them with the peaches she's preserving (she'd earlier stored them in the flour). He'd made a similar gesture earlier when he closed Samuel's hand; Samuel had been pointing at the picture of the narcotics officer who had committed the murder and thus had been endangering his own life. If the first gesture was protective, its echo is entrusting. He would, although recovering, accept her protection and her ways—he would put himself in her hands. This scene is followed by his acculturation to farm life, his declaration of love (jokingly offered as a line from a TV commercial:

"Honey, that's *great* coffee!"), and the appearance of Daniel. While Rachel fends Daniel off on the porch swing, John stares at them from down the path, looking for all the world like a bowlegged cowboy about to challenge his rival to draw. After a rapprochement at the carpentry bench, John and Rachel meet in the barn, where he gets his car working again; its radio comes on, and they dance to Sam Cooke's "What a Wonderful World (this could be)."

This "golden oldie" transports Book back twenty years to his adolescence. With all the authority of a seventeen-year-old he declares to Rachel, "This is great! This is the *best!*" The song, built on a classroom metaphor, begins, "Don't know much about history. Don't know much biology." As they start to dance, with John taking the lead, they move between giddy excitement and terror. The terror arises from their awareness that, unlike teenagers, they can't dissociate history from biology. This can't be just a casual sexual encounter for them: they are caught between their longing to take each other and their awareness that that taking would require radical relinquishment of culture and values. Eli catches them dancing and scolds Rachel, temporarily giving the conflict a renewed cast of adolescent transgression. Later in the evening, John encounters Rachel bathing half nude. He is now helpless; she, prideful and remote. The next morning he apologizes, "If we'd made love last night I'd *have* to stay. Or you'd have to leave." In fact, they are only able to make love near the end of the film, when it has been determined that he will be going.

Each has had to discover the disjunction of passion and commitment in the life thus far led: for John passion has been possible if commitment is denied, for Rachel commitment has been at the price of precluding passion. This disjunction has paralyzed development for each of them, and it is socially supported—this is what is allowed to men and women in their cultures. In *The Last Wave* Weir took the separation of biology and history as a given: Anglo Australia was represented as divorced from passion, which was located in the disowned aborigine, and consequently as sterile. In contrast, the protagonists in *Witness* move toward an informed and informing passion. Commitment returns passion from its dissociated biological existence and allows it to inform and create personal history. To return to our narrative: in witnessing Rachel's naked pride, John realizes that she is not a creature of his creation; in witnessing John's helplessness, Rachel is made aware of her responsibility for the encounter (her passionate capacity to arouse him). The witnessing here is not the child's passive viewing as traumatized victim (such as Samuel's viewing of the murder), but rather an active witnessing in which experience is sought for its transformative potential. In seeing her pride, through the eyes of his passion, John can discover that a woman he cares for has a will of her own. In seeing John's helplessness, while aroused in her passion, Rachel can now become aware of the force of her passion. This is important learning for each of them.

The film takes a further step in exploring the impact of cultural values on learning. The police society values the commitment of personal loyalty, the Amish value commitment to a suprapersonal ethical system. The internalization of each of these loyalties shapes the personality organization of the community members, and yet these loyalties must be both honored and transcended. Thus, both societies seem oppressive to us, and both offer the opportunity for a crucial encounter. Both protagonists wrestle with those issues with their mentors: Schaeffer was originally Book's partner and trainer, while Eli is Rachel's preceptor.

Loyalty is a sustaining value in the police community. In the face of corruption, there is both an implication that loyalty requires collusion and an argument that dirty cops "lost the meaning"; the demands of personal loyalty hold sway. Loyalty is confirmed through implicit homosexual bonding, and it is the perverse aspect of the bonding that threatens to make the loyalty perverse. In an extraordinary moment in the climactic scene, Schaeffer has Rachel hostage and is pointing his gun at Book, who is now unarmed. Despite having the upper hand, we hear him pleading with John, "You really fucked up now, you idiot!" John's crime in Schaeffer's eyes is his violation of their perverse bond. The problematic of male bonding has been a recurrent Weir theme. Here we have a clearer statement of its role in the cultural transmission of loyalty, and of the potential transformation of that loyalty in a heterosexual encounter. (The boys' fate at Gallipoli could be understood as resulting from the absence of such a transformation.) For John Book, generative love gives new dimensions to the loyalty first fostered in a same-sex culture, sparing him the fate of being an iconoclast vigilante.

Unrelenting commitment to fundamental values in the face of a hostile world is a core issue for the Amish. "Wherefore come out from among them and be ye separate," Eli quotes from the Bible. The irony, of course, is that the Amish abide no deviations. Arguing for pacifism, Eli tells Samuel, "There's never only one way." Rachel is faced with the problem of integrating conscience and communal commitment, and it is precisely the strength of her education that enables her to grapple with these issues. This also seems to be a broader issue for Weir—the relation of ends to means—in our nuclear age. I take the recurring presence of rain and water in his films as a reminder that the rain falls equally on all of us. (In the wake of a nuclear power plant disaster, we have been reminded that we all share one atmosphere.) The theme of holocaust haunts antipodal Australia (the traditional last refuge from fallout since *On the Beach*); *The Last Wave* is apocalyptic. Weir again touches this preoccupation with the grain storm that drowns one gunman in the silo. Our inability to regulate our violence threatens us with expanding catastrophes. Weir is suggesting that neither the cultural solution offered by the police nor that offered by the Amish is sufficient in itself: for the one, "whacking" is a sanctioned sadistic outlet, and for the other, "whacking" is turned back on the self. Their interpenetration offers the possibility of informed, committed passion.

John and Rachel find their way to an integration of passion and commitment through being open to novel experience in which internalized culture can be put to the test. Analogous issues are operative for Weir in the making of the film. Unlike all his earlier films, *Witness* was not Weir's project. Producer Edward Feldman selected Weir to direct the film because he believed that foreign directors could look at America in a fresh way. For Weir, Feldman was an "old-time show-biz man," action oriented. By contrast, in *Gallipoli* Weir had wanted to make a war film in which a single bullet was fired, and he had virtually succeeded. To work with Feldman meant both accepting collaboration in the shaping of the film and opening up his established style. The two struggled with the dramatic construction, at Weir's insistence leaving out a scene of a man being kicked to death by a mule, and including a feistier ending to satisfy Feldman. That Weir allowed his approach to the cinema to be challenged in this way contributed to the deepening passion in this film, a direction in which he had already been moving with *Year*. The scenes of Jill seducing Guy as he drove through the roadblock and John and Rachel's dancing in the barn are a dramatic shift from an approach in which a romance could be made with a single embrace. Earlier in the film, Rachel and Eli had brought John's (decidedly non-Amish) car into the barn to hide it, and in a haunting silhouette we see Rachel pulling the barn door closed. Finding the courage to risk taking Book in is mirrored by Weir's concessions to the melodramatic Hollywood style, in the service of opening up his filmmaking.

Witness has been Weir's most popular film, but at the same time it has disappointed some of his admirers, who find its concerns banal and fear that Weir is being ground into pablum by the Hollywood mill. Is it the fulfillment of his growth as a director to turn out a slick genre product, they ask? *Witness* fails to stimulate unconscious fantasy and conscious reflection for them, in the way that *Picnic, The Last Wave,* and *Year* did; this film doesn't stay with them the way the earlier films did. I have not argued here that *Witness* is a better artistic product than the preceding films, but I do make the claim that in specified ways it represents a maturation of technique. This brings us to the problematic area of the relationship between creativity and maturity, a psychoanalyst's nightmare. Is it possible that emotional maturity and artistic creativity are separate lines of development in the individual, lines that intersect at points but run independently, rather than the one being a function of the other? That might be a consoling thought for those moments when analysts worry about analyzing away creativity (and a humbling thought for those inclined to think the opposite).

Since Weir's oeuvre is still in creation, it is possible that future films will continue to elaborate the issues developed above. It is also possible that filmographies recapitulate ontogeny on a broad scale, making this essay only a specific illustration of a wider principle in film, and perhaps in the arts generally. I shall close with a brief further consideration of the relationship between witnessing and bearing witness. Filmmaker and psychoanalyst share the capacity to create projective vehicles (the film and the transference) through which they put themselves vividly in the center of another's experience. The viewer and the patient experience themselves at first as witnesses—something is being done in front of them or to them, they are watching a public or private spectacle. What is less clear to them is that their response is projective—this is so for any experiencing of a work of art, but more vibrantly so at the cinema—in that it calls upon aspects of their own past experience. No witnessing can be simply naive; every witnessing requires bearing witness. The patient's discovery that this is so is the heart of the analytic process. The viewer, however, is at liberty to resist this discovery, to treat the viewing as a passive escape. The good filmmaker knows that confrontation can occur without acknowledgment and is not discouraged. In claiming that he is making his films for the elderly lady who wants her sense of wonder back, Weir feigns being a conjurer. But the apparitions he creates touch us because they materialize the spectral concerns that haunt us. The ghosts we witness bear witness to the mysteries that confound our lives.

Note

1. The first two of the five films are *Homesdale,* not released in America, and *The Cars That Ate Paris,* released only in a radically reedited version here (without Weir's involvement) as *The Cars That Ate People. The Plumber* has not been in theater distribution but is available in videocassette, as are *Picnic* and *The Last Wave.*

References

Bennetts, Leslie. "East and West Meet Amid Mystery in Peter Weir's New Film." *New York Times* 16 December 1982, Sec. 2, pp. 23, 28.

Blos, Peter. "When and How Does Adolescence End?" In *Adolescent Psychiatry*, edited by Sherman Feinstein and Peter Giovacchini. Vol. 5. New York: Basic Books, 1977.

Cavell, Stanley. *Pursuits of Happiness: The Hollywood Comedy of Remarriage.* Cambridge, Mass.: Harvard University Press, 1981.

Dempsey, Michael. "Inexplicable Feelings: An Interview with Peter Weir." *Film Quarterly* 33 (1980):2–11.

Erikson, Erik H. "Identity and the Life Cycle." *Psychological Issues* 1 (1959), no. 1.

Fonda-Bonardi, Claudia, and Fonda-Bonardi, Peter. "The Birth of a Nation: An Interview with Peter Weir." *Cineaste* 11 (1982):41–42.

Mathews, Sue. *35mm Dreams: Conversations with Five Directors about the Australian Film Revival.* Australia: Penguin, 1984.

McFarlane, Brian, and Ryan, Tom. *Cinema Papers* 34 (1981):322–29.

Stratton, David. *The Last New Wave: The Australian Film Revival.* London: Angus & Robertson, 1980.

5   Stanley Cavell and the Plight of the Ordinary

Timothy Gould

This essay takes off from some of Stanley Cavell's conclusions about skepticism, film, and the ordinary. I consider first some selections from throughout the range of his reflections, each of which points to a central concern with the theme of passivity. I will then consider in more detail a crucial angle in Cavell's approach to Wittgenstein and conclude with a look at some scenes from Hitchcock's *Shadow of a Doubt*.

To understand Cavell's work one must sooner or later come to grips with the following discoveries, claims, and projects: (1) Cavell's discovery that skepticism can be understood philosophically as a particular denial of the human voice, a denial that is understood and undermined in the writing of Ludwig Wittgenstein and otherwise responded to in the work of Martin Heidegger; (2) Cavell's increasingly detailed picture of skepticism as something that can be studied in fictions that represent or dramatize an effort to deny the all but undeniable; (3) Cavell's characterization of the movies as providing us with what he calls a "moving image of skepticism," an image, I take it, that shows us—recurrently and poignantly—the insubstantial but nearly insuperable distances between our thoughts and the subjects and objects that they claim to be about; and, finally, (4) there is his recent claim that under certain circumstances, "the threat to the ordinary that philosophy names skepticism . . . show[s] up in fiction's favorite threats to forms of marriage, namely in forms of melodrama and tragedy."[1] In the lecture that opens this volume—and implicitly in the last chapter of *Pursuits of Happiness*—he unmasks this threat as a type of revenge.

Cavell's work, almost from the start, bears the markings of his conviction that these claims about skepticism and the ordinary are all about something that one might learn to think of as a single field for investiga-

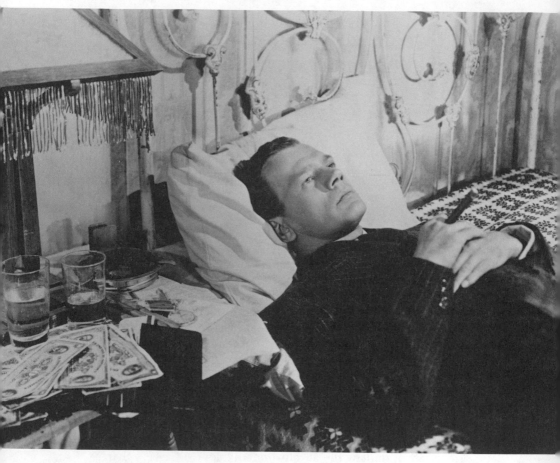

Uncle Charlie (Joseph Cotten) broods in Alfred Hitchcock's *Shadow of a Doubt* (1943).

tion. His confidence in the singleness of this field is not meant to deny that the investigations may themselves be irreducibly plural. The confidence points rather to his capacity for repeatedly taking his bearings and following the track of his thoughts. Thus, his faith in his writing predicts and even works to embody the divisions and the divisiveness that may be occasioned by his particular results. In what follows, I am supposing that Cavell's work not only constitutes such a single field of study but allows for and anticipates the possibility that other approaches to this field can be made. In particular, I am supposing that students of these subjects and objects can cross this territory on the way to their own studies.

I am not assuming, however, that there exists some recognizable spot among the disciplines of the humanities from which to monitor the connections among Cavell's questions or the single-mindedness of his progress. Still less do I assume that there is some obvious spot from which to ask whether these various things that he calls skepticism can usefully be taken to name a single threat to our existence (one, perhaps, with different aspects or one that may emanate from different regions). *Searching* for such a spot seems to me to be a worthwhile project, though not one to be completed in the space of an essay. From the side of professional philosophy, the question of the connectedness of Cavell's versions of skepticism is likely to be secondary to the question of whether his work (since, say, the 1960s) is really philosophy at all. Outside philosophy, there is perhaps a wider and more usable range of reactions to his preoccupation with skepticism, and I will not try to characterize this range in general terms. It still seems common, however, for those in the other humanistic disciplines to assume, for instance, that there must be some kind of answer (in the sense of "solution") to the skeptical question; or else that the question must be irrelevant to the practices of interpretation and criticism;[2] or else that the question should be given up for lost, or as outmoded, perhaps by developments in Continental thought.

Whatever the difficulties in locating Cavell's work in relation to traditional disciplines (and, perhaps, to some not-so-traditional disciplines such as film studies or women's studies), they are less formidable than the difficulties and the instabilities that lie *within* the topics and questions that he has brought to light. And nothing is more fundamental to Cavell's procedures than the idea that we cannot get under way with the questions of skepticism apart from an understanding of what keeps us from posing such questions—that is, apart from an understanding of just these difficulties and instabilities. High on the list of such obstacles is the question of whether the skeptical question is after all a good one, which means, in part, whether it is possible or sensible for a normal human being to ask it. (This worry was a theme of Descartes's and an obsession of Hume's, long before Wittgenstein and Cavell made it their own.) Here, as elsewhere in philosophy, unearthing the obstacles to thinking is not merely a preparation for philosophy but a piece of its distinctive business. This side of Cavell's procedures sounds to me like a significant echo of psychoanalytic practice, as if this were one of his ways of inheriting Wittgenstein's understanding of his methods as therapies (see *Philosophical Investigations,* no. 133). And at least since *The Claim of Reason,* Cavell has been explicitly characterizing some of the agencies that block philosophy from certain topics and certain methods as something like modes of resistance (and, more recently, like modes of repression). I am inclined to follow him in this, while recognizing that the relation between this use of the idea of resistance and the psychoanalytic use remains mostly unmapped, if not exactly unexplored.

The idea that there are resistances to philosophy and to thinking that are internal to philosophy will naturally be opposed by most professional philosophers. But I think the idea would also seem foreign to some opponents of professional philosophy—for instance, to Richard Rorty, for whom it appears that philosophy can have no resistances apart from the professional quirks and fashions and rebelliousness that the discipline displays at a given moment. The extent to which, in Rorty's work, the historical shape of a discipline is defined by the rebellion of a particular generation has not been much examined. The idea extends to his treatment of "Father Parmenides," and of "bad brothers" such as Derrida. This particular idea of philosophy as family romance, while intriguing, does not get out the questions about what the fantasy is in the service of. I think we would especially want to know something of the erotic attachments, as well as the more overt and politicized aggressions, that make for generational change (and sometimes, of course, for generational continuity) in various disciplines.[3] I will come back to this problem in my discussion of Wittgenstein.

The idea of resistances internal to philosophy is linked by Cavell to the possibility of isolating certain resistances in thinking about film. Beginning with *The World Viewed,* Cavell has taken these two regions of resistance as very closely linked, as generally illuminating each other, and sometimes as essentially identical (see 41, 165, 189, and passim, and *Pursuits of Happiness,* 41–42, 73–80). One important link between these regions can be made by investigating the various forms of passiveness that each region contains. Cavell has insisted on this link with increasing explicitness in recent years, and I want to dwell on it.

Cavell continues to abide by his early sense that what calls for thinking in the movies (and to some degree in all photography) is pretty much the same thing as what for most people seems to epitomize the thoughtlessness of moviegoing. It is, after all, not just intellectuals who are prepared to interpret, or redescribe, the condition of moviegoing as one that offers us entertainment or an escape. Sometimes more spectacular concepts are deployed, such as that of film as commodity, as fetish, as purveying something for the male gaze, as constituted by cinematic codes, or as itself constituting a language. In most of these cases, the condition of viewing in question is regarded as a kind of drawback, something to be apologized for, or overcome, or despised, or explained in some more or less elaborate theory. In Cavell's account, the idea of the condition of viewing as thoughtless, while not necessarily a false one, is understood as a sign of the intolerance of passivity, and the idea thus seems designed to prevent us from accurately appreciating the movies' power of seduction. The standing temptation, subjected to such seductiveness, is to convert our knowledge of it into disdain or into a theory about its power over others, from whose scope we are to some extent exempted. But this seductiveness cannot be understood in this way, or in any way that comes short of knowing its power over us. The need to bear up under this temptation in thinking about film makes this another region of knowledge and criticism whose home, in Cavell's terms, is in acknowledgment.

A related series of questions opens up when we ask what we are called upon to think about in this condition of viewing. The condition is already part of the "moving image" of skepticism with which the movies provide us:

> Not only is there a reasonable possibility, it is a fact that here our normal senses are satisfied of reality while reality does not exist—even alarmingly, *because* it does not exist, because viewing it is all it takes. Our vision is doubtless otherwise satisfiable than by the viewing of reality. But to deny, on skeptical grounds, just *this* satisfaction—to deny that it is ever reality which film projects and screens—is a farce of skepticism. . . . The basis of film's drama, or the latent anxiety in viewing its drama, lies in its persistent demonstration that we do not know what our conviction in reality turns upon. To yield here to the familiar wish to speak of film as providing in general an "illusion of reality" would serve to disguise this latent anxiety—as does the conclusion of philosophical skepticism itself.[1979b, 188–89]

Cavell also says that the condition of viewing offers us a mechanical explanation for our sense of hiddenness and unknownness and that it therefore offers the opportunity for looking out at the world, "feeling unseen." This last phrase means not only that we feel ourselves to be unseen and therefore in the condition of voyeurs but also, I take it, that we can, in viewing, allow our feelings and even the very capacity for feeling to remain unseen. This is one place, by the way, where we could begin to link film's treatment of skepticism to the idea of living your skepticism with respect to others (see *The Claim of Reason*, 451–78).

What we are called upon to think about in our condition as viewers must also take into account what we wish to see. In "The Acknowledgment of Silence," in *The World Viewed*, Cavell speculated on the power of the movies to affect the constellation of our memories, suggesting that it must have to do with the movies' power to make us small (1979b, 154). He was thinking of the "gigantism" of the movies' figures, and he mentions Hitchcock's *Saboteur* as one of the few movies that directs our attention to that fact. (A character gets chased across the stage in front of the screen at Radio City Music Hall.) But this thought of "gigantism" surely hints at other scenes of viewing, scenes from when we were small, or perhaps from times when we fear that we will become small, and when what we want to see involves the big people, the grown-ups. I find confirmation for my sense that ideas of the primal scene are already on Cavell's mind at this stage in the fact that his preceding paragraph addresses the question of the "casual, permanent seductions" of childhood (including prominently one of Rousseau's).

A further stage of his investigations explores our passivity as viewers in relation to the passivity of the subjects of photography, especially the photography that constitutes the "material basis" of the movies. That passivity, acting on us at a distance, is said to be at the same time what is mythically described by Nietzsche as the action of women (or, as Cavell modifies or moderates Nietzsche, as the action of the feminine side of human character). That passivity is also, Cavell claims, the principal condition that is studied in the movies.[4] The distance created by film's screening of its subjects, allowing them to act in their own absence, permits hiddenness and safety on our side. But it also gives us the chance to study and appreciate the visibility of others, to see what their exposed existence amounts to. These themes are taken to a still higher pitch in the Weigert lecture, where the sufferings and knowledge of women are placed at the origin of both movies and psychoanalysis.

Cavell's entanglements with psychoanalysis have become increasingly explicit over the years, and his work provides one of the few remaining sources of an instructive controversy about the relation of philosophy to psychoanalysis. Cavell wants to hold open the question of this relation, and he wants to demonstrate exactly how hard it is to keep this question open. For this he will get no thanks from professional philosophers, since the only open question for most of them in this regard remains the question of whether psychoanalysis is a science. That the knowledge it offers could be in competition with philosophical knowledge seems as likely as, for instance, the idea that Wordsworth's ode "Intimations" is a poem whose philosophical ambitions are worth taking seriously. For the reader who is already engaged in the issues of psychoanalysis, Cavell may leave more room for maneuvering. He is, after all, not the only critic nowadays who insists on the possibility that it is the work and not the critic that occupies in the first place the position of the therapist—for instance, in enacting a version of therapeutic silence. In regard to the movies, this implies that we are to resist the temptation to analyze directly the situation of the moviegoer, apart from analyzing the specific power of the movies that we are ourselves drawn to think about.

Here I cite one example of the kind of theorizing that, however fascinating in itself, would tend to stall our critical powers:

> All vision, all spectacle is, in the unconscious, the primal scene, that is to say the relationships of the parents between themselves. . . . When one regards a film, one is in the dark, one has the screen in front of one, one is in the screen and the screen is in one. *This total lack of barrier,* this very great pregnancy of the image, makes the cinematographic spectacle, *whatever the contents of the film,* something lived at a certain level as a way not only of being at the primal scene but of participating there, of being inside. One could well think there of the voyeuristic impulse, so active among psychoanalysts, as rendering them peculiarly sensitive to the art of cinema [my emphasis].[5]

This version of the sometimes overwhelming immediacy of the movies' presence has nothing to say about the nature of the distance that the screen puts between us and the primal scene and the nature of the fictions that this distance enables us to crave and to be satisfied by. I would add, somewhat tentatively, that the fantasy of participating in the primal scene seems to me to be a manic fantasy, which is more likely to be a defense against voyeurism—or a denial of it—than an explanation of it.[6]

Turning now to the question of passiveness in philosophy, I note that Cavell has for some time relied on the idea of receptiveness as the mark of a certain kind of thinking (1981b, 132; 1981a, 185). This receptiveness is the other side, one might almost say the better half, of the ways that a human being thinks in response to a sense of victimization, which is to say, resentfully, reactively. This line of thought descends most famously, I suppose, from Zarathustra's idea that the spirit of revenge is the source and content of the human being's best reflections. (See Zarathustra's discourse "On Redemption" and also the first essay of *On the Genealogy of Morals.*) Nietzsche sees this spirit as animating our existence and consequently our philosophers. He interprets one of the central starting points of modern philosophy, the idea of the will as the faculty of human activity (in opposition to the faculties of knowledge), as mostly a guise of human passivity.[7] Heidegger picks this theme out in *What Is Called Thinking?* but rejects the idea that this passivity has anything to do with the current understanding of the "psychological," much less with what psychoanalysis might say on the subject. Heidegger quietly takes issue with Nietzsche (or with a certain idea of Nietzsche's) by suggesting that a truer sense of passivity in thinking must give over certain ideas of active originality in favor of a certain kind of listening.[8] Perhaps not surprisingly, Heidegger is often interpreted as simply rejecting metaphysics as, for instance, in error or as repressive and as pursuing an incomprehensible singularity. Analytic philosophers, on the other hand, are still inclined to think that he embraces metaphysics as a cover for his meaningless singularity.

Cavell's handling of these themes owes at least as much to Emerson as to Nietzsche and Heidegger, and it also owes something to the experience of the movies and of writing about the movies. A number of paths meet at this juncture. There is, of course, Emerson's attention to the dangers of reading and of influence, as in a central thought of "Self-Reliance" that "genius is always sufficiently the enemy of genius by over-influence." At the same time, Emerson tells us that the right reading, "sternly subordinated," may also be a requirement of thinking, and Cavell has gone as far as to take the capacity for discipleship to be a part of the philosophical mind in the twentieth century. A sense of discipleship is, for instance, one way in which the will to the systematic, and hence a capacity for a certain discipline, can work itself out after the collapse of philosophical system building.[9] These topics have yielded much insight in relation to questions of literary or poetic priority, but I think they have been less explored in relation to questions about the continuities and discontinuities of thinking.

Cavell follows Emerson in addressing other passivities that are related to, but not exhausted by, the passivities of influence. Chief among these is willingness for a certain subjection to one's thoughts. In a passage that follows the one in which he calls our thinking a "pious reception," Emerson has this to say:

> Our truth of thought is therefore vitiated as much by too violent direction given by our will, as by too great negligence. . . . We only open our senses, clear away as we can all obstruction, and suffer the intellect to see. We have little control over our thoughts. We are the prisoners of ideas. They catch us up for moments into their heaven and so fully engage us that we take no thought for the morrow, gaze like children, without an effort to

make them our own. By and by, we fall out of that rapture . . . and repeat
as truly as we can what we have beheld. ["Intellect," in *Essays,* first series]

The inclination to thinking must include the willingness to be lost in
thought, given over to the need or the inclination for thinking. It seems
to me that many readers have underestimated Emerson's appreciation of
what it takes to "clear away . . . obstruction," as they may have overesti-
mated the palatability or genteelness of the ecstasies in question. In any
case, the idea of imprisonment shows another possibility for the sense of
victimization. Emerson expands on this idea in "The Poet": "The inac-
cessibleness of every thought but that we are in, is wonderful. . . . Every
thought is also a prison; every heaven is also a prison. Therefore we love
the poet, the inventor, who in any form, whether in an ode or in an
action or in looks and behavior has yielded us a new thought. He unlocks
our chains and admits us to a new scene." This theme of being delivered
over to your own thought is thus related to the need for other sources of
thought and the consequent danger of those independent sources.

One problem about passivity in these forms of thought is that we do
not know whether finding ourselves lost in thought is something that we
do or something that happens to us. Cavell points from here toward
related problems in other areas (or in what we may at first take to be
other areas): is "working through" a resistance something one does or
something one allows to happen? Is letting the work teach you how to
read it something you do with the work or something that you allow the
work to do with you?[10] Working through these interchanges of active and
passive, of reading and being read, of speaking and being spoken for, is
not a preliminary to the work of thinking and therapy. It is often enough
the substance and the form of the work. On such interchanges our
thinking will turn, if it is to turn at all.

A final place where I locate the theme of passivity in thinking is in the
first (and title) essay of *Must We Mean What We Say?* Its opening
sentence goes like this: "That what we ordinarily say and mean may have
a direct and deep control over what we can philosophically say and mean
is an idea which many philosophers find oppressive." At the end of the
paragraph an early diagnosis of a (philosophical) resistance makes its
appearance: "Eventually, we will have to look at the sense of oppression
itself: such feelings can come from a truth about ourselves which we are
holding off" (1–2). And at the end of the essay, he comes back to the
sense of confinement and the antithetical (Pascalian) wish for the ability
to sit quietly in a room:

Philosophy, they will feel, was not always in such straits; and it will be
difficult for them to believe that the world and the mind have so terribly

altered that philosophy must relinquish old excitements to science and poetry. There, it may be claimed, new uses are still invented by profession. . . . No wonder the philosopher will gape at such band wagons. But he must sit still. [41–42]

Cavell does not say much more about what motivates the philosopher's reluctance to tolerate the ordinary, nor about how such motivation is related to human motives in more ordinary frames of mind. Nor does he speak directly of a wish to repudiate the world that has so terribly altered or—even more to the point—of a wish to repudiate a world that bears the features of our own alteration. But much of his later work investigates the forms and consequences of such wishes.

I want now to examine in some detail Cavell's account of Wittgenstein as providing the means for undoing philosophy's efforts to repudiate the world of the ordinary. I will then consider Hitchcock's depiction of what I think of as a parallel effort of repudiation. I take up Cavell's study of Wittgenstein first, in part because I think that most readers outside professional philosophy will find it hard to believe that Wittgenstein's work is resisted by professionals as much as Cavell's treatment suggests. Still harder to take, perhaps, is Cavell's idea that interpreting the resistances of professional philosophers has something to tell us about the tasks of interpreting the mind and its more interesting efforts to embody itself.[11]

I will not provide much evidence that Wittgenstein is resisted by professional philosophy. One piece of evidence that I would insist on is the prevalence of the idea that Wittgenstein is primarily concerned with defending common sense or something like the common beliefs of the plain man. This might even be thought of as the principal mechanism of professional resistance to Wittgenstein. But it is admittedly a good deal harder to say what the appeals to ordinary speech are designed to accomplish. In any case, Cavell is certainly not alone in his sense that, for all the private changes wrought by Wittgenstein's later writing in the works and lives of individual readers, this writing has not yet had an appropriate public effect on the English-speaking philosophical culture.[12] At certain moments, it is hard for a reader of Wittgenstein not to sense this, however hard it is to articulate that sense. To think this is not necessarily to think, for instance, that hundreds and hundreds of philosophers have failed to appreciate some special doctrine or the intricacy of a particular thesis or investigation that Wittgenstein is supposed to have advanced. It is rather a collective failure to see the point or the importance of an aspect of the enterprise as a whole.

A next step in the direction that I am exploring would be to consider the possibility that the partialness of Wittgenstein's reception is not a case of accidental ignorance or of a simple if massive bout of misreading. From here, we may consider the possibility that there is something in Wittgenstein's writing that naturally and, so to speak, actively resists the efforts of the profession to understand it because, in the first place, it resists professionalization. That is, it resists comprehension or accommodation within the relatively stable, precise, and—perhaps above all—*teachable* procedures or paradigms that philosophers are trained to follow. This idea—which is already at work in the foreword to *The Claim of Reason*—casts the resistance between Wittgenstein and the profession as, to some extent, something he wished to provoke.

If the resistance between Wittgenstein and the profession is mutual and if, on the other hand, those who are not professionals are unlikely to find themselves addressed in *Philosophical Investigations,* the situation Wittgenstein helped create seems very close to comic or tragic. The situation might be more intimately instructive if the professionalization of philosophy is recognized as a viable, if by now somewhat stunted, embodiment of a genuine impulse to philosophy. This recognition is what I take Cavell to have dramatized in *The Claim of Reason,* at a level of detail that can still seem daunting. His way of locating Wittgenstein's efforts to refuse professionalization is not readily separable from his account of the main burden of the *Investigations.* I take Cavell's diagnosis of professional resistance to Wittgenstein to be for the most part latent in his analysis of the skeptic. It is therefore worth noting that skepticism, in Cavell's account, is itself a phenomenon that cannot be reduced to the adventures or misadventures of a particular profession. (This is another main point of Rorty's disagreement with Cavell.) The skeptic is a possibility of philosophy, of any mind trying to reflect on itself and on the extent of its relations to others. I will there leave open—as Cavell's book leaves open—the question of how far a particular diagnosis applies to the contemporary professional scene.

Following Cavell's account, I want to pick up his idea that Wittgenstein's accomplishment is in part defined by his discovery of ways of writing philosophy that are fully, if no more than intermittently, attentive to the human voice. (See especially *The Claim of Reason,* 5, 27–28.) These ways of writing are understood as recoveries of the voice at once from philosophy—that is, from the philosophical efforts to deny or to shun the voice—and also *for* philosophy, or for what is now left of it to us. Cavell's way of thinking of Wittgenstein's attention to the voice, and to our agreement in the language of what we ordinarily say, interprets this agreement as what he calls our attunement in speech. This thought indicates the path Cavell takes toward his interpretation of skepticism—in particular, of skepticism as the will to forego this attunement. Before we take a further step along this path, I want to consider briefly one of the moments in which Wittgenstein himself gives an account of his procedures.

The point of achieving in writing a relationship to ordinary speech is to remind us of what Wittgenstein calls "the *kind* of statement we make about phenomena." (The word *phenomena* is in this case a misleading translation of *Erscheinungen*. This might better be translated as "appearances," but that word inevitably produces difficulties.) These reminders are designed to achieve, or achieve again, an understanding of the "'possibilities' of phenomena." These procedures and the understanding at which they aim constitute a good reason why his investigation is a grammatical investigation or why he thinks to call it that. I suppose it is obvious enough that what we ordinarily call "grammar" also has to do with "kinds" of statements (e.g., assertion or question or imperative or exclamation) and the possibilities that such classifications may help to clarify (e.g., asserting or questioning or demanding or exclaiming). But then it is not quite right to think of "grammatical" as being used by Wittgenstein in a straightforwardly "technical" sense, any more than it is right to think of "criterion" as belonging to a technical vocabulary that Wittgenstein perversely refused to acknowledge. (This point is enforced in the first chapter of *The Claim of Reason*. A possible contrast to the term "criterion" is with, for instance, the phrase "secondary sense," which is used in part 2 of the *Investigations* [216].) Some pieces of Wittgensteinian grammar are very close to being ordinary pieces of grammar—as some of what he calls criteria are close to ordinary criteria—and it would take an investigation of considerable scope to arrive at the differences and hence to appreciate the similarities.

Undertaking a grammatical investigation depends on being able to recall or bring to mind what we ordinarily say in order to bring to mind what we already know about (the possibilities of) things. But in Wittgenstein, as opposed to some other philosophers of "ordinary language," the achievement of the ordinary is more than a methodological requirement, or perhaps it would be better to say that its methodological potential is seen in another light. I suggest that one route to Cavell's reading of Wittgenstein lies in appreciating the connection between the idea (in section 116) of the ordinary language game as the home (or even "homeland": Wittgenstein talks of the word's *Heimat*) and the much later remarks that "every sign by itself seems dead" and "in use, [the sign] is alive" (sec. 432). Here we can look to the ordinary as the home not just of the words but of the possibilities of the phenomena (the things and events) that come to light in the recollection of those words and their occasions. Here I want to describe Cavell's account of Wittgenstein (and especially his undermining of the skeptic) as inspired by a knowledge of the life of our language.

A couple of warnings or qualifications must be made here. It does not follow from the suggestion that we cannot know of the life of our language apart from knowing its home in the ordinary, that we can know, for instance, that all extraordinary uses of words are dead. What we know, what we must know, is that they no longer have what Wittgenstein calls their "original home." Their home is to be discovered, and so far they remain homeless.[13] On the other hand, words can be described and experienced as going dead, and if they could not, it would make no sense to speak of the knowledge of the life of words (or of signs, or of other physiognomies). How is this supposed to happen? How can it be overcome, especially by so methodical an activity as "assembling reminders for a particular purpose"? In Cavell's account, the need for these reminders expresses the knowledge that our words, in reflection—in philosophizing—have indeed gone intermittently dead. In getting what Wittgenstein calls "away" (from our ordinary grasp, into metaphysics), they achieve a kind of emptiness that might measure their deadness to us. On this reading, bringing words back to the ordinary is like bringing them back to life, back to where we may become alive to them.

Now we are in a somewhat better position to see the role of skepticism in Cavell's account of Wittgenstein. For Cavell casts skepticism as the willingness to embody in words—most often, I suppose, in writing—a kind of will to emptiness in our common speech. In terms specifically devoted to Wittgenstein, this is diagnosed as a will or willingness to forego the attunement in speech, the agreement in what we ordinarily say. Whichever way you turn, this willingness contains a repudiation of the naturalness of speech (for instance, in theories of the conventionality of language) and of our presentness to the ordinary world in which that speech is at home. It is at the center of Cavell's vision that the willingness to repudiate the ordinary world is at once the most common and the most intellectual (or intellectualized) form of the wish to repudiate the world as such.

The first consequence of Cavell's account is that skepticism can be understood as a kind of failure of voice, though it is a failure that is likely to understand itself as a kind of success or at least as the beginning of intellectual progress. Some take it to be the discovery of a certain kind of problem about knowledge, others take it to be a useful course of study for advancing a certain technical precision about the problems of knowledge, and still others take it to be a model of intellectual conscientiousness. (These options are, of course, not exclusive). More recently, versions of skepticism have become imbedded in depictions of the world as constituted by the unending—but nevertheless sporadic and unaccountable—play of interpretation.

To characterize Wittgenstein's work as containing recoveries of voice from the philosophical denials of it will seem to some to be characterizing his accomplishment as literary. In light of my remarks about the knowledge of the life of our words, and about the possibilities of homelessness, I would not exactly deny this characterization. (And characterizing it as "literary" serves to emphasize that the idea of voice in question here can, and sometimes must, be understood as a function of writing and therefore not as fundamentally in opposition to writing.) One trouble with this idea is that there are now those for whom such a thought seems to be a commonplace, if perhaps a desirable commonplace, as well as those for whom the thought seems (merely) outlandish and obviously irresponsible. But Cavell's interpretation is to be distinguished from various current ideas of philosophy as a genre or species of literature. Sorting out these various ideas would require coming to terms with the fact that there are differing and indeed conflicting ways in which philosophy can be understood as a "set of texts"—to use Cavell's initial formulation—rather than as a "set of *given* problems" (1979a, 4–5, Cavell's emphasis). This in turn will require understanding something more of what Cavell means by "given" in this formulation and also what he means by implying that the profession of philosophy possesses a genuine, though self-encapsulating, alternative way of proceeding, exactly in its confidence that the set of philosophical problems *is* given and hence fixed.

This sense of an alternative to the idea of philosophy as a set of texts, an alternative that is usable and instructive and always, each day, to be overcome from within, has everything to do with the various kinds of subjection to the conditions of thinking that I mentioned in the first part of this essay. I am trying to characterize Cavell's sense that the traditions of thinking in the West harbor a vision of discipline, in addition to what we might describe as various disciplinary fantasies. The possibility of discerning in the thought of the past the right discipline, the right "subordination" (to use Emerson's word), and even the right dejection, signals a point at which Cavell's writing begins to move away from Wittgenstein's preoccupation with fragments of a handful of writers (including his own fragments). It is territory more familiarly associated with Heidegger, and it may be that there is room here for accommodation between Cavell and, for instance, Derrida. Only from an understanding of such subordination to what seems like the past (or the pastness) of philosophy can one come to appreciate what I might call the truly insubordinate. (From the perspective of Rorty, all three of them keep going back to texts that must sometimes seem about as promising as the burial grounds of tribes whose superstitions are now at best merely picturesque.)

However we may sort these issues out, we will need to understand the way in which Cavell casts philosophy not in the first place as the production or the dissemination of a text or as a genre or canon of writing but as a kind of reading. (It is reading, as Emerson says, that is the "best type of the influence of the past.") And whatever we find to be anarchic or playful or dismantled in a philosophical reading must, for Cavell, take its measure from the ways in which reading is at the same time the principal mode of acceptance of "an endless responsibility for one's own discourse, for not resting with words you do not happily mean" (1983, 35). Such a responsibility, with its requirement of an autonomous responsiveness to itself—to the internal conditions of its own communicability—can seem to professionals to be more irresponsible than the most continental playfulness. My impression is that this side of Cavell's work strikes others as unduly solemn and devoted to a kind of authority that the humanities should rather seek to be rid of.

A second consequence of Cavell's interpretation bears closely on the issue of the limits of philosophy and, perhaps especially, the limits of what counts as a topic or issue of philosophy. The point of achieving voice, as I said above, has as much to do with recovering the life of the language as it has to do with dismantling the traditional concepts and problems of philosophy. Cavell's interpretation of Wittgenstein makes explicit and to my mind inescapable something that other readers have sensed obscurely or reluctantly, namely, that we do now know in advance what philosophical nonsense, or theory, will look like or sound like. We must seek it in the knowledge that anyone might come to possess (or, more probably, come to deny) that his or her use of a word or a figure or a tone has become empty. There is no longer a special place or disciplinary structure to house the particular knowledge that might result from what philosophers call the analysis of our concepts. This is a further stretch of the still-unmeasured distance between Wittgenstein and his Anglo-American inheritors in the profession. It is all too easy for them to assume two things. First, we *do* know, and essentially in advance of our investigations, at least the rough location of the nonsense that it is philosophy's job to criticize, in particular that it will be located somewhere around the traditional problems of philosophy or their modern equivalents. And second, Wittgenstein's practices (the appeal to the everyday uses, the achievement of a perspicuous representation, the knowledge of grammar) are, or ought to be, reducible to some more or less recognizable form of the analysis of our concepts. From this point, it is only a single step to the idea that, as P. F. Strawson confidently put it in *The Bounds of Sense,* "philosophical reflection" just is *equivalent* to "the stage of conceptual self-consciousness" (1966, 44). Whatever else this idea represents, it is a remark that is, I believe, intimately unresponsive to the methods and aspirations of Wittgenstein's philosophizing. It would be truer to the spirit of this work to describe Wittgenstein as seeking what Cavell has called the "de-sophisticated" and what I might characterize as a recovery of an unself-consciousness in our daily use of words.[14]

In turning to Alfred Hitchcock's *Shadow of a Doubt*, I want to consider in its light some further questions about the ordinary and the repudiation of the ordinary. First of all, it seems clear to me that a full-scale reading of this movie would include some comparison to what Cavell has called the comedy of remarriage and what he has more recently begun to excavate as the genre of the unknown woman. Such a reading is beyond the scope of this paper, but it is worth bearing in mind these remarks from the Weigert lecture.

> The idea in *Pursuits of Happiness* that marriage, through the concepts of repetition and devotion, invokes the ordinary or everyday amounts to the suggestion that marriage so conceived is narrative's guise for studying whatever it is philosophy studies in turning aside the threat of skepticism. It follows that where comedy pursues the happy achievement of the ordinary conceived as marriage then what attacks this comedy is what attacks this achievement, so that what is studied in philosophy as skepticism is what is studied in narrative as tragedy and melodrama.

I assume that no one who has seen *Shadow of a Doubt* would deny that Uncle Charlie (Joseph Cotten) is a threat to life. He is, by the same token, a threat to marriage, or at least to his own marriages, apparently a whole string of them. He is also self-consciously an opponent of the ordinary—so he declaims to his niece, at a climactic moment of the movie at the same time that he insists on taking her as in her very essence a representative of the ordinary. And whatever else the movie shows him to be, he is certainly a threat to his niece. Here is a brief account of the plot to help the reader better place the moments that I discuss.

> The movie's narrative opens on an urban scene, the camera moving indoors to discover Joseph Cotten lying on a bed, indifferent to the money that lies nearby. Eluding the two men who are tailing him, he sends a telegram announcing his arrival to his sister and her family, ending it with "a kiss for little Charlie from her Uncle Charlie." We cut to some views of a small town, and then to Teresa Wright—the niece Charlie—lying on a

bed and wondering aloud to her father whether anything can save their family from a life of domestic routine. She decides to invite her uncle for a visit. As she composes a telegram to her uncle, she learns that his telegram has already been received.

The uncle's visit makes the household livelier. Dinner becomes an occasion, overcoming Charlie's anxiety that her mother's life consists of nothing more than "dinner then dishes then bed." But Charlie's suspicions are aroused by her uncle's behavior (tearing a story out of the local newspaper, giving her a ring engraved with others' initials), along with the arrival of two men who turn out to be detectives. She confirms her suspicions (and ours) by checking the newspaper at the library and observing that the initials in the ring correspond to the latest victim of the Merry Widow Murderer, the object of a nationwide search. She sleeps till dinnertime, which is a far less pleasant affair than before. There are more revelations of Charles's character—and his rhetoric. Charlie leaves the house, in anger at one of her father's conversational remarks about murder.

Her uncle catches up with her, denounces her suspicions and her ordinariness, and manages to get the ring back. (He does not deny the truth of her suspicions so much as her right to have them.) He appeals to her sympathy, playing for time. The next day, after church, they learn that another suspect has been killed in an accident with an airplane propeller. The police are now certain that he was the killer.

Charles still feels endangered by Charlie's knowledge, and he makes two attempts on her life, both of which are set up to look like domestic accidents. The first is apparently a warning (he saws off part of an outside staircase), but the second attempt is serious and scary. He sets a trap for her in the family's garage, which he fills with carbon monoxide fumes. Charlie wakes up to see her uncle bending over her, and repeats her demand that he go away. (She has previously told him, "I don't want you here. . . . I don't want you to touch my mother.") After a speech to the woman's club, Charles returns to the house and is about to give a toast when Charlie makes an entrance down the front staircase, having reclaimed the ring. The camera tracks in to the ring on her finger, following his gaze but taking us closer than his gaze could normally go. Shaken but still in control, he responds with an announcement that he is leaving the next morning, an announcement that evidently destroys his sister's composure. On the brink of incoherence, she pleads that his departure will be unbearable.

He does leave, grapples with Charlie on the departing train, and plunges to his death in front of an oncoming locomotive. The final sequence shows Charlie on the steps of a church, not listening to the minister's conventional, uncomprehending praise. She tells the younger detective (who has previously proposed to her) that she could not have managed without someone who knew. He says the world isn't as bad as Uncle Charlie believed: "But sometimes it needs a lot of watching. It just goes crazy now and then, like your Uncle Charlie." They look away from each other as the minister finishes his eulogy.

Is the niece Charlie really a representative of the ordinary? Often, when one thinks about a Hitchcock movie, it can seem as if he has preempted the gestures of interpretation. Hitchcock does this frequently, perhaps most frequently with psychoanalytic interpretations in mind. There are, for instance, the virtuoso displays of symbolism (the fireworks in *To Catch a Thief,* the gun slowly penetrating the frame of the woman's consciousness in both versions of *The Man Who Knew Too Much;* the incriminating wine stains discovered by Claude Rains in *Notorious*). Sometimes he offers an interpreter within the fiction of the film, for instance, the unperturbed psychiatrist as local know-it-all at the end of *Psycho* or the breathtakingly sensible Thelma Ritter in *Rear Window,* who asks Jimmy Stewart (already confined to a wheelchair) if his peeping activities are really worth a poker in the eye. And later in the film Stewart himself, as if picking up on the consequences of looking, remarks on the subject of the same windows that there's some pretty private stuff going on over there. Sometimes the sheer absorptiveness of the plot (which is not the same as its being filled with "action" or "suspense" as these are conventionally understood) invites the sense that its intricacies are all in the service of our viewing pleasure, the sources of which we need not inquire about too closely.

In the case of *Shadow of a Doubt,* the ideas of the ordinary and the extraordinary are so blatantly present from the beginning that they can thwart as much as invite our attention. As William Rothman has pointed out in his book *Hitchcock: The Murderous Gaze,*[15] the movie begins with scenes right out of film-noir, scenes that suggest precisely a dark side of city life that is not part of the daily round for most of us. We are then shifted to a series of near-cliché shots of small-town sunny California and to pictures of a homelife that manages to be at once zany and wishfully ordinary. (There are moments when it can seem as if Hitchcock were prophesying the brittle family comforts that television would start to offer us a decade later.) And then there are the detectives, pretending to be investigating a "typical" American family. Charlie (Teresa Wright) says it makes her feel funny to be picked as an "average family." The romantic detective says that "average families are best," but then denies that he thinks Charlie is average, as if recognizing that *average* is not a word people want to hear. (At the same time, he exhibits the fact that average is what some of us apparently want to be.) Charlie goes on to identify the condition of not seeming average with not feeling down in the dumps, as she had a few days ago, that is, before Uncle Charlie arrived.

The movie harps explicitly on the extraordinary bond between the uncle and the niece. Rothman singles out the parallel opening shots, which approach each of the main characters at the same angle, worlds apart, lying in bed and evidently lost in thought. These shots link their worlds, as well as them. Hitchcock seems from the beginning to have worked to undermine any position from which we could confidently try to sort out the ordinary from the extraordinary or to isolate the art and artifice that go into the depiction of the average and the typical. The issue of the typical (for instance, of the typical mother, baking a typical cake) becomes entwined with the issue of the phony documentary and thus with issues about photography. Rothman is very useful on Hitchcock's undermining of "documentary" authority, in the person of the detectives. This satire on photographic authenticity is played off against the moment when the photographer takes Uncle Charles's picture against his will and the companion moment when Uncle Charles's sister (Charlie's mother) produces a childhood photograph of Charles, thus refuting his claim never to have been photographed. The power of the photograph goes beyond the pretensions of the documentary, but its role in documenting and in failing to document our lives is something a good director will account for, one way or another.

The range of Hitchcock's references and themes offers some hints about what kind of issue the ordinary becomes in his hands. And one thing we are shown, unforgettably, is that what is and isn't ordinary may be the subject of a struggle. (The struggle goes beyond the relatively obvious facts that some people take the ordinary for granted and others use it as a cover for their projects.) That just such a struggle is a possibility for the movies is something we might have expected from Cavell's account of the ordinary as best discovered in its loss. Where there is the threat of loss, there is a possibility of struggle, and consequently the possibility of fictions about that struggle and that loss.[16]

That the movie has to do with a struggle about the ordinary is made explicit at one of its climactic moments. Confronted with the evidence of the ring with the incriminating initials, and sensing that Charlie has somehow been pursuing her sense of a special connection between them, Uncle Charles delivers what Rothman has called the most shocking of his speeches. (I remembered the feel of this speech, without very many of the words, for almost a decade.) This glamorous uncle, a man of the world who has captured the imagination of his niece, stops at no rhetorical or emotional trick to enforce his view of things and to undermine her capacity for an independent view of the world and of him. Her independence needs to be suppressed all the more since he apparently feels at times, as she does, that they are like twins. He has already exploited this in a way that both affirms and denies the bond, making his words all the more poisonous. Rothman reconstructs the speech like this:

You think you know something, don't you? There's so much you don't know. So much. What do you know really? You're just an ordinary little girl living in an ordinary little town. You wake up every morning of your life and you know perfectly well that there's nothing in the world to trouble you. You go through your ordinary little day and at night you sleep your untroubled, ordinary little sleep filled with peaceful, stupid dreams. And I brought you nightmares. You live in a dream. You're a sleepwalker, blind. How do you know what the world is like? Do you know the world is a foul sty? Do you know that if you rip the fronts off houses you'd find swine? The world's a hell. What does it matter what happens in it? Wake up, Charlie. Use your wits, learn something!

Confronted with the vicious brilliance of this speech, Charlie not only finds little to say but also is deprived of the position from which her words could have any independent weight. Charlie leaves the bar where the encounter has occurred, and Charles follows, twisting his words to one more notch of ironic meanness. He shifts to an appeal for a little time, on the grounds that a public revelation of what he is would kill her mother. Besides, he adds, "I can count on you. You said yourself we're no ordinary uncle and niece."

What marks Charles as a skeptic is, in the first place, his portrayal of the ordinary as a place of limited knowledge, interpreted in part as a willful lack of imagination. The question I want to focus on is, what enables him to use this idea to serve his purposes? I am not now asking why skepticism is such a good mask for nihilism that it functions even when the nihilism is just about being laid on the table. I am asking rather what makes young Charlie so vulnerable to the power of these words to smother her.[17] Why does she have to accept as hers the plight that he offers: you are ordinary (and can do nothing on your own), *and* you are extraordinary (because you are bound to me and I am no ordinary uncle). The consequence of this situation is not that she is neither the one nor the other but that she is both. According to him, she must live against her nature, away from the ordinary life that is the only one that is hers to live.

I suggest that part of the picture she must fight against in his words is something that she had already accepted about herself. She has taken herself, or a certain capacity in herself, to be representative of the ordinary. That at least is how I am interpreting her opening speech to the effect that she and her family (and especially her mother) are in a "terrible rut." To my ear, the idea of one's ordinary life as being in a terrible rut is a pretty good contemporary facsimile of a Wordsworthian picture of the everyday as dominated by the "weight of custom," and it is perhaps even closer to Blake's idea of a "dull round." I am not asking that young Charlie be taken seriously as inheriting a Romantic problem about the everyday, though it would be worth thinking through exactly what we understand as disbarring her from this inheritance. (I am not at the moment interested in pursuing the idea that the thought of the Romantics has approximately the intellectual force of the daydreams of a dissatisfied adolescent. This is, however, a picture that is common enough among philosophers and, I suppose, among other American intellectuals.) I take her to be at the start of a train of thought that, if she were given the chance to follow it out, would let her know to what end her thinking had been awakened.

It is reasonably clear that her beginning to think has something to do with the awakening of desire. She herself remarks that she's beginning to sound like a "spinster," which suggests that her thoughts are a compromise between this awakening of desire and the fear that the desire will not be satisfied. Again, I do not ask that someone credit her idea that being down in the dumps is what makes a person seem average as the beginning of a theory about how the everyday is to be renewed. But surely her general direction is the right one: being down in the dumps—or, let us say, a certain silent depression or melancholy—*does* transform the ordinary into the average and leaves us in the rut of the commonplace.

There is, it seems to me, no special reason why her thoughts and wishes should bring with them such terrifying realizations. Perhaps she should not have located the source of renewal outside herself or taken the object of her desire to be the thing that was to "save" her and her family. But if that is an error, it is as common as asphalt. ("Who has thought most deeply, loves what is most alive," Hölderlin says, and he does not seem to think that this is an argument why Socrates ought to have loved himself better than he loved Alcibiades [1980, 66–67].) The moral of the story cannot be "Don't let your wishes make you skeptical about your and your family's position in the everyday course of things." The drama of the story turns rather on showing us that when we are drawn out of the ordinary we do not know how far we will be able to live with what materializes as the other side of desire and the other side of what we took ourselves to know. The world of the ordinary, and hence the world itself, may become accessible to us only when we are threatened by its loss. But understanding this threat and acknowledging that we have wished for it are likely already to estrange us, and we do not know in advance if we can get back to the world.

It is against this uncertainty, this shadow of doubt that hangs over the end of the movie, that I want to glance at the impressive scene where Teresa Wright comes down the staircase to the party, wearing the ring that she has taken back from her uncle. (He had taken it back from her just before his denunciation of her in the bar.) The moment bears comparison with the moments that Cavell has characterized as the arias of divorce (in the genre of the unknown woman), relating them to the self-affirmation within the discovery of the cogito. As in *Gaslight,* the moment involves a man's recognition of a woman's jewelry (the possession of which has raised some doubts and some anxiety), but the more immediate comparison is, I think, to *Vertigo,* as Rothman notes. There, Kim Novak more or less unconsciously puts on the pendant that so to speak belonged to her in the past, in her masquerade as another man's wife.[18] In letting herself be recognized as the blank screen on which Jimmy Stewart has twice materalized his fantasies, she enacts a kind of negative cogito: love me for myself, as the nothing I now am, and not for the fantasied something that I then was; and love me for my willingness to let you be the re-creator of that past and hence the author of my present. And his rage turns on her, forcing her to relive the fantasy one more time, from the outside, so to speak, but not less fatally for that. Teresa Wright, on the other hand, seems wholly awake and in startling possession of herself. It is a wonderful moment, but it is still equivocal. Rothman's account brings home inescapably that the scene is an all but public declaration that they are somehow already married, or anyway indissolubly betrothed. But the literal meaning of the gesture is that she is telling him to go away, reminding him that she knows something. One of the things she knows is where this ring comes from, and I think it is not too much to say that she has realized what sort of relationship produces a ring like this. So the moment also declares a kind of solidarity with other women. ("Someone was happy wearing this ring," she says when it is first given to her.) At the same time, she knows that she is, by this gesture, isolating herself.

The other thing she is doing at that moment is admitting that she doesn't (or must not any longer) care whether the public revelation about her uncle destroys her mother. As it happens, her gesture becomes the occasion for her uncle's declaration that he is leaving the next day. And that declaration proves devastating to her mother, whose voice dissociates into helpless nostalgia and blatant revelation. ("We were so close growing up. . . . Then you know how it is. You sort of forget you're you. You're your husband's wife.") At this, Charlie weeps, and Rothman is surely right that she is weeping also for herself. I can't help thinking that part of what makes Charlie weep is the fact that both her earlier efforts to spare her mother pain and her current willingness to risk her mother's pain are beyond her mother's knowledge. I think that something like this must be part of the reason that the mothers of the female leads are absent from the remarriage comedies. It may be hard to take when a mother interferes with the daughter's desire or when her own desires go on dictating the course of events. But when the mother's desires, still incestuous and unacknowledged, make the daughter's specific existence irrelevant, the forward movement of the drama can scarcely survive. In *Shadow of a Doubt,* the scene fades out on this note, leaving only the catastrophe.

A last piece of speculation may be in order. Granting my suggestion that Charlie has already accepted a piece of her uncle's description of her as a representative of the ordinary, can we say any more about what the uncle represents? It is, of course, not enough to say that he represents a possibility of skepticism, even if we add that it is a monstrous possibility. I would like to point here to his wish to avoid being photographed, as if, beyond his suspiciousness, a primitive fear of the photographic were coming to light. His denial of the existence of the childhood photograph combines this fear with an implied denial of his having had a childhood. Cavell remarks on this denial as part of the monster's sense of himself as a victim. (See *The Claim of Reason,* part 4.) Nor is it enough to say that he is portrayed as a kind of dandy and thus as a sort of debased or decadent version of a romantic hero. This helps to explain his attractiveness to his niece and also why we are tempted to think of him as having a kind of genius, if only for emptiness and destruction. I would not want my interpretation to reduce our reaction to his enormities. But there are hints or questions that perhaps ought to be pursued.

The hint that I will examine is contained—but also, I believe, slightly displaced—in Rothman's description of Charles's ability to hear and to heed, however perversely, the calls of lonely women (234–35). I take Hitchcock to be commenting on the nature of this ability (or of this fantasized ability) in the moment following Charlie's impassioned plea on behalf of the widows: "They're alive, they're human beings!" Looking directly at the camera, Charles responds: "Are they, Charlie? Or are they fat, wheezing animals?" Just before, he had described them as "proud of nothing but their jewels" and as "smelling of money." It seems to me obvious enough that these details betray a disgust at the sexuality of these woman and specifically a disgust at the smells and noises of arousal. Such arousal would be something he thinks of himself as having to endure (for the sake of his career, you might say), and it can also be understood as a disguised memory of the childhood that we saw him work to deny. If this interpretation of him is accurate, it suggests why he can seem both impassive and perhaps even a little gratified at his sister's display of herself. She both is and is not one of his victims, and his disgust at his victims presumably includes the desire to make them produce such displays and such helpless noises. And finally, this reading makes it still more appropriate that Charlie's eloquence on the staircase is silent.

Charlie's silence is at once part of the promise and part of the pain of this movie. In place of a conclusion, I would like to let her silent declaration stand as echoing ambiguities and uncertainties in my reflections on Cavell's work. To banish the skeptic's banishment of the ordinary is finally to accommodate the knowledge that we had already been willing to banish the world. We must let go of the wish to respond to the skeptic's provocation, accepting instead what there remains to be in-structed by. This will take silence as well as resolve. In Charlie's case, we know that the resolve takes courage and that the silence is appropriate because her uncle has left her with no room in which to speak and with no words at her disposal. But how are we supposed to know that our resolve is not just another form of intransigence and that our silence is, like hers, an achievement of voice, however transient the occasion? In the comedies of remarriage, the achievement of voice is displayed in the readiness for conversation. This befits a genre that turns upon an offer of forgiveness and wants an end to the cycling of revenge in favor of the repetitions of the everyday. In *Shadow of a Doubt,* the cycle is not ended but interrupted. Consequently, we cannot know that the conversation will resume, that Charlie will speak again in a normal voice. But neither do we know that she will not.

Notes

1.   This was a principal theme of the Tanner lectures, delivered at Stanford in April 1986. I am grateful to Stanley Cavell for a typescript of the second of these lectures. In the discussion period at Stanford, Cavell returned to *Shadow of a Doubt* (and to *Notorious*) as possible points of reference for the genre of the unknown woman. I would also like to thank Cavell, Garrett Stewart, Kathleen Whalen, Natasa Durovicova, and Joshua Wilner for their comments on an earlier draft of this essay.

2.   Some recent objections to "theory" as irrelevant to "practice" in general might be considered here. We would also have to consider how far the concep-tion of theory and of certainty as requiring an Archimedean point "outside" the space of our beliefs is a conception already formed by a skeptical inspiration, however apparently antiskeptical (or antitheoretical) the conclusions are. It is, after all, just this picture of a point above or below common belief that animates Descartes's response in the Second Meditation to his own prior skeptical medita-tions. See also Cavell, "The Division of Talent," in *Critical Inquiry* (1985).

3.   See Rorty's *Consequences of Pragmatism* (1982), especially p. 92, and also "Deconstruction and Circumvention" (1984). At the same time, Rorty speaks of the "philosopher's own scholastic little definitions of 'philosophy'" as "intended to exclude from the field of honor those whose pedigree is unfamiliar" (1982, 92). This is also a sort of romance—as indicated by the phrase "field of honor"—but a different romance, one whose relation to the family romance is still unclear. Perhaps for Rorty both are essentially mere disguises for the gritty facts of position, money, and prestige.

4.   See "On Makavaev on Bergman," in *Themes out of School*, pp. 137–38. The passage from Nietzsche is from section 60 of *The Gay Science;* the same passage is discussed by Derrida in *Spurs* (42–47).

5.   Janine Chasseguet-Smirgel, *Pour une Psychanalyse de l'Art et de la Créativité*, my translation. She also suggests an analogy between being at the movies and listening to a patient, which makes me speculate that there must be an analyst's fantasy of having interesting patients to correspond with the patient's fantasy of producing interesting material.

6.   This idea about the fantasy of participation (both actively and passively) in the primal scene was, I believe, first put forward by Bertram Lewin. See, for instance, the investigations of elation and the hypomanias in his collected papers.

7.   Cavell emphasized this in a seminar in the spring semester of 1973 and again in *The Claim of Reason*, especially pp. 384 and 400. See also my "What Makes the Pale Criminal Pale?" (1986).

8.   See *What Is Called Thinking?*, pp. 89 and 95. This translation is useful, but it sometimes omits without comment significant pieces of the German. I have elsewhere characterized Heidegger's relation to the past of philosophy as equally a mode of incorporation ("On Heidegger's Track," 1985, pp. 231–33). Both modes or both fantasies of relationship to past thought tend to deny or to assume the importance and the occasions of reading in philosophy and likewise tend to deny ambivalences about what is being incorporated. This denial of ambivalence was a reason for my choosing a term such as incorporation, which has, of course, resonances in psychoanalytic thought, as well as with later Heideggerian cruxes such as the *Verwindung* of metaphysics and the *Ereignis*. For a student of American thinking, reading is likely to be the place where the passivities and activities of influence get worked out, both theoretically and practically.

9.   This was underscored first in "The Availability of Wittgenstein's Later Philosophy" (1976) and most recently in the second of the Tanner lectures. The capacity for discipleship will contain new topics for the sense of victimization, as well as the possibility of wise passiveness, on both sides. I think of this as related to the difficulty of calculating whether the speaker of the following words in "Self-Reliance" is master or disciple: "Who has more obedience than I masters me, though he should not raise his finger." This dialectic of obedience and mastery—of listening and being listened to—seems to me also addressed by Derrida in *Writing and Difference*, when he is getting ready to take on Foucault: "The disciple . . . feels himself indefinitely challenged, or rejected or accused; as a disciple, he is challenged by the master who speaks within him and before him . . . he is also challenged by the disciple that he himself is." The relation of this

dialectic to the one we presume that the master is undergoing and, on the other hand, to the narcissistic dialectic of mirroring that Derrida goes on to invoke, has not yet been worked out.

10.   Cavell makes this (apparent) paradox explicit in "The Politics of Interpretation," collected in *Themes out of School*. The analogy to the problems of psychoanalytic therapy also occurs there, and he is also fairly explicit about the nature of the passiveness involved. See also *The Claim of Reason*, p. 352, on the question of whether knowing your self is something active or something passive. For more on the overcoming of false pictures of passivity and activity in reading, see my "Reading On: *Walden*'s Labors of Succession," forthcoming.

11.   This is the point at which Richard Rorty sticks, in his review of *The Claim of Reason*, "From Epistemology to Romance," reprinted as essay 10 of *Consequences of Pragmatism*. See especially pp. 177–81.

12.   That others involved in Wittgenstein's work have seen this was brought home to me in conversations with B. R. Tilghman. It was an implicit theme of his paper at the Inter-American Congress of Philosophy (Guadalajara, November 1985). See also the opening chapters of his book *But Is It Art?*, a principal target of which is Arthur Danto's claim in *The Transfiguration of the Commonplace* to have absorbed and gone beyond Wittgenstein's representations of the ordinary.

13.   The homelessness of uncommon speech in Jonathan Edwards (and in David Hume) is a theme of my doctoral dissertation, "Natural Notions, Uncommon Speech" (Harvard, 1978). This dissertation was directed and encouraged by Cavell.

14.   This thought might help us understand the connection between Cavell's reading of Wittgenstein and his concern with theater and theatricality and other forms of self-consciousness in the arts and in philosophy. But I cannot, within the scope of this paper, connect these possibilities of self-consciousness and the possibilities of emptiness that I have been emphasizing as central to his account of Wittgenstein.

15.   *Shadow of a Doubt* is one of the five films that Rothman gives readings of. I know of no work on film that surpasses the thoroughness and detail of Rothman's work. My remarks are indebted to his book and to his lectures at Harvard in 1976 and 1977, and to conversations that date back even earlier. Much (but not I think all) of what I am doing in this last section is making explicit what is latent in his account.

16.   See Cavell's essay in this volume. This also suggests why the ordinary cannot, in this movie or in general, be equated with innocence. Where innocence has to struggle with a certain kind of knowledge it is no longer exactly innocent. But that we might struggle for the ordinary, or find ourselves in a quest for it, is exactly the possibility that is at stake in Cavell's work. The sense that the ordinary is a matter of innocence—of, let us say, unimaginativeness—is explored in Hume and in Thomas Mann's *Tonio Kruger*. Wittgenstein addresses this issue when he responds to the interlocuter's question about whether certainty is only achieved by closing your eyes in the face of doubt (*P.I.*, 224).

17.   The attempt to poison her with the fumes from the exhaust of a car

seems to acquire part of its scariness from the fact that he has in effect already tried to poison her.

18.   Though really it "belongs" to the historical/fictional woman on which the fiction of a troubled wife is modeled. The spiral of Hitchcock's speculations—as of Jimmy Stewart's—is difficult to capture.

References

Cavell, Stanley. "The Availability of Wittgenstein's Later Philosophy." In Cavell (1976).
———. *Must We Mean What We Say?* Cambridge: At the University Press, 1976.
———. *The Claim of Reason: Wittgenstein, Skepticism, Morality, and Tragedy.* New York: Oxford University Press, 1979a.
———. *The World Viewed.* Cambridge, Mass.: Harvard University Press, 1979b.
———. *Pursuits of Happiness.* Cambridge, Mass.: Harvard University Press, 1981a.
———. "Thinking of Emerson." In *The Senses of Walden.* San Francisco: North Point Press, 1981b.
———. "Genteel Responses to Kant?" *Raritan* 3 (Fall 1983):39–61.
———. *Themes out of School: Effects and Causes.* San Francisco: North Point Press, 1984.
———. "The Division of Talent." *Critical Inquiry* 2 (June 1985):519–38.
Chasseguet-Smirgel, Janine. *Pour une Psychanalyse de l'Art et de la Créativité.* Paris: Payot, 1971.
Danto, Arthur. *The Transfiguration of the Commonplace.* Cambridge, Mass.: Harvard University Press, 1981.
Derrida, Jacques. *Writing and Difference.* Translated by Alan Bass. Chicago: University of Chicago Press, 1978.
———. *Spurs: Nietzsche's Styles.* Translated by Barbara Harlow. Chicago: University of Chicago Press, 1979.
Emerson, Ralph Waldo. *The Selected Writings of Ralph Waldo Emerson.* Edited by Brooks Atkinson. New York: Modern Library, 1940.
Gould, Timothy. "On Heidegger's Track: A Response to a Portrayal by George Steiner." *Soundings* 68 (Summer 1985):229–52.
———. "What Makes the Pale Criminal Pale?" *Soundings* 69 (Summer 1986):526–29.
———. "Reading on: *Walden*'s Labors of Succession." *The Thoreau Quarterly,* (1986):131–34.
Heidegger, Martin. *What Is Called Thinking?* Translated by J. Glenn Gray. New York: Harper & Row, 1968.
Hölderlin, Friedrich. "Socrates and Alcibiades." In *Poems and Fragments,* translated by Michael Hamburger. Cambridge: At the University Press, 1980.
Lewin, Bertram. *The Psychoanalysis of Elation.* New York: W. W. Norton, 1950.

Nietzsche, Friedrich. *Thus Spoke Zarathustra.* In *The Portable Nietzsche,* edited and translated by Walter Kaufmann. New York: Viking Press, 1954.

———. *On the Genealogy of Morals.* Translated by Walter Kaufmann and R. J. Hollingdale. New York: Vintage Books, 1968.

———. *The Gay Science.* Translated by Walter Kaufmann. New York: Vintage Books, 1974.

Rorty, Richard. *The Consequences of Pragmatism.* Minneapolis: University of Minnesota Press, 1982.

———. "Deconstruction and Circumvention." *Critical Inquiry* 11 (September 1984):1–23.

Rothman, William. *Hitchcock: The Murderous Gaze.* Cambridge, Mass.: Harvard University Press, 1982.

Strawson, P. F. *The Bounds of Sense: An Essay on Kant's Critique of Pure Reason.* London: Methuen, 1966.

Tilghman, B. R. *But Is It Art?* New York: Oxford University Press, 1984.

Wittgenstein, Ludwig. *Philosophical Investigations.* 3rd ed. Translated by G. E. M. Anscombe. New York: Macmillan, 1958.

6   The Shows of Violence

Irving Schneider

But my claim is that in the case of films, it is generally true that you do not really like the highest instances unless you also like typical ones. You don't even know what the highest are instances of unless you know the typical as well. —Cavell

Describing the hallucinations he suffered in his psychotic break of 1900, Clifford Beers wrote in his 1908 memoir *A Mind That Found Itself* (Beers 1921, 30), "I imagined that these visionlike effects, with few exceptions, were produced by a magic lantern controlled by some of my myriad persecutors. The lantern was rather a cinematographic contrivance. Moving pictures, often brilliantly colored, were thrown on the ceiling of my room and sometimes on the sheets of my bed. Human bodies, dismembered and gory, were one of the most common of these. All this may have been due to the fact that, as a boy, I had fed my imagination on the sensational news of the day as presented in the public press. Despite the heavy penalty which I now paid for thus loading my mind, I believe this unwise indulgence gave a breadth and variety to my peculiar psychological experience which it otherwise would have lacked. For with an insane ingenuity I managed to connect myself with almost every crime of importance of which I had ever read."

Writing at the dawn of movie history, Beers was already dealing with the connection between violent movie images and violent mental images. In attempting to account for their relationship, he speculated on the excitatory power of the mass medium of his youth, the public press. In our own time, one of the most shocking events of violence to focus our attention once more on the relation between movies and personal fantasy and behavior was the attempted assassination of President Reagan by John Hinckley Jr. A major source of concern in the investigation of the events was the implication that Hinckley's action had been inspired by his exposure to a motion picture, Martin Scorsese's *Taxi Driver*.

The Hinckley case points up the difficulties in establishing a link between one stimulus—what is presented by TV or movies—and an act,

137

in this case a violent one. We know from the court and psychiatric testimony that Hinckley had seen *Taxi Driver* at least eighteen times, mostly in 1976, before President Reagan was on the national scene. In the movie, Travis, played by Robert de Niro, stalks a candidate with intent to shoot, but is kept at a distance by a Secret Service man. When Hinckley stood outside the Washington Hilton in March 1981 he noted to himself with some surprise that he had gotten closer to the president than Travis had, and this seemed to loosen some of his inhibitions about the act. Additionally, he thought Reagan smiled at him, and this further loosened his inhibitions.

This sequence of events makes a pretty good case for the morbid effects of a movie on a susceptible individual. But the story gets more complicated. What may have been the greater influence on Hinckley's act was Mark Chapman's shooting of John Lennon in December 1980. Hinckley was at the Lennon vigil, was deeply involved in the mourning, and in his bag carried a copy of *Catcher in the Rye,* which had also been in Chapman's bag. At this point, a book and a life event are also implicated. In fact, many who studied Hinckley feel that it was the life event more than anything else that removed the barrier.

Movies were also implicated in Lee Harvey Oswald's shooting of President Kennedy. There was some speculation at the time that two movies he had seen in October 1963 might have influenced his decision: *Suddenly* (1954), in which Frank Sinatra plays a political assassin, and the 1949 *We Were Strangers,* a John Huston film in which John Garfield plans to execute a dictator. An incident that occurred while Oswald was in the Soviet Union in January 1962 further indicates his sensitivity to political violence and the media. He heard from an important source about an attempt that had been made on Soviet Premier Khrushchev's life in Minsk, but the attempt was never reported in the Soviet Union. Oswald commented to others that if something like that had happened in the United States it would have been all over TV and radio. As another parallel to the Hinckley story, some analysts think that the trigger event that presaged the Kennedy assassination was the shooting of Medgar Evers in Mississippi in June 1963, which reportedly excited Oswald.

In both dramatic cases we find a susceptible individual, a movie, and a significant life event. There is, of course, a legitimate question as to what might have been the principal cause of the violent acts, but those who distrust the popular media have tended always to blame violence on simple imitation or incitement by the media. The defect in much of the research in this area is that it, too, focuses on but one factor, one influence. The results of such inquiries have too often ranged only from the moralistic to the predictable. At least three factors have to be considered when one studies the effect of something like a movie or TV program. One is the nature of the stimulus: what is it that the person is reacting to? Second, whom is it acting on—what do we know about the person or population we are studying? Third, what is the setting—the environment in which the behavior is being studied and to which members of the audience return after the film?

An experience I had with a different Scorsese film illustrates this complexity. I saw *Raging Bull* in two contrasting environments. The first time was on New York's 42nd Street, which has one of the world's greatest concentrations of movie theaters, most of them devoted to action films, and which is one of the world's best places to see movies. In the film, the boxer Jake LaMotta is pathologically suspicious of his wife's fidelity, and as a result ends up driving her away. In this 42nd Street theater there were several middle-aged men, apparently poor, some black and some white, sitting near me, and they were talking back to the screen, supporting LaMotta's suspicions: "Don't trust her," "You can't trust a woman," "Put it to her," and so forth. I saw the film a second time in a theater in suburban Washington, D.C. The audience was quietly horrified by LaMotta's aggressive behavior. Same movie, different audience, different theater atmosphere, different response.

Fears about the potential for movies to cause crime and sexual delinquency go back to the earliest years of the medium and are well summarized in Robert Sklar's *Movie-Made America* (1976, 122–40) and Garth Jowett's *Film: The Democratic Art* (1976, 74-107). Movies have been described as the first of the modern mass media. Their earliest appeal was to the lower-class and lower-middle class working men and women in the cities, and there is a sense that the concern about effects was really a disguised concern of those in power about what people of different class and background might be learning and doing. As has often been the case in censorship battles, the concern was expressed in terms of protecting women and the young. Early movies often mocked the pretensions of the rich in seeking to protect the children of the poor from their ostensibly bad environment. One of the most effective depictions of this occurs in the modern segment of D.W. Griffith's *Intolerance* (1916), a sequence later released as a separate film, *The Mother and the Law.*

One has to read the testimony and court decisions of the early part of the century to get the flavor of class prejudice involved in the struggle to control movie content. The models for suppressing films, interestingly, were the Pure Food and Drug Act and meat inspection legislation passed during Teddy Roosevelt's presidency. If government could prohibit products that could harm the public—for example, defective drugs or meats—why not inspect movies before people were allowed to consume them? Ergo prior restraint.

As I have suggested, the concern about the effects of movies has usually involved their possible effect on people who were thought to have little impulse control, people who were not fully socialized. Thus, what those in power have been concerned about have been the destabilizing effects of the media on children, adolescents, women, immigrants, poor people, and minorities. Often the pressure for censorship has come when materials have become available to the masses, as, for example, when suit was brought in England against the distribution of *Lady Chatterley's Lover* after a cheap paperbound edition was published.

Early conclusions on the subject consisted of prejudices presented as scientific evidence. In 1909, for example, Jane Addams, the renowned director of Chicago's Hull-House, attacked movies for the dangers they presented in provoking neurosis, delinquency, sexual license, antisocial behavior, bad health, and attempted murder (Jowett 1976, 79). In 1919, a physician testified before the Chicago Motion Picture Commission hearings that moviegoing caused nervousness, St. Vitus's dance, and bad eyesight in children (Sklar 1976, 124). He continued, saying that it very definitely increased the use of glasses, led to physical disturbances, and over a period of years would turn neuroses into organic disturbances for which nothing could be done. Before we too easily mock this sort of testimony, however, we should look at current "evidence" being presented before pornography and rock lyrics commissions.

In an attempt to produce some hard scientific evidence on the effects of movies on youngsters, from 1929 to 1932 the Payne Foundation funded a series of studies by a group of psychologists, sociologists, and educators. Twelve books emerged from these studies, the best known of which was a popular summary volume of the work titled *Our Movie-Made Children* (Forman 1935). The conclusions were that movies could cause all sorts of criminal, sexual, and antisocial effects. One of the strong sex movies alluded to in the study starred Melvyn Douglas and Lupe Velez; the most powerful stimulus to a life of crime was *Little Caesar;* and the most imitated actor in the slums was Jimmy Cagney. Ironically, many of these findings were based on studies in Chicago, the city with the longest history of censorship. Sklar (133) cites a mocking article by Charles C. Pettijohn, Will Hays's right-hand man, in which he reviewed the effects of censorship on life in Chicago. Everyone can see, he said in 1926, that movie censorship had made it "the nicest, cleanest, most orderly, crime-less city in the world today."

While the movies cited in the Payne Foundation studies certainly had an effect on the audience, the defect of the research was something that has already been alluded to—the fact that it focused on the movies alone, not considering them in any broader context. More modern studies have attempted to correct some of the earlier methodological errors.

In the days since the Second World War, there has been an acceleration of research on the effects of the media, and this has come to deal almost exclusively with the relationship between television and violence (film research, by some division of the territory, has come to center almost exclusively on the effects of pornography).

In 1972 the Surgeon General's Scientific Advisory Committee on Television and Violence published its report on the relationship between television watching and aggressive and violent behavior of viewers. Its major conclusion, a cautious one, was that "there is a convergence of the fairly substantial experimental evidence for a short-run causation of aggression among some children by viewing violence on the screen and much less certain evidence from field studies that extensive violence viewing precedes some long-run manifestations of aggressive behavior. . . . A good deal of research remains to be done before one can have confidence in these conclusions" (Surgeon General's Committee 1972).

A good deal of research *has* been done in the decade since that report. Indeed, 90 percent of all research on television has appeared in the last ten years, over 2,500 titles. These studies have been reviewed and summarized in a 1982 update on the Surgeon General's report published by the National Institute of Mental Health (NIMH) (Pearl et al. 1982).

As one examines the many studies one can find defects, shortcomings, or limitations in almost all of them, but once again they converge in the direction of supporting a causal relationship between televised violence and later aggressive behavior. This is true both of laboratory studies and the more difficult field studies.

David Pearl, chief of the Behavioral Sciences Research Branch of the NIMH, has summed up a number of laboratory studies and suggests that aggressive behavior is more likely to occur when the TV violence has these characteristics: the violence pays off, is not punished, is shown in a justifying context, is socially acceptable, appears realistic, appears motivated by a deliberate intent to injure, is expressed under conditions similar to the viewer's environment, and involves a perpetrator who is similar to the viewer (Pearl 1981,4). It all adds up to a perfect description of televised football, but I don't think that is what the report intended.

Most studies of media and violence cited in the Surgeon General's report have studied the short-term effects, and as indicated, they have found a positive correlation. In contrast, a large-scale, technically sophisticated study sponsored by NBC came to somewhat different conclusions (Milavsky 1982). This study found that in the elementary school and high school children they studied there was some evidence of short-term effects of TV violence, but the findings for long-term effects were negative. The conclusion was that short-term effects do not cumulate and produce stable patterns of aggressive behavior in the real world.

Other studies have dealt with the ways in which people's attitudes are affected by watching television. It has been shown that people who watch a great deal of TV tend to be more suspicious and distrustful of others, and also think there is more violence in the world. A disproportionate percentage of victims on TV are the powerless and have-nots, including older citizens, and there is some evidence of an increase in fearfulness in these groups as a result of TV viewing.

Other interesting attitude-change studies have shown that children's attitudes are changed if adults discuss a program with them. Violent shows can lose their power if seen with or discussed with adults. If true, these findings provide some scientific support for movies' PG-13 and R ratings, which allow children to view violent or sexual material when accompanied by an adult.

Apart from explicitness of images, however, commercial television is an inherently violent medium. In dramatic shows, there is a need for some sort of emotional bang prior to every commercial break in order to hold on to the audience, and this is immediately followed by the quick emotional grab of each commercial. Such build-up and excitation is repeated several times an hour, a process made even more insistent by the competition between networks for viewer attention. The recurrent process must have at least some short-term emotional effect on the audience akin to the aggressive behavior and fearfulness researchers have described as a consequence of watching depictions of violence.

In nonfictional television programming, too, even when there are no explicitly violent images, an atmosphere of violence exists. In the realm of news, for example, editors have a number of stories from which to choose in putting together a program. To get air time a news correspondent needs to present a punchy, dramatic story that has a sense of urgency about it that will capture the attention of both editor and viewer. The result, too often, is a program in which one crisis follows another. It is no wonder then that frequent viewers see the world as a violent place, and no wonder that watching TV for long periods feels like a ride on an emotional roller coaster, independent of specifically violent content.

But violence often *is* a major component. When we look at the recent crop of violent films, and consider what the TV networks are selling in the face of all the reported research, it is tempting to strike out at those who inflict the products on us. But we must resist that temptation and bear in mind, to paraphrase a critic (Michelson 1971, 241), that these exist not so much because unscrupulous fiends produce and sell them, but because violence is a part of our nature.

Before reflexively criticizing television for its emphasis on violence, we must remember that TV is the most consumer-sensitive medium ever. Shows rise and fall on the basis of continuing consumer polls, and yet season after season a "Miami Vice" and its copies go on the air. If violence persists, then, it must be because it is what the public wants. Makers of exploitation films—Roger Corman was the master—are similarly tuned in to their market. If their products did not make money, they would change them. But these products do make money, and lots of it. A look, for example, at the three top-grossing movies of the week this essay is being written reveals the following titles: *Cobra* ("Crime is a disease. Meet the cure"); *Poltergeist II* ("They're back"); and *Top Gun* ("Two hours of pure POW . . . the screen explodes"). The first two received terrible reviews, the third mixed.

In the face of such popularity of violent shows, it is unlikely that censorship or control will eliminate their appeal, for the appetite for violence is certainly not a new one. It has a long history of popular appeal. When one looks back at bible stories, myths, ancient sports, Shakespeare, fairy tales, and public punishments, Michelson's caveat is borne out: violence is part of our nature. Under pressure, the borderline between the acceptable and unacceptable may shift back to those less explicit films of the thirties, or it may, with future technology, advance toward increasingly graphic representations, but the effects of these products and the interest in them will persist. So while researchers continue to study effects of such films and programs, it behooves us to try to understand what it is in us that seeks out and responds to them.

It is important to make clear at this point that what are being included here under the general rubric of violent movies are a number of different film genres, each of which has its own rules, conventions, and typical content apart from the depiction of violence, which is common to all. Some of the more popular genres in which violence figures prominently have been the horror, Kung Fu, Blaxploitation, science fiction, war, crime, car chase and slasher movies.

Film critics have analyzed genre from a variety of perspectives: social, political, psychological, psychoanalytic, historical, semiotic, and technical. The horror film, for example, has been discussed by Robin Wood (1979) as representing the return of repressed sexuality; by Harlan Kennedy (1982) as a manifestation in the eighties of atavistic throwbacks reflecting the political climate; by Tony Williams (1980) as proposing monstrous reactions to the patriarchal family's repressiveness; and by Linda Williams (1983), in a feminist reading, as reflecting the similar status of woman victim and monster as twin threats to vulnerable male power.

The cult horror classic *Last House on the Left* provides evidence for all of these readings, but it raises another important question. In a story almost unbearable to watch, it tells first of a couple of teenage girls who, in a condition of total helplessness, are tortured, raped, and killed by a gang they encounter when walking in the woods. Then, by coincidence, the gang unknowingly takes refuge in the home of the murdered girls' family. When the family members accidentally learn of the crime, they take grisly revenge on the torturers.

One reviewer wrote of the film: "Is it a remake of Bergman's *Virgin Spring* illustrating the sickness of life in modern-day America? Is it a coarse, repulsive exploitation film for sickos? It's both" (Weldon 1983, 415). This comment revives the old high art versus low art controversy, which has cropped up whenever censorship or control have been debated. Is a depiction in a Bergman film that will be seen only by an elite audience safer than a vernacular version of the same story aimed at those who are judged to be in poorer control of their impulses? Movies have always managed to incorporate the high and the low in their canon, but this creates what Cavell (1979, 6) calls the nightmare "for the fastidious writer about film who takes an indiscriminate attention to movies as a manifestation of bad taste and of a corrupt industry and society, rather than as a datum in understanding the appetite for film."

Rather than attempting in this paper another analysis of each of the genres, or pursuing the deeper meanings in the story lines, I want to pursue the questions raised by Michelson and Cavell and look instead at the audience that is attracted to these films, speculating about their motivations and satisfactions. It has often been true in film criticism that the films that best lend themselves to analysis are those that have not been especially successful commercially, a discrepancy that can throw doubt on some elegant formulations. The most complete understanding of a film comes from sitting with a live audience, observing and sharing its reactions, and then joining that experience with one's own speculations.

A look at the audiences in New York's 42nd Street theaters that I mentioned earlier is quite instructive. Of the many theaters on the block only a few show pornographic films, and the people who attend these are quite different from those at the action films. The audience at porn films tends to be older, whiter, and quieter; they attend alone and sit at least a seat apart from one another. Whatever their fantasy life, it is hard to imagine any of them committing a violent act.

In the more numerous theaters that show action movies, one enters another world. Instead of the solitary viewer, couples, groups, and families predominate (the presence of young children sitting with parents and watching wrenching violence is always disconcerting). Most of the audience is black or Hispanic, and rather than sitting in silence, they engage in loud and continuous commentary on the action on the screen. When the action slows—as it must in even the most frenetic film—for a romantic scene or an expository passage, the audience becomes restless and distracted. They walk around, talk or shout to their neighbors, and hoot the inaction on the screen. Once the action resumes, they are engaged again. Clearly, the audience is there for the action, and the more violent it is, the greater the response. One may feel uneasy about the effects the show may have on those who are watching it, but since it is unlikely that anyone goes to the movies in order to be incited to commit violence, we must again ask ourselves, what is the appeal? Why do audiences repeatedly seek out these gut-wrenching entertainments?

One doesn't have to go to 42nd Street to see audiences in action. In many neighborhood theaters, when the gorier and more frightening of the recent violent films—the mad slasher movies—are shown, the audience often consists predominantly of high school boys and girls who seem to attend largely to prove that they can take it. For boys especially, as occurs so regularly in the rest of the animal kingdom, it is a form of mating display. The gorier the movie the better the opportunity to prove how tough one is. My friends and I still talk about the first time we went to a double feature of *Dracula* and *Frankenstein* and how scared we were of what was occurring on the screen; but each of us was even more afraid to be the first to back out. This motive for experiencing violent films, one of several I will be citing, might be dubbed a rite of passage. Primitive societies frequently have frightening rituals that mark the initiation into puberty, and perhaps in the absence of more formal rituals, this one serves our society.

Another related motive for seeking out violent images is what has been called desensitization, learning to reduce one's responses to frightening stimuli. For example, one study found that boys who regularly looked at violent programs showed less physiological arousal when they looked at new violent programs (Feshbach 1969, 461–72). Another study demonstrated that students exposed to a stressful film reacted with less anxiety to another stress-inducing film than did those not so prepared (Pillard et al. 1967, 35–41). Exposure to anxiety-producing materials in these studies seemed to lower the response to subsequent stressful material. For people living under conditions of stress, as do ghetto dwellers, who constitute a significant audience for action movies, viewing these movies may help them cope with their environments, a media equivalent of the *dozens*, that grim ghetto game of stoically enduring insults.

The ceremonial and desensitizing aspects of attending a violent movie only partly explain why moviegoers return again and again for each new film. Another plausible explanation comes from Joseph Gelmis, writing in *Newsday* (1983), when he describes the horror flick as the most obvious example of what he calls the pharmacological cinema. Anyone who has sat through a frightening or violent movie knows that it produces powerful visceral effects—all sorts of tightenings, churnings, and quickenings. These reactions may in fact constitute the equivalent of a drug high, and for those seeking the experience, the appropriate movie is readily and regularly available. Gelmis's suggestion of pharmacological effects also receives support from the experience of many people with attention deficit disorders or hyperactivity, who, like hyperactive children calmed by amphetamines, are able to sit transfixed through these films. To counter the tolerance-producing effects of desensitization, new varieties and levels of gore and explicitness are continually devised so that each new film may promise a new and relatively cheap high.

Above and beyond the significance of the rite of passage, desensitization, and pharmacological motives for going to violent movies, however, lies a further attraction. In focusing so much on the gore as the major attraction of stories of violence, a significant dimension of these productions is overlooked. To recognize it, one needs to look at the plots of these movies and note the pattern that begins to emerge. The dominant themes one finds over and over again are powerlessness, humiliation, and revenge. Though humiliation and revenge may be most prominent in a film such as *Rambo,* and powerlessness in *Night of the Living Dead* and other monster and science fiction films, the themes most often are linked. Usually, someone who is humiliated and powerless takes his revenge on the people, institutions, or authorities who have contributed to his condition. He or she strikes out against police and corrupt officials in the Clint Eastwood and Charles Bronson movies, villains from abroad in the Chuck Norris and Sylvester Stallone films, women in the mad slasher films, and men in the rapist and women's prison films.

One of the most successful of the violent genres, the Kung Fu movie, has in fact been referred to as "the cinema of revenge." The basic Kung Fu methods are said to have been developed at a time when the peasantry were not allowed to arm themselves with conventional weapons. The martial arts became the equalizer in the battle of the underdog against powerful authority figures.

The principal appeal of the horror movie, the violent movie, the action movie, and the movie of revenge is to people who have grown up humiliated. Just in growing up and being socialized, everyone has experienced feelings of humiliation and powerlessness, and for this reason— for all of us—violent movies have an appeal. It is in delineating the universal experience of humiliation that psychoanalysis has made a great contribution. The Oedipus complex has provided a blueprint for the understanding of family politics. Using Harold Lasswell's classic definition of politics—who gets what, when, how—we can understand the oedipal situation as an attempt on the part of the child to escape the immediate threats of powerlessness and humiliation by developing strategies for eventually gaining power. Usually the child is successful, but one of the consequences of the oedipal strategy is the common proclivity to identify with the aggressor or the underdog. This tendency is especially well served by the violent film genres.

Psychoanalytic interpreters of popular culture, by concentrating so completely on the psychological, and more specifically on the family romance, have been inclined to overlook or ignore the impact of social, economic, and political forces on our entertainments. Yet the fact is that some disadvantaged groups of people—minorities, the poor, the underemployed, the physically and sexually abused—have experienced far greater humiliation in their lives, and for them the shows of violence have much greater appeal. One can get a palpable feeling for this attraction by comparing the audience response to movies in different parts of the community, as I described with respect to *Raging Bull*.

Political forces have propelled the shows of violence into the mainstream in recent years. As we have tried as a nation to come to terms with a series of humiliations, we have seen the growth of a national cinema of revenge. From our defeat in Vietnam to our current sense of impotence in dealing with terrorism, we have begun to turn increasingly to fantasy or PR victories. The supreme humiliation of being the most powerful nation on earth and yet being unable to use any of that power against our perceived enemies has found expression in a series of revenge movies populated by men fighting alone and against all odds to defeat the forces of evil empires. At a time when politicians campaign and win elections by running against our own government even as they constitute that government, the new movie heroes—Stallone, Schwarzenegger, Norris—show their contempt and distrust of our own institutions and officials in their solo battles. Corrupt senators, cowardly leaders, and dishonest police are staples of the Rambo films and their many clones, and they provide whatever justification is needed for the explosions of violence that punctuate the films (one reviewer of *Cobra* noted that the violent rogue cop played by Stallone kept in his office a picture of President Reagan, the consummate antipolitician politician, and wondered if that lent support to the view that pictures can cause violence).

The humiliation and powerlessness we experience within the family, in society, as a nation, and against the forces of nature thus have all found their expression in the violent films of our time. From *Friday the Thirteeth* to *Red Dawn* to *The Terminator*, we find helpless people fighting back against the enemy within and outside our society, meeting violence with violence. As Freud noted in *Civilization and Its Discontents,* civilization cannot exist without repression; thus, it is unlikely that we will ever be free of the need to seek revenge, at least through art, against the forces that attempt to police our impulses.

So long as revenge is sublimated through art, good or bad, society rests easy. It is when art is perceived as shouting fire in a crowded theater that the forces of repression gather strength and freedom is threatened. Violent movies have upset Horace's dictum that "Medea must not butcher her children in the presence of the audience" (Alloway 1971, 71). How this will affect us and where it will lead are the unanswered questions.

Note

Since writing this paper I have come across Robert J. Stoller's *Observing the Erotic Imagination* (1985). In it, Stoller propounds the theme of humiliation and revenge as central to the development of sexual perversions. The following quote links the argument of his book to the point I am making in this paper: "Were we to study the role of humiliation in provoking psychopathology, we would find it at work wherever sadism and masochism appear—for example, in paranoid (sadistic) or depressive (masochistic) responses. My guess is that humiliation shapes erotic life only when the attack is aimed at those parts of the body/psyche concerned with erotic or gender behavior" (31).

References

Alloway, Lawrence. *Violent America: The Movies, 1946–1964.* New York: Museum of Modern Art, 1971.

Beers, Clifford W. *A Mind That Found Itself (1908).* New York: Doubleday, 1921.

Cavell, Stanley. *The World Viewed.* Cambridge, Mass.: Harvard University Press, 1979.

Feshbach, Seymour. "The Catharsis Effect: Research and Another View." In *Violence and the Media,* edited by Robert K. Baker and Sandra J. Ball. Washington, D.C.: Government Printing Office, 1969.

Forman, Henry J. *Our Movie-Made Children.* New York: Macmillan, 1935.

Gelmis, Joseph. "The Assault by Screen Violence." *Newsday,* 1 May 1983.

Jowett, Garth. *Film: The Democratic Art.* Boston: Little, Brown, 1976.

Kennedy, Harlan. "Things That Go Howl in the Id." *Film Comment* 18 (March/April 1982): 37–39.

Michelson, Peter. *The Aesthetics of Pornography.* New York: Herder and Herder, 1971.

Milavsky, J. Ronald, Kessler, Ronald C., Stipp, Horst H., and Rubens, William S. *Television and Aggression: Results of a Panel Study.* San Diego: Academic Press, 1962.

Pearl, David. Statement to Subcommittee on Telecommunications of the Committee on Energy and Commerce, U.S. House of Representatives. 21 October 1981.

Pearl, David, Bouthilet, Lorraine, and Lazar, Joyce, eds. *Television and Behavior, Summary Report*. Rockville, Md.: U.S. Department of Health and Human Services, 1982.

Pillard, Richard C., Atkinson, Kim Wells, and Fisher, Seymour. "The Effect of Different Preparations on Film-Induced Anxiety." *Psychological Record* 17 (1967): 35–41.

Sklar, Robert. *Movie-Made America*. New York: Vintage Books, 1976.

Surgeon General's Scientific Advisory Committee on Television and Behavior. *Television and Growing Up: The Impact of Televised Violence*. Washington, D.C.: Government Printing Office, 1972.

Stoller, Robert J. *Observing the Erotic Imagination*. New Haven: Yale University Press, 1985.

Weldon, Michael. *The Psychotronic Encyclopedia of Film*. New York: Ballantine Books, 1983.

Williams, Linda. "When the Woman Looks." In *Revision: Essays in Feminist Film Criticism*, edited by Mary Ann Doane, Patricia Mellencamp, and Linda Williams. Frederick, Md.: University Publications of America, 1983.

Williams, Tony. "American Cinema in the 70s: Family Horror." *Movie* 27/28 (Winter 1980/Spring 1981): 117-26.

Wood, Robin. Introduction to *American Nightmare: Essays on the Horror Film*, edited by Andrew Britton et al. Toronto: Festival of Festivals, 1979.

7   *Kiss of the Spiderwoman*

Micheline Klagsbrun Frank

Given the current popularity of romance and adventure on the movie screen, it would seem unlikely that a film that takes place within the walls of a prison cell, focused on two main characters, both male, would last long in mainstream theaters. The Success of *Kiss of the Spiderwoman* testifies to the excellent acting of Raul Julia and William Hurt, but principally to the extraordinary power of the movie, on various levels. Not only does it express certain primitive yearnings and complexes that resonate within all its viewers but also, through its self-referential aspect (the way that movies are included within the movie itself), it illuminates the power of cinema in general. Furthermore, it explores the concepts of male and female, self and other, in a way that is intimately connected with psychological and developmental issues on the one hand and philosophical matters on the other.

The Power and Place of the Cinematic Experience

The power of cinema derives from the primitive nature of the viewing experience, recalling earliest infantile life. This idea now seems accepted in current thinking about film, yet the exact nature of the experience is often not specified. It seems to me to have two crucial characteristics: (1) confusion between internal and external phenomena, and (2) confusion between active and passive viewing.

Obviously, the situation in which movies are viewed is conducive to regression: the room is darkened, the surroundings shrink to a cushioned chair, the rest of the world disappears. The self of the viewer also disappears; to some extent viewers become invisible, focusing their attention on an image that is both external to them and yet in some way internal.

150

Molina (William Hurt) and Valentin (Raul Julia) in Hector Babenco's *Kiss of the Spiderwoman* (1985).

The situation of feeding is the one that for me provides the closest analogy: viewers are fed by the movie, "drinking it in" like the infant at the breast. Freed from the anxiety of having their cannabalism visible to others, they are able to view devouringly.[1]

Several writers have emphasized the similarities between movie viewing and dreaming (e.g., Eberwein 1984, Lewin 1963), but to me this overstates the passive side of movie viewing insofar as it implies that the state is akin to sleep. One cannot deny the immobility of the audience and the related hypnotic quality of film (partly physiologically induced). It is equally undeniable that in the infant, the sated condition of falling asleep after feeding extends the blissful feeding state into a state of union, with total loss of boundaries. In addition, there are many parallels in structure and function between dream and film. But to step from these to an analysis of film viewing as "a revival of the dreamlike state of infancy . . . the dissolution of the ego results in a merger of viewer and object" (Eberwein 1984, 34), is to ignore the active component that characterizes both feeding and film viewing and to overlook the "potential space" (Winnicott 1971) between baby and mother, which is all-important in this context. We are not completely one with the universe, and in an altered state of consciousness in the movie theater, but like the staring infant, we are receiving and incorporating, assimilating and organizing, exploring, feeling through different senses, comparing, maintaining or remaining aware of our sense of self and other (though this may fluctuate). We are not up on the screen, are not Meryl Streep and Robert Redford, but we are in constant relation to them and may at moments become closely identified with them. This is not the same as a dream, which happens to *me,* in which I am the central character with the action taking place around me. There is also an element of choice or voluntary censorship in movie viewing. I can close my eyes, put my fingers in my ears, walk around, or leave, none of which is possible during the dream.

We view the movie with an intensity and involvement that makes what we view partially ours, yet not entirely. The fusion of subject and object is not complete; it rather has to do with a "creative relation to the world" (Milner 1952). It takes place in Winnicott's "potential space," a third human state that is neither internal nor external but "intermediate." The baby's experience of mother's reliability is what allows the process of separation from her to begin: paradoxically, the "absence of a space between" (Winnicott) allows the potential space to take shape. At the same time that the baby begins to separate out "me" from "not-me," "separation is avoided by the filling-in of the potential space with creative playing, with the use of symbols, and with all that eventually adds up to a cultural life" (Winnicott 1971, 109). Although in the earliest instance of creativity the mother "places the actual breast just there where the infant is ready to create, and at the right moment" (Winnicott, 11) so that the infant feels he has "created" it, creative apperception (including enjoyment and appreciation of the arts) is based not on a state of merger with mother but precisely at the end of that state, when the baby begins to separate. There is a space, a tension, a give-and-take between audience and spectacle. The active component is exploratory, a playful grasping of the world that is being presented and a creative investment of that world with associations and feelings. The excitement has to do with "the precariousness of magic itself" (Winnicott, 47).

Within *Kiss of the Spiderwoman,*[2] Molina narrates movies to Valentin, initially as a way of entertaining himself, of making a prison existence tolerable, and of establishing contact with his fellow inmate. As the movie develops, the movies begin to function as comforters, easing pain, allowing Valentin to fall asleep, like the bedtime stories, songs, and transitional objects that are used to help children fall asleep. The movies also provide a fantasy for Valentin that is both different from his own troubled fantasy life and yet sufficiently relevant to it to provide relief from its unpleasantness and pain. Again this seems to parallel the function of the bedtime story, which can perform its own particular alchemy on the problems and unfulfillments of real life.

The Kiss

There seems no question to me that this is a highly poignant movie, even a melodrama (as in Cavell's genre of melodrama), in which yearning for the unattainable is a basic structure of experience. Molina yearns to be loved by a "real man," yet the catch is that no real (heterosexual) man will ever be attracted to him. Beneath this yearning lies the impossibility of his existence. He is not, I believe, a true homosexual, but a woman inside a man's body. (I shall return to this later). Valentin's existence is doomed in a different way. Only political revolution, a radical upheaval of the outside world, can save him, and this is far from likely. For them as a potential couple, love is no less impossible. Indeed, it seems to me to be of the essence of melodrama that the couple be separated forever by a tragic ending that at the same time binds them together forever. A paradigm might be the legend of Apollo and Daphne: after lengthy pursuit he catches up with her, but at the precise moment of his embrace she turns into a tree, thereby escaping him forever and yet remaining captive, rooted to the spot and bound to him forever.

Cavell speaks of the genre of melodrama as presenting the dark side of the "remarriage comedy" genre, and I would extend this to characterize it as being most clearly about separation, about the unattainable object, which must at some level be the breast and the earliest experience of blissful union. A poem by Marvell (published 1681), is most apt here (reproduced in part):

The Definition of Love

My Love is of a birth as rare
As 'tis for object strange and high:
It was begotten by despair
Upon Impossibility.
. . . .
And yet I quickly might arrive
Where my extended Soul is fixt,
But Fate does Iron wedges drive,
And alwaies crouds it self betwixt.
. . . .
And therefore her Decrees of Steel
Us as the distant Poles have plac'd,
(Though Loves whole World on us doth wheel)
Not by themselves to be embrac'd.

Unless the giddy Heaven fall,
And Earth some new Convulsion tear;
And, us to joyn, the World should all
Be cramp'd into a *Planisphere.*

As Lines so Loves *oblique* may well
Themselves in every Angle greet:
But ours so truly *Paralel,*
Though infinite can never meet.

In the metaphysical conceit of this poem, the lovers become the opposite poles of the earth's axis. Paradoxically, they are forever joined and forever separated.

After Molina's death we are taken to the prison hospital, where Valentin is half-dead from brutal torture. Given morphine by a sympathetic intern, he drifts into a final dream in which he continues a movie that Molina had been telling him, the story of the Spiderwoman. Though separated forever, the two men become a couple in fantasy—they create themselves as a couple. Molina creates himself in his dreams as the ideal Spiderwoman, the beauty he wants to be, adulated yet alone, in search of her perfect man, who is one day washed up onto the beach of her prison cell; Valentin, hearing the story, gives the woman the face of Marta, his unattainable woman, the taboo woman that he really wants.

And so Molina becomes Marta, becomes the woman Valentin really wants, and in the last dream, continued by Valentin where Molina left off, they kiss as they kissed good-bye in the cell, a long Hollywood kiss.

The Spiderwoman

One moment is crucial to this film. As in *Letter from an Unknown Woman* (see Cavell in this volume), a switch in camera angle seems to provide a key. In an early, highly erotic scene, Molina is telling a movie, moving like a woman, sliding his hips, tossing his hair. He lies back on the floor, opening his thighs, and suddenly the camera is also lying on the floor and we see Valentin from Molina's viewpoint. The camera's assumption of the female angle produces a shock. It seems to me that this is rare in movie sex scenes, where the camera is usually at the same level as the lovers, viewing from the side; or darting around voyeuristically to catch nice arrangements of flesh; or stationed from the man's viewpoint, watching the woman undress; or coming down toward her (or, more rarely, watching her come down toward him). The switch in angle has a double-twist impact: the woman with whom the camera is identifying here is inside a man. For women in the audience, this creates the disturbance of identifying with a sexually attractive man. I both identify with his movements, recognizing them as my own, as feminine, and am attracted to him physically. This is why the eroticism is crucial here, producing a clash, making a conflict suddenly acute. Somehow the eroticism and the confusion are at a pitch in this scene, compared to the actual lovemaking, which is almost an anticlimax, a more standard Hollywood climax, and less provocative.

I am making a vital distinction here between the homosexual and the woman-inside-a-man, a distinction that has been addressed most fully by Robert Stoller in almost thirty years of writing on the subject (see especially Stoller 1968, 1975, 1976, 1985). Stoller defines core gender identity as "the sense we have of our sex—of maleness in males and of femaleness in females . . . a part of, but not identical with, what I have called gender identity—a broader concept, standing for the mix of masculinity and femininity found in every person" (Stoller 1976, 61).[3] Core gender identity, fixed by the age of two or three, includes the earliest stage of gender development, which is also the phase of merger with mother. "Sensing oneself a part of mother—a primeval and thus profound part of character structure (core gender identity)—lays the groundwork for an infant's sense of femininity. This sets the girl firmly on the path to femininity in adulthood but puts the boy in danger of building into his core gender identity a sense of oneness with mother (a sense of femaleness)" (Stoller 1985, 16). Thus, Stoller reverses the traditional Freudian ethos of masculinity as the secure, well-founded, stable identification and femininity as problematic (both because of the girl's "inferior," less visible genitals, and because her first "love object" is homosexual, i.e., her mother). For the female baby, the original intimacy with mother is no problem for future identification, but for the male, Stoller hypothesizes that "a trace, a touch of uncertainty that their masculinity (identity) is intact" persists throughout life. The second stage of gender development takes place at the oedipal level, along the general lines described by Freud.

Stoller's theory is founded primarily on his extensive clinical studies of "primary transsexual males," through which he also explores masculinity in general. He explains:

> In the rare case, despite biologically normal sex and proper assignment, core gender identity can still be shifted from that expected. . . . I believe this occurs in the excessively intimate and blissful symbiosis found in the most feminine of boys (transsexuals), those who believe they are in some way females (while still not denying their anatomy or sex assignment). . . . There is no evidence that these infants were traumatized in the symbiosis or subjected to frustrations that could cause intrapsychic conflict as seen in effeminate homosexuals. [1976,64]

The behavior of these boys is exclusively feminine, accentuated but without caricature. Stoller continues:

> My data suggest that this femininity is not the result of preoedipal or oedipal conflict, but is rather the product of the failure of the infant to sense himself as separate from the mother's female body; the process is nonconflictual—is, in fact, an extremely gratifying experience in an excessively prolonged mother-infant symbiosis. [1976,69]

While trying to make sense of my intuitions concerning the Spiderwoman, I turned to Stoller's writings and was struck by the relevance of his ideas. His concept of the "male primary transsexual" (1985), as distinct from "male secondary transsexuals" (defined as "men requesting sex change"), seemed to fit Molina perfectly. In Puig's novel, Molina refers to himself as "this girl," "this woman," and gives himself a "real" name, Carmen. He distinguishes himself and his closest friends from the other "fags": "We're normal women, we sleep with men." His feminine style is evident in the way he makes the cell habitable, decorating, setting up house, and in his mothering of Valentin, feeding and telling stories, cleaning and diapering him during the diarrhea episode. His movements, the clothes he prefers, his gracefulness are those of a woman.

In the book, he tells himself a "a totally romantic" film (not shared with Valentin), the tale of a blind man, an artist, who sees what's really important, not superficial appearances. In this story, the ugly servant girl lives alone with her sadness, content with a glimpse of her hero and his beautiful fiancée. Then the hero is scarred in battle, with Valentin's scar, making him as ugly as the servant girl and similarly rejected by society. Together they achieve happiness because when out of sight of the rest of the world they become magically beautiful to each other. Even in internal fantasy, where he can dream of himself with a man, Molina dreams of a man-woman romance and identifies with the woman, specifically with this outcast girl whose hopeless love is magically fulfilled.

In his discussion of the transference of male transsexual patients, Stoller further notes "a great silence," which he takes, along with other features, to be "the recapitulation of an infancy and childhood in which father was absent and mother treated her beautiful son as if he were a *thing,* an ideal feminized phallus that she had grown from her own body and then kept all-too-attached in the unending symbiosis" (1976, 69–70). The parallel is striking between this image and that of the Spiderwoman, whose web "is growing out of her own body, the threads are coming out of her waist and hips, they're part of her body, so many threads that look hairy like ropes and disgust me, even though if I were to touch them they might feel as smooth as who knows what, but it makes me queasy to touch them" (Puig 1979, 280). This passage also makes it clear that the Spiderwoman is the Phallic mother, primitive and omnipotent.

Stoller elaborates his theory to encompass "the forms that masculinity typically takes in cultures everywhere—the macho belligerence that degrades women" (1985, 17), which he takes as evidence of male anxiety about primary femininity. Less emphasized in the movie than in Puig's novel, this tendency is evident in Valentin, particularly in his nightmare, in references to the guerrilla girl who loves him—"a girl treated like a thing . . . a girl who gets used up and tossed aside, a girl to dump semen into" (Puig 1979, 128–29). This nightmare appears in italic type, as do flashes of imagery, like a strand of unconscious subtext woven through the book. At one point the images emerging from Valentin's unconscious evoke the brutality and oppression of the Nazi regime, with associations of racial inferiority and brain measurement:

> a dog's cortex, a mule's, a horse's cortex, a monkey's, a primate's cortex, a chick's from suburbia hanging out at the movies when she's supposed to be in church . . . impassive gaze of the learned executioner down upon the poor innocent cortex of a chick from suburbia, of a fag from suburbia . . . the poor rolling head of the fag from suburbia . . . the narrow little

forehead encasing the brains of that poor chick from suburbia, and who
gave the order to have her guillotined? the learned executioner obeys an
order which comes from no one knows where.[187–88]

These images point up the macho structure of the revolutionary, the
potential Nazi core within the victim of oppression, echoed by the Nazi
propaganda movie recounted by Molina.

The story of this relationship can be read as a triumph for femininity,
as Molina's love brings out the tenderness in Valentin and overcomes the
barrier to intimacy that protects the male from the pull back into symbiosis. In a rare portrayal of a primary transsexual as a human being and
not a freak, *Spiderwoman* opens up questions for its whole audience.
What is a man? What is a woman? Where are my own responses? What
am I? The extreme instance highlights the potential femininity in all
men and, indeed, the bisexuality in all human beings. The question of
gender is addressed directly in the text, thus:

V: And what's masculine in your terms?
M: It's lots of things, but for me . . . to be marvelous-looking, and
     strong, but without making any fuss about it, and also walking very
     tall . . . walking absolutely straight, not afraid to say anything. And
     it's knowing what you want, where you're going.
V: That's pure fantasy, that type doesn't exist.[61]

Molina's definition of a man is pure fantasy because it refers to what was
essentially missing in his childhood—the "powerful paternal force"
(Loewald 1951). Stoller quotes Loewald on the "positive non-hostile
aspect of the father figure . . . with whom an active, non-passive identification is made, an identification which lies before and beyond submis-
sion as well as rebellion" (15–16). This preoedipal identification, which
prepares for and feeds into the Oedipus complex, is markedly absent in
male primary transsexuals, Stoller notes. It may also be that Molina's
definition is pure fantasy because it includes phallic uprightness and
strength together with feminine qualities, exemplified by Molina's idol,
the resolutely heterosexual waiter who occasioned this discussion: "It was
poetry, one time I saw him do a salad . . . like he caressed the lettuce
leaves, and the tomatoes, but nothing softy about it—how can I put it?
They were such powerful movements, and so elegant, and soft, and
masculine at the same time" (61).

The discussion continues, with a clash of masculine and feminine
modes—Molina pointing out Valentin's competitiveness and Valentin
retaliating with "You can't carry on a discussion, there's no line of
thought to it." Molina counters by asking for Valentin's definition of a

man, receiving a nonanswer: "Mmmm . . . his not taking any crap from anyone. . . . But no, it's more than that . . . it has to do with not humiliating someone else . . . you've caught me off guard. I can't seem to find the right words. Some other time, when my ideas are a little clearer on the subject, we can go back to it" (63). This evasion, from the otherwise articulate Valentin, implies that his masculinity rests on the type of macho defenses elaborated by Stoller, of which Valentin is not proud. For him, the "man" of the movie, the answer to "What is a man?" is unsure.

When he is finally released from prison, Molina takes on an assignment from Valentin, passing a message to the revolutionaries by telephone. He knows that he is likely to be followed by the authorities, that the mission is highly dangerous, and we suspect he anticipates that it will cause his death. Indeed, he dies trapped, as in life, between two camps, a victim of both the police and rebels. By his heroic act, standing tall in these circumstances, he becomes, by his own definition at least, a man. But this raises the question How desirable is this goal? What is the point of this person's "becoming a man"? It's a death, or waste of life, on two levels—the death of the person and the death of the woman-inside-the-man. Puig seems to be echoing Valentin: by eliminating Molina at the moment in which he becomes his own ideal man, the combination of masculine and feminine virtues, he tells us, "That's pure fantasy, that type doesn't exist."

If we agree with Stoller that the task of the developing male is to separate himself from his mother's female body and feminine behavior, then we can place Molina at the far end of a continuum that includes all men. Taking this movie to be at least partly about the power of movies, as it derives from the primitive nature of the movie-incorporation experience, then part of the power of the film is that its central character expresses the same theme through his being. His essence is a yearning for that "too-intimate, gratifying, unending symbiosis" (Stoller 1976, 71) that was his for a most unusual length of time. In Wordsworthian terms, since he spent a longer time amid the clouds of glory than most of us, he is a fit guide to that region, and this is why he himself is addicted to movies and holds the power of moviemaking, web spinning, lullaby creating. Through him we are led into a second level of fantasy life: his need for movies reflects our own—the need to submit to the pull, to suspend our selves, or at another level, to enjoy more of the pleasures of life ("What kind of cause is it that doesn't let you eat an avocado?"). A highly tentative speculation could attribute the genesis of Molina's storytelling powers to the delay in separation from mother. Although Winnicott places the critical stage for development of the "potential space" at the point at which the baby is beginning to move toward autonomy, he draws no conclusion as to the effect of prolonged fusion. Possibly an extended period of bliss would raise the stakes in the separation process; although a substantial *potential* space would have been created, the pull toward remaining merged would be so much greater than usual that the need to fill in that space would result in more productive creativity.

The Fly

The logic that where there exists a spider there must also be a fly rescues us from sentimentality about this film. The paradox is contained in the title and our associations thereto: the kiss—seductive, erotic, fascinating—draws us in; the spider—repulsive, poisonous—traps us and sucks us dry. Molina is supposed to be eliciting information from Valentin for the authorities, who are "softening him up" by poisoning his food (hence the diarrhea). In the written text, Molina's unconscious imagery portrays him as a nurse, assigned to a patient on the critical list "and she doesn't know how to keep him from dying or killing her." "The nurse trembles, the patient looks up at her, asking for morphine? asking to be caressed? or does he just want the contagion to be instantaneous and deadly?" (172–75). There are several hints at his duplicity: "the strict nurse, the very tall cap stiff with starch, the slight smile not without cunning . . . the treacherous somnambula" (162, 168). Yet other references to contagion show his fear that he will "catch" death from this patient, that his love for Valentin will prove fatal.

There are two points in the story at which the fly " pours out" a mixture of physical diarrhea and confession. The first (in the book but not in the movie) follows Valentin's first episode of stomach pain, which Molina tries to alleviate by telling a movie about a racing car driver and a beautiful older woman. During the narration, Molina suddenly says, "You know something . . . you never talk about your mother." Valentin's response is diarrhea, which Molina cleans up. When they return to the conversation, Valentin replies:

> V: My mother is the kind of woman who's very . . . very difficult, that's why I don't talk about her much. She's never liked my ideas.
> M: Upper-crust like.
> V: You might say that.
> M: A little like the film I'm telling you.
> V: No . . . you're crazy.
> M: Well then, more or less.
> V: Not at all. Aghhh . . . hurts so much. . . . [121]

After this exchange Molina quickly finishes the story, pointing out the similarity with Valentin's life situation, concluding "oh, and I forgot to tell you how when at the end they free the father there's a shootout with the cops, and the father is mortally wounded by them, and the mother reappears, and they end up together, the son and the mother I mean, because the other woman doesn't stay, the one who loves him, she goes back to Paris'' (122). Thus, the difference between the two characters is emphasized: an idealized woman of superlative beauty and power is a figure for both, yet the dynamic of Valentin's story is clearly distinguishable as oedipal.

The nightmare that follows the racing car driver movie uses the same characters because they fit Valentin's life. He is the well-born hero who sympathizes with the guerrillas, who loves a poised, beautiful woman obviously reminiscent of his mother; he's also the hero who exploits the poor guerrilla girl who loves him. His disgust and guilt at his sexual exploitation of this girl are followed by footnotes from Anna Freud on the earliest repression of prohibited sexual impulses leading to impotence, frigidity and guilt obsessions.[4] Sigmund Freud is also quoted on how an unresolved Oedipus will spoil future sexual experiences because they will always be associated with guilt.

Valentin's true confession is wrenched out of him by Molina's song: "Dearest . . . night brings a silence that helps me talk to you, and I wonder . . . could you be remembering too, sad dreams . . . of this strange love affair. My dear . . . although life may never let us meet again and we—because of fate—must always live apart . . . I swear, this heart of mine will always be yours . . . my thoughts, my whole life, forever yours . . . just as this pain . . . belongs . . . to you'' (137, footnoted with a quote from Fenichel on identification with the compelling mother, especially when father is absent). Ironically, all the most brutal forms of torture inflicted by men could not get it out of him, but after the song, and more cramps, he describes his relationships with his girlfriend-comrade, and then: "Something really terrible, something despicable . . . what I really like is . . . is the other kind of woman. Inside I'm just the same as all the other reactionary bastards . . . with Marta, I don't feel attracted to her for any good reasons, but because . . . because she has class . . . that's right, class, just like all the class-conscious pigs would say'' (144–45). Marta has all the qualities he idealized in his own mother but cannot accept—they are listed in the unconscious subtext: "a bright woman, a beautiful woman, an educated woman . . . of impeccable taste . . . young and at the same time mature . . . who knows how to give orders to servants . . . how to organize a reception for a hundred people'' (144–45).

The Web

For the majority of males, all the characteristics, occupations, attributes that Western culture defines as feminine, exemplified by Molina, become feared and rejected as part of the little boy's push away from the blissful merger with mother. In normal male development, the encouragement of masculine impulses leads to "symbiosis anxiety" (Stoller 1985) that functions as a "protective shield" within.

Two points in Stoller's writing here lead to a different plane of discussion, which I would now like to enter. He refers to "symbiosis anxiety" as a protective shield within the boy, implying the need for protection not only from outside influences but also from an inner core—"the already-constructed core of impulses toward femininity" (1985, 183). In the same passage he specifies the fear of intimacy "of entering, even more than their bodies, into women's inner selves." At this juncture, the echoes of Cavell's writings become too loud to ignore, and I find myself pulled irresistibly toward an attempt to integrate these thoughts with aspects of his essay in this volume.

Cavell asks, "Why does psychoanalysis first realize itself—through the agency (that is, through the suffering) of women, as reported in the *Studies on Hysteria* and in the case of Dora, the earliest of the longer case histories? The second question is: How, if at all, is this circumstance related to the fact (again, granted the fact) that film—another invention of the last years of the nineteenth century . . .—is from first to last more interested in the study of individual women than of individual men?" For the man, woman is quintessentially other, both from a philosophical viewpoint and, as representative of the unconscious, as the hidden primitive core of being that must remain sealed away. The man is fascinated with and attracted toward whatever recalls the earliest experiences of bliss, and what must remain unknown.

Woman is not only the unknown, according to Cavell, but has a special access to knowledge. Starting from the notion that "philosophical skepticism is inflected, if not altogether determined, by gender, by whether one sets oneself aside as male or female," Cavell moves to an even more radical possibility, "that philosophical skepticism, and a certain denial of its reality, is a male business." The "fanaticism" of doubt is personified by Leontes, who doubts that his children are his—a doubt that is uniquely male. In response to this doubt, a patriarchal society imposes the Name-of-the-Father (to use a Lacanian phrase) arbitrarily on its children.

Although Cavell doesn't extend his argument this far one could posit that this "gender asymmetry" is recapitulated at the physical level of sexual intercourse. If the female response to skepticism is "I know the other exists because he has been inside my body," then receiving the penis and holding it inside would seem to reaffirm this. Molina, who receives Valentin's penis, is again the woman in this context. The skeptic might question further here: Why is being inside the woman not, for men, a refutation of skepticism? I believe that the answer would be that it *is* an antiskeptical experience and works as well as it can (contributing to the satisfaction of intercourse), yet it cannot be the equivalent of the woman's experience. The woman's nonskeptical assurance of herself and her world can be directly related to female *jouissance* (a Lacanian term connoting sexual pleasure and enjoyment that is not "used up" or ended in discharge), an experience somehow closer to the "pure female element of Being" (Winnicott 1971, 80, see later discussion) than to the male mode of object relating and being-at-one-with. The fact of female *jouissance* would seem to offer another opportunity for the male to refute skepticism as he sees that he can cause pleasure in the other, yet this opportunity is rejected, as Cavell turns even this into a male doubt, "Is her satisfaction real and is it caused by me?" At the same time, Cavell quotes Lacan's belief in "the *jouissance* of the woman in so far as it is something more" (Lacan 1975, 71) as meaning "What there is (any longer?) of God, or of the concept of the beyond, takes place in relation to the woman." Her knowledge is that of the mystic, the ecstatic, probably not verbalizable.

Lacan has always emphasized woman as unknown, as "the other" (*l'objet "a"*, small "a") and *l'Autre*. In his seminar *Encore* (1975), he takes up the question that Freud "expressly left aside, the *Was will das Weib?* (the What does woman want?)" (75). The answer is "Encore," seemingly spoken by Saint Teresa on the seminar cover, of whom Lacan writes, "you only have to go and look at the Bernini statue in Rome to understand immediately that she's coming, no doubt about it" (70).[5] But this attempt to pin down a moment of certainty belies his basic feeling that woman is a mystery, essentially unknowable. Phallic satisfaction, according to Lacan, gets in the way of the man's potential possession of the woman. Repeatedly, through his series of lectures, "the phallic order and phallic enjoyment are shown to be a kind of failure: a failure to reach the Other, a short-circuiting of desire by which it turns back on itself. The phallic order fails because, although unable to account for the feminine, it would, nonetheless, operate as a closure, attempting to create a closed universe that is thoroughly phallocentric" (Gallop 1982, 34).

To invoke the name of Lacan opens up a whole new (but closely related) area of discussion, principally "the Discourse of the Other," which can only be alluded to here. He integrates the different levels at which the concept of "object relation" operates, from the "stade du miroir" (1966), the fascinating image that is both self and other, providing a source for future identifications, to the play of logic and epistemology, where the lack of the object becomes the basis for language itself. What I have called "yearning" seems to be closely related to Lacan's concept of *desir*. Developmentally, the occasional absence of the object leads to desire. The desire for primal unity can be expressed as the desire for annihilation of difference: to use Lacan's mathematical metaphor, the primordial "one" or unity is actually "the not-nothing-not-something of zero" (Wilden 1968, 191). The child progresses from this zero state "to the status of 'One,' who can therefore know two. The subject *is* the binary opposition of presence and absence, and the discovery of One—the discovery of difference—is to be condemned to an eternal desire for the nonrelationship of zero, where identity is meaningless" (Wilden, 191).

Cavell's concern with skepticism, with the problem of the existence of other minds, can be partly translated into the essential aloneness of the characters he examines. In *Letter from an Unknown Woman*, the crucial question, "Are you lonely out there?" (answered "Yes, very") is called out to the woman from another room. In *Spiderwoman*, Molina is by nature alone, trapped as the Spiderwoman, neither one gender nor the other; even in his relationship with Valentin, a secret is always between them. After his release from jail, his loneliness as a marked man, progressing inevitably toward his death, is emphasized by the tracking of the camera. The camera takes long shots of his solitary figure sitting by the window, tracks him from afar amid his former friends, from whom his experience in jail has psychically removed him. He dies alone, trapped between hostile forces of guerrillas and police, his noble gesture misunderstood. Yet as the woman, through the passion of his love for Valentin, he has redeemed his life. Somehow we feel it has been made worthwhile.

In discussing Lacan's concept of *desir,* Wilden notes that "Desire, as an absolute, is fundamentally the Hegelian desire for recognition" (1968, 189). This relates to Molina's desire to be recognized as a woman, requiring a heterosexual man to recognize his desire. In examining the terrible poignancy of the end of the movie, I tried to imagine what reparative ending might have alleviated it, and came up with the return of Molina (alive) to prison, not to be reunited with Valentin but simply so that Valentin would see him recaptured and *recognize* the extent of his love and heroism. I sense a parallel here with *Letter from an Unknown Woman*, with the way that the woman's final letter reveals her true self to the man, reveals the extent of her love, so that he must acKNOWledge her. I also think of the last view of Stella Dallas, standing in the rain, watching her daughter's wedding through the window, unacknowledged in her sacrifice yet happy, sustained by her love. In this regard, the ending of the written *Spiderwoman* is gentler than the movie. It's made clear that Valentin does know of Molina's sacrifice, and also comes to see him as a very sad, very beautiful woman.

Male and Female

Just as one who doubts the paternity of his children must be male, the one who causes the doubt, who undermines the Name-of-the-Father, is always female. In the works of Lacan and his followers and critics, the position of woman and the female emerges as constantly subversive, outside the system. Although I have chosen not to focus on the political side of *Spiderwoman*, the setting of the drama in a prison cell places Molina, as female, outside society, with the revolutionary. In Puig's book, citing Freud, Otto Rank, Wilhelm Reich, and Herbert Marcuse, among others, he implies a similarity in political position between women and homosexuals. A state run by men, with women as child producers without political power, is shown to be historically a state that fosters sexual repression (by associating sex with sin, justified only by the procreation of children) and rejects all forms of sexual behavior outside the genital and heterosexual.

There are, of course, numerous descriptions that imply woman's "inferior" status. For example, there is Lacan's famous statement, "The phallus is the privileged signifier" (1966, 692). Irigaray discusses woman's language: "The fluid . . . is, by nature, unstable. . . . Woman never speaks *pareil* [similar, equal]. What she emits is flowing [*fluent*], fluctuating. Cheating [*flouant*]" (1974, 52). The privilege of the phallus is also the preference for the solid, the rigid, "the metaphysical privileging of identity" (Gallop 1982, 39), as opposed to the flow, which "allows itself to be easily traversed by flows on account of its conductibility . . . mixes with bodies in a like state . . . renders problematic the distinction between the one and the other" (Irigaray 1974, 52). According to Irigaray, the paradigm object for Lacan is fecal—"solid, distinct, countable" (53). For Valentin, his solid masculine identity is gradually undermined as he is "softened up" by poison and by his relationship with Molina, until the explosive diarrhea scenes, when his confession pours out.

A further dimension to the consideration of male and female elements comes from Winnicott, who speaks of gender identification at the earliest stage, of male and female modes of relating to the breast. "The element that I am calling 'male' does traffic in terms of active relating or passive being related to, each being backed by instinct . . . by contrast, the pure female element relates to the breast (or to the mother) in the sense of *the baby becoming the breast (or mother), in the sense that the object is the subject.* I can see no instinct drive in this" (Winnicott 1971, 79; Winnicott's emphasis). The sense of being (which predates being-at-one-with, as, for Lacan, zero predates one) is the "female element" in both men and women. "The male element *does* while the female element (in males and females) *is*. Here would come in those males in Greek myth who try to be at one with the Supreme Goddess" (Winnicott 1971, 81; Winnicott's emphasis).

The Supreme Goddess, the Phallic Mother, the Spiderwoman—all have in common the fusion of male and female qualities. Descending from the mythological plane to the real, this fusion is enacted through sexual intercourse, ideally "not simply the mingling of two opposites, which keep their opposite identities, but an intermingling of two opposites, a contamination of the opposition, a risking of difference and identity" (Gallop 1982, 126). Psychoanalysts also have pointed to the fusion of sexual identifications during intercourse: for example, "the excitement accompanying the partner's orgasm also reflects an unconscious identification with that partner and, in normal heterosexual intercourse, a sublimated expression of homosexual identifications from both pre-genital and genital sources. . . . Such an intense double identification during orgasm also represents a capacity for transcendence, for entering and becoming one with another person in a psychological as well as physical sense" (Kernberg 1974, 222–23). Both the "risking of difference and identity" and the transcendent merging are illustrated in the lovemaking between Molina and Valentin, as in this extract:

M: Just then, without thinking, I put my hand up to my face, trying to find the mole.
V: What mole? . . . I have it, not you.
M: Mmm, I know. But I put my hand to my forehead, to feel the mole that . . . I haven't got.
M: For just a second, it seemed like I wasn't here . . . not here or anywhere out there either . . . like it was you all alone. . . . Or like I wasn't me anymore. As if now, somehow . . . I . . . were you. [219]

Through this intermingling, Molina can finally become the perfect woman, as fantasied by Valentin, who can be the superhero male.

The written *Spiderwoman* text provides a flow of parallel ideas, with several strands interwoven (story and related movie, theory and narrative, conscious and unconscious). I think of my essay in similar terms. As an example of what has been described as "feminine" writing, it proceeds not as an argument toward closure, but as an exploration, a loosening of boundaries, a bringing together of diverse ideas, "risking contamination" through interpenetration. The Spiderwoman's final advice to

Valentin, in the last morphine dream, is to know when to stop analyzing, "and I answer her that it's good this way, that it's the very best part of the film because it signifies . . . and at that point she didn't let me go on, she said that I wanted to find an explanation for everything, but that in reality I was just talking from hunger although I didn't have the courage to admit it" (280). She may be telling us that her mystery, and the mysteries of art in general, are beyond complete explanation.

Notes

1. "The breast" and "nursing" are summary terms I use to include all aspects of intimate contact between mother and baby: holding, warmth, pressure, skin contact, rocking, stroking, heartbeat, smells, pulses, rhythms, kissing, sights and sounds, etc. Nursing is the primary organizer of the baby's world.

2. Throughout this chapter the movie and written text (Puig 1979) are used interchangeably. The text is barer than a stage play, devoid of description or direction, leaving the images of the movie unaltered. The book contains additional material, but the essence of the two seems to me identical.

3. "Masculinity or femininity is defined here as any quality that is felt by its possessor to be masculine or feminine. In other words, masculinity or femininity is a belief—more precisely, a dense mass of beliefs, an algebraic sum of ifs, buts and ands, and not an incontrovertible fact" (Stoller 1985, 11).

4. The footnotes in the *Spiderwoman* book are substantial enough to be considered as a subtext. In them, Puig catalogs and describes social, political, and psychoanalytic theories, and recounts the Nazi movie. Often the relation between the footnotes and main text on any one page seems peripheral and must be closely examined.

5. Lacan uses *jouissance,* with reference to its legal sense, as "enjoyment" of something that cannot be used up—i.e., sexual pleasure that does not end in discharge. However, he alludes also to the word's colloquial meaning, "to come" or to achieve orgasm, which is how his reference to Saint Teresa is usually translated. I find that at least two points cast doubt upon this translation: first, Lacan's next sentence aligns Saint Teresa with the mystics, whose *jouissance* is ecstatic but not physical, and second, the sculpture itself seems to capture a moment of anticipatory ecstasy (as Cupid stands over Saint Teresa pointing his arrow at her) more related to the onset of "coming" than to a climax. The ambiguities inherent in this moment of apparent clarity imply that the female experience and the mystic's knowledge remain beyond the reach of verbal analysis.

References

Eberwein, Robert. *Film and the Dream Screen*. Princeton: Princeton University Press, 1984.

Gallop, Jane. *Feminism and Psychoanalysis: The Daughter's Seduction.* London: Macmillan Press, 1982.

Irigaray, Luce. "La 'Mecanique' des fluides." *L'Arc* 58 (1974):49–55.

Kernberg, Otto F. "Mature Love: Prerequisites and Characteristics." In *Object Relations Theory and Clinical Psychoanalysis.* New York: Jason Aronson, 1976.

Lacan, Jacques. *Ecrits.* Paris: Seuil, 1966.

————. *Le Séminaire: Livre XI. Les quatre concepts fondamentaux de la psychanalyse.* Paris: Seuil, 1972.

————. *Le Séminaire: Livre XX. Encore.* Paris: Seuil, 1975.

Lewin, Bertram. *Dreams and the Uses of Regression.* New York: International Universities Press, 1963.

Loewald, Hans W. "Ego and Reality." *International Journal of Psycho-Analysis* 32 (1951):10–18.

Milner, Marion. *On Not Being Able to Paint.* London: Heinemann, 1950.

————. "Aspects of Symbolism in Comprehension of the Not-Self." *International Journal of Psycho-Analysis* 33 (1952):181–95.

Puig, Manuel. *Kiss of the Spiderwoman.* Translated by Thomas Colchie. New York: Knopf, 1979.

Stoller, Robert. *Sex and Gender.* Vol. 1. New York: Science House, 1968.

————. *Sex and Gender.* Vol. 2. London: Hogarth Press, 1975.

————. "Primary Femininity." *Journal of the American Psychoanalytic Association* 24 (Supplement) (1976):59–78.

————. *Presentations of Gender.* New Haven: Yale University Press, 1985.

Wilden, A. *The Language of the Self.* Translation of *The Function of Language in Psychoanalysis,* by Jacques Lacan, New York: Dell, 1968.

Winnicott, D. W. *Playing and Reality.* London: Tavistock Publications, 1971.

8 Ingmar Bergman's *Cries and Whispers:* The Consequences of Preoedipal Developmental Disturbances

Bruce H. Sklarew

In *Cries and Whispers* the sisters Maria and Karin dutifully return to their family mansion to keep vigil for their dying sister, Agnes. The devoted housekeeper, Anna, embraces Agnes with intimate care. The film presents the interactions among the four women in the vulnerable state created by the dying and death of Agnes. Acute mourning engenders a regression that uncovers the women's struggles with intimacy, homosexuality, and sadomasochism.

This chapter focuses on the influence of the mother on the preoedipal conflicts and subsequent character development of the three sisters. Bergman reveals how difficult it is for each sister to establish intimacy, a cohesive self, and mature feminine identity because of preoedipal struggles to survive an inconsistent, narcissistic mother. This paradigm was probably not Bergman's conscious intention, but his intuition delivers powerful, poignant, and internally consistent characterizations.

One of Ingmar Bergman's most powerful films, *Cries and Whispers* leaves viewers with a shattered feeling of heaviness and despair, unraveled as if they had had a sad and bewildering dream. Bergman (1972) introduced the film to the cast in a story form later published in *The New Yorker:* "As I turn this project over in my mind, it never stands out as a completed whole . . . it resembles a dark, flowing stream: faces, movements, voices, gestures, exclamations, light and shade, moods, dreams. Nothing fixed, nothing really tangible other than for the moment, and then only an illusory moment. A dream, a longing, or perhaps an expectation, a fear, in which that to be feared is never put into words." Although couched in the form of a story, the film, like a dream, stresses visual images more than dialogue and uses rhythms and choreographed movements.

169

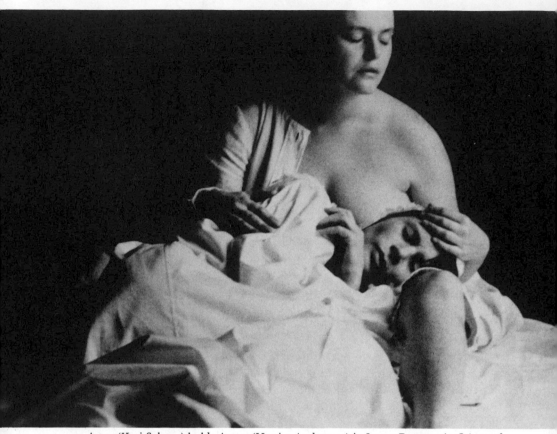

Anna (Kari Sylwan) holds Agnes (Harriet Andersson) in Igmar Bergman's *Cries and Whispers* (1972).

Bergman was plagued for six months by an image of three women dressed in white walking around and whispering in a red room, and he didn't know why. "If people talk with each other, I get terribly curious. I couldn't understand why these damned women were there. I tried to throw it away; I tried to write it down; I tried to find out what they said to each other, because they whispered. And suddenly it came out that they were watching another woman who was dying in the next room." The images haunted Bergman; he tried to reject them, but they would not go away—as the film's images do not for its viewers. He was both curious and disturbed by the contrast between the women's innocence and purity (symbolized by virginal white clothes) and their passions of blood (symbolized by red rooms, dresses, wine, fade-outs—and actual blood). The film's images recall the paintings of Edvard Munch: the sickrooms of his dying sister and his intense, mysterious women (*The Scream, Red and White, The Sick Child, Woman in Three Stages*).

The fade-outs and the interiors of the remote eighteenth-century mansion—"built as a retreat for a cast-off mistress"—are shades of red. Bergman has said, "The whole thing is something internal . . . ever since my childhood I have pictured the inside of the soul as a moist membrane in shades of red." The external image of the soul was that of a faceless, huge, red monster (Cowie 1982, 276). Mellen (1973) has said that Bergman defines women as instinctual, passive, submissive, and trapped within the odors and blood of their genitals. Bergman's view of women is similar to Freud's (no longer accepted by contemporary psychoanalysts) in its emphasis on damaged and defective genitals, masochism, a poorly developed superego, and a lack of capacity for sublimation. The feminine traits accentuated by Deutsch (1944) fit the three sisters: masochism (Karin); passivity (Agnes); and narcissism (Maria). Karin, for example, is unfulfilled in her motherhood and finds no sexual pleasure with men. Instead, she mutilates her genitals, and in a horrifying display humiliates and terrifies her husband. Intimacy is closely linked to blood; both scenes of husband-wife interaction result in blood on the face from self-inflicted injuries. Karin smears her face with blood after cutting her genitals, and Joakim, Maria's husband, brushes his bloodied hand along his face after stabbing himself.

The film presents a bleak view of women and men. To Bergman, the four women represent various facets of women's yearnings and lack of satisfaction—their hopes dashed by lies, their "tissue of lies." He has said that the four women depict aspects of his own mother. "Like the sisters in *The Silence,* they seem to be a part of a single soul" (Cowie 1982, 277). The men are inadequate and isolated, used and humiliated as objects for the rage of Maria and Karin. Choosing men who are cold and ungiving like their mother, the sisters displace their rage onto them. The striking absence of the father makes him a seeming nonentity in the family, but his influence is pervasive.

Contemporary psychoanalytic views of female development include Weil's (1970) delineation of the interaction between the infant's endowment and the earliest maternal attunement in the symbiotic stage, which leads to a basic core containing directional trends for later development. "At the beginning and even more so at the height of symbiosis, the specific initial core, which ranges from considerable harmony to considerable disharmony, becomes discernible" (443). Trends from the core suggest inferences in the nascent person about the dawning ego (such as object relatedness, resiliences, anxiety potential) and the balance between libido and aggression. In discussing the preoedipal and oedipal phases, Freud (1933, 134) observed: "We are no doubt justified in saying that much of both of them is left over for the future and that neither of them is adequately surmounted in the course of development. But the phase of the affectionate pre-Oedipus attachment [to the mother] is the decisive one for a woman's future: during it preparations are made for the acquisition of the characteristics with which she will later fulfil her role in the sexual function and perform her invaluable social tasks." Stoller (1976) believes that a gender identity and a feminine self-representation develop between the ages of eighteen months and three years, and that they are subsequently almost irreversible. Mahler (1974) agrees that during separation-individuation the development of feminine identity contributes to the shape and solution of crucial oedipal conflicts. Blum (1976, 171) discusses "The preoedipal development of cohesive self and object representations, of identity and gender identity, and the postoedipal evolution of a feminine and maternal ego ideal." Stoller, Mahler, Blum, and Galenson and Roiphe (1976), each from their own perspective, emphasize the influence of the preoedipal period on later development.

Bergman speaks of the inability to connect as "the unreasonable and never satisfied longing for fellowship, the clumsy attempt to do away with distance and isolation." Although his women have apparent intimacies, they all seem to be at cross-purposes, evoking a sense of ships passing in the night. *Cries and Whispers,* and *The Silence* and *Persona* as well, could be retitled *Touching* or *Hands and Faces.* All the women express their yearning for intimacy by touching: as a prelude to heterosexuality (Maria with the doctor), as an attempt to find maternal intimacy (the dying Agnes with Anna), as a solace for pain (Agnes with the doctor), as a way to comfort (Agnes with her mother), and as a stimulus to longing and fears of homosexuality (Maria and Karin). By touching, Maria melts Karin's masochistic defenses and leads her to entrapment and subsequent rejection. Cries and the touching of faces revive the usual activities and developmental messages of the early months of life, the most plastic phase of the preoedipal period. Their marked persistence into adulthood, however, suggests maternal deprivation or an alternation between connectedness and deprivation, which leaves character scars on all three sisters. "In infancy, the hand carries oral tensions from the mouth to the body, where it reinforces the stimulation exerted by the bodily care of the mother. If the maternal care is deficient, the adult hands carry the tensions of both the yearning for maternal love and the hate and the attempts at entrapment from the unfulfilled yearnings" (Rose 1980)—a clear description of Karin's agitated and clumsy hands. The film is replete with orality—Maria's finger on her lip with a hint of sucking, twirling her hair, and biting the doctor's finger; the gluttony of the doctor and Karin's husband; Agnes's gaspy breathing with open mouth; Karin's mouth and tongue movements; and Anna's biting into an apple, inviting Agnes to her breast and hovering watchfully, as though she devours with her eyes.

The wordless but highly animated, ecstatic exchange between Maria and Karin delivers the film's most hopeful scene, gesticulating joy and intimacy. Silent except for an unaccompanied cello (the Saraband from Bach's *Suite #5 in C minor*), it articulates the preverbal mother-child intimacy. However intense their dance, this pair is also reenacting the greater intimacy of Anna and Agnes. One could imagine a single image that condenses the entire film: the embracing Agnes and Anna at the center, Maria and Karin circling them at stand-off distance, their backs turned to the intimate pair but glancing at them over their shoulders, the fear on their faces covering an intense inhibited longing. The mother, the minister, and the husbands wander at the periphery.

The impending death of Agnes brings her two sisters dutifully to her bedside and revives memories of their mother, who died when the sisters were in their teens. In flashbacks, their mother (played by Liv Ullmann, who also plays Maria) is an attractive, narcissistic, isolated, preoccupied woman who seems cold and uncaring. Symbolized by a nonfunctioning clock with a flute-playing shepherd, the mother fails to lead her flock. Agnes describes her as a woman plagued by "ennui, impatience, and longing." In Bergman's story (1972, 66–67) the adult Agnes poignantly describes her in a diary entry. These later memories reflect aspects of early development—screen memories.

> Mother is in my thoughts nearly every day. She loved Maria because they were so alike in every way. I was too like father for her to be able to stand me. When Mother spoke to me in her light, excitable way, I didn't understand what she meant. I tried terribly hard, but never managed to please

her. Then she would get impatient. She was nearly always impatient, mostly with Karin. I was sickly and puny as a child, but Karin was always being scolded, because Mother thought she was so clumsy and unintelligent. Mother and Maria, on the other hand, had so much to talk about. I often used to wonder what they were whispering and laughing about, and why they got on so well together. They always had little secrets, and they used to tease me and Karin.

I loved Mother. Because she was so gentle and beautiful and alive. Because she was so—I don't know how to put it—because she was so present. But she could also be cold and indifferent. When I used to come and ask her for affection, she would rebuff me and be playfully cruel, saying she hadn't time. Yet I couldn't help feeling sorry for her, and now that I'm older I understand her much better. I should like so much to see her again and tell her what I have understood of her ennui, her impatience, her panic and refusal to give up.

I remember once—it was autumn—I came running into the drawing room; I suppose I had something important to do (one always has at the age of ten). Then I saw Mother sitting there in one of the big chairs. She sat there in her white dress, quite still, looking out of the window with her hands resting on the table. She was leaning forward slightly in a peculiar, stiff way. I went up to her. She gave me a look so full of sorrow that I nearly burst into tears. But instead I began to stroke her cheek. She closed her eyes and let me do it. We were very close to each other that time.

Suddenly she came to herself and said, "Just look at your hands, they're filthy. Whatever have you been up to?" Then, overcome with affection, she took me in her arms and smiled at me and kissed me. I was dazzled by these riches. Just as suddenly, she began to weep and begged my forgiveness over and over. I didn't understand a thing; all I could do was hold her tightly until she freed herself. Her face changed and, giving her little laugh, she dabbed her eyes. "How ridiculous," was all she said, then she got up and left me with my tumult.

One can assume that the absence of the mother's husband contributed to her loneliness, depression, preoccupation, and sadism. Except for her warmth toward Maria as a narcissistic extension of herself, perhaps because Maria resembled her, the mother failed markedly to provide empathy and a "safe anchorage" (Mahler et al. 1975); she was inconsistent, mercurial, and deaf to her children's cries, audible or not.

The "cries" in *Cries and Whispers* are the cries for help, the unarticulated yearnings of the needy infant. In her "resurrection" Agnes pleads, "Can't anyone help me?" and when the doctor arrives, "Is someone out there? I hear someone." Karin also asks about the sounds out there, and risks "crying" for the sake of continuing closeness with Maria after Maria has penetrated her armored walls. Maria "cries" to be soothed via her seductiveness with the doctor and with Karin. Anna "pleads" to be fulfilled as a mother. She nurses Agnes as the replacement for her dead daughter. Anna begins her resurrection dream by saying, "Don't you hear the crying? I hear an endless crying."

The "cries" for help express the yearnings for closeness and attachment, for intimacy. The "whispers" are the torment of the frustrated longings, the hovering unattainable fulfillment. Beyond the unfulfilled dyad, they represent an intimacy that exists but from which one is excluded, the jealousy in the triadic relationship. The despair and helplessness felt by many viewers may derive from these barely audible and unfulfilled yearnings.

Bergman recreates the mother's alternations between acceptance and rejection with scenes of hopeful expectation followed by scenes of dashed hopes. Since the viewer is intermittently subjected to the same kind of hope and frustration that the sisters may have experienced with their mother, he or she, like them, may despair. In the opening shots, images of a cold, lifeless statue are alternated with ones of a life-bearing tree; their sudden juxtaposition foreshadows the later sequences and symbolizes the elusiveness and ambivalence of the mother, the source of life. In the bedroom scene the doctor manipulatively leads Maria to expect adulation by speaking to her beauty, but sadomasochistically dashes her expectations by sneeringly detailing her aging discontent, then declaring their alikeness in selfishness, coldness, and indifference. Maria juxtaposes an Easter (resurrection) invitation with implied infidelity to her husband. After the caring bathing scene and the reading from *The Pickwick Papers*, Agnes shudders in the agony of her pain. Agnes's diary further describes sudden alternations of mother's affection and rejection.

In addition to the thematic presaging in the opening images, the flashbacks of the four women punctuate the film, providing an internal structure. Each sequence begins with a close-up of the woman with one side of the face illuminated, and ends in a red fade-out. Maria's and Karin's flashbacks are similar. Both include a dinner table scene, a bedroom scene, and a bloody interaction with their husbands. Both present self-inflicted bloody injuries: Karin cuts her vagina with a glass shard, and Maria's husband plunges a knife into his abdomen. These scenes of sadomasochistic humiliations contrast with Agnes's mixed memories of her mother that include touching and intimacy and with Anna reading about the seeming bliss of the four women in the garden scene.

With a particular emphasis on the influence of the mother on the three sisters, a detailed analysis of the four women follows.

Agnes

Distant and critical toward Agnes, the mother impairs this middle daughter's separation-individuation and development of a sense of self and of feminine identity, leaving her unable to relate intimately with a man. Her view of herself as being too like father for mother to stand her further impairs her femininity. Lacking intimacy, except with Anna, she fantasizes and elaborates intimate memories. What is unfulfilled in reality, she tries to achieve in fantasy. Ironically, as her unused uterus develops cancer, her abdomen enlarges, symbolizing a fantasied but unfulfilled pregnancy—a macabre symbol of growing life and death. In her parents' bedroom, clocks with cupids slice off her living seconds and she dies in her conception bed: to be the only birth in your life is tantamount to death, to not living at all. "She complains little and does not think that God is cruel" (Bergman 1972). Agnes is a saintly martyr—all-good, forgiving, and overly grateful for her sisters' limited warmth. She protects her mother from the knowledge of her disappointment and rage at mother's neglect and sadistic teasing by alternating affectionate displays with humiliating withdrawal. This character stance both expresses her sympathy, love, and need to be loved and serves as a massive reaction-formation initiated to ward off her envy, jealousy, and rage toward mother and toward Maria and mother for their whispered intimacies and consistent connection. "They always had little secrets and they used to tease me and Karin." Her next words—"I loved Mother. Because she was so gentle and beautiful and alive"—illustrate her reaction-formation of transforming envy and rage to "love." In the same passage, her rage at mother's being "playfully cruel" is changed to an opposite, pity: "Yet I couldn't help feeling sorry for her."

The mother's alternation between affection and rejection is further portrayed in the diary. While Agnes was stroking her mother's cheek, the mother abruptly chastised her for filthy hands. "Then, overcome with affection, she took me in her arms and smiled at me and kissed me. . . . 'How ridiculous,' was all she said, then she got up and left me with my tumult."

Agnes's overappreciation of the crumbs of affection from Maria and Karin illustrates Anna Freud's (1946, 133) description of the defense of altruistic surrender "of one's own instinctual impulses in favor of other people." Vanity, libidinal wishes, and ambition are projected onto another, and by identifying with the other, one's own instincts can be gratified vicariously. Yet Agnes is not without a capacity for sublimation, as illustrated in her painting, music, reading, and diary writing. In many ways she is portrayed as a latency child.

Agnes's substitute mother, Anna, provides a comforting intimacy and soothes her bodily pain. Anna is the idealized, all-giving, "good" earth mother, the perfect servant, split from the narcissistic "bad" real mother.

Karin

Desperately tormented in agitated depression, the oldest sister, Karin, struggles with enraged, envious, and jealous feelings toward Mother and Maria in another way. Instead of reaction-formation and altruistic surrender, Karin resorts to turning against the self, self-punishment, sadomasochism, and depression. "Always being scolded because mother thought she was so clumsy and unintelligent," Karin introjected mother's denigration into her superego. She isolates affectionate feelings, protectively presenting a cold remoteness and a sour disposition. Her staccato speech, strangulation of words, and striking of Anna reflect her conflict with her rage. Karin's intense guilt and need for punishment for her rage render her unable to enjoy warmth. She degrades Maria by expressing hatred for her and her absurdity. And Agnes was "disgusting with her limpness and her meddlesomeness and her old-maidishness . . . and her ridiculous artistic ambitions" (Bergman 1972).

Bergman describes Karin's marriage as "charged with hatred—a mutual hatred that is almost tangible, without mercy or letup. Neither of them has taken a deep breath of relief for the last fifteen years. You could almost speak of the loyalty of total hatred. They owe each other nothing." Strikingly, Karin combines her rage with a sexual current and finds gratification in sadomasochism. In the sadomasochistic flashback scene in which Karin mutilates her vagina with a glass shard, Bergman depicts the physical pain that is the necessary condition for the sexual pleasure of the erotic masochist. Here, Karin's rage at her husband is turned inward, and the psychic pain mixes with masochistic orgiastic pleasure. The tongue movements and grimacing smile evidence the intense sexualization. She can torment her husband with what he desires by smearing her face with blood because she has already endured suffering. Karin threatens her husband with the same violent castration that she inflicts on her genitals. She equates intimacy with destructiveness. Her "tissue of lies," then, refers to her female genitals. (The shape of the glass shard ironically resembles a butterfly, symbol of purity and innocence.) "There is a void felt by women, and by men, who suspect that their feminine nature, like Persephone, has gone to hell. Whenever there is such a void, healing must be sought in the blood of the wound itself. It is alchemical truth that no solution should be made except in its own blood" (Hall 1982, 68).

In the original story, Karin, before her flashback, fixes her eyes on a painting of the ascetic contemplative Saint Teresa in the third stage of prayer and displays a sarcastic, sexualized smile. Bernini's sculpture *Ecstasy of Saint Teresa* is his near-perfect attempt to render mystical experience credible. Saint Teresa described how "the angel pierced her heart with a long barb of gold. . . . The exquisite joy caused by this incomparable pain is so excessive that the soul cannot want it to cease."

In her chronically depressed, wary state, Karin shows an intense wish-fear of intimacy and merger. Her torment and her marked emotional isolation are only momentarily penetrated by Maria's need for closeness and sadistic manipulation. Their shared grief leads to regression and increased vulnerability to revived archaic conflicts and yearnings for intimacy. After Agnes's death, Karin displays a borderline state as evidenced by looseness of associations, unrelatedness, voice alterations, and mood lability. Karin and Maria search for merger in a symbiotic union with their mother through their attempts at touching, holding, and stroking each other. The juxtaposition of heads in two-shots of Maria and Karin, Anna and Agnes, and Karin and Anna visually represents merger. But merger also is feared, because it involves the threat of losing oneself in the other, devouring or incorporating the other or being devoured or incorporated—a form of death. Maria and Karin turn to sadomasochism to regain more clearly defended boundaries. They alleviate feelings of emptiness and fear of annihilation through the stimulation of the painful sadomasochism. In the regression, their search for intimacy stimulates homosexual yearnings that are also feared. Their sadomasochistic interactions with their husbands further evidence a failure to reach oedipal level development and feminine identity.

Karin's restrictive and punitive superego inhibits femininity and interferes with maternal fulfillment. In saying "I don't love you" as she turns away from the dead Agnes in Anna's dream, she reveals the negative side of her ambivalent struggle with loving feelings.

Maria

Pleasure-seeking, beautiful Maria is the favored, indulged, perhaps engulfed youngest daughter—narcissistic like her mother, freer, but emotionally shallow and manipulative. In her first scene, with its hints of thumb sucking, she even looks like a young girl. One sees a dollhouse and a photograph of her mother, with whom she yearns to recapture her childhood intimacy. Maria searches for a common identity, or an incorporating merger with mother. Bergman conveys this idea through the photograph of Liv Ullmann, who also plays Maria. Maria's hysterical and sadomasochistic character structure and narcissism interfere with a concerned relatedness to others.

Agnes writes in her diary: "It is early Monday morning and I'm in pain. My sisters and Anna are taking turns to sit up. Kind of them. I needn't feel so alone with the dark." But the sitting-up Maria is asleep and is not chagrined when awakened by Anna. In Anna's resurrection dream or hallucination, Maria withdraws from Agnes. After provoking her husband to despair and a suicidal attempt by telling him the doctor has stayed overnight, she gazes in immobile, removed horror rather than help him. In the story Joakim begs for help, and Maria shakes her head, saying, "No." He pulls out the knife and sobs. Bergman then describes Maria's conflicting mental images. In one she lovingly rescues him; in the other she forces "the knife deeper into his chest with all her strength, in a moment of stinging satisfaction." Her sadism is foreshadowed in her playfully biting the doctor's finger when he nods no to her overture in their initial scene and is repeated in her verbal humiliation of Karin. By saying, "I can't possibly remember every stupid thing," in response to Karin's overture to continuing closeness during the departure scene, she sadistically dissolves their intimacy. This near repetition of her mother's saying "How ridiculous" after closeness with Agnes clearly represents Maria's identification with her entrapping mother as described by Agnes.

Maria hostilely seduces both men and women. Approaching the doctor by touching his face as she also does with women, she indicates that she may use heterosexuality as a displaced way of searching for the warm and tender homosexual gratification that she yearns for but finds threatening. The intimacy of touching another woman represents her reliving of the early erotic attachment to mother. The arousal of these yearnings, along with the fear of death, as portrayed in Anna's dream, leads Maria to flee in terror from Agnes's seductive death grip.

Anna

Apart from, and perhaps as a foil to, the three sisters and their mother is Anna. In contrast to their clearly drawn character types, Anna's character and motivations are complex and ambiguous. She seems to epitomize the pure, all-giving, earth mother who not only asks nothing for herself but even relinquishes her claim, though under pressure, accepting as a memento something of Agnes's (perhaps a transitional object). Anna represents the loving mother longed for by each of the sisters. Her maternal role is set early in the film as we see her breathe life into the fire with her blossoming cheeks. Because Agnes serves as a substitute for Anna's child, who died at age three, Anna's devoted caring intensifies. In death, Agnes actually wears a bonnet as though she is the resurrected child. Anna holding Agnes, both women draped in white, suggests the pietà: Anna becomes Mary; Agnes, Agnes Dei, the lamb of God: Christ, whom the minister describes as suffering for us, being worthy of agony, and advocating our cause. Of the four women, Anna and Agnes are the closest to the experience of death. With the pietà image, Bergman suggests that in the presence of death their relationship seeks to satisfy an unexpressed and profound longing for love that is ultimately unconditional and sacrificial, as only idealized maternal or divine love can be.

But Anna's seemingly omnipresent devotion also puzzles and assails Karin and Maria as a provocative tyranny of goodness that neither can provide for their own families. Because of their experience with faulty mothering, they are jealous of Anna and fail to comprehend her maternal devotion to Agnes. They maintain a hostile, unappreciating distance. Anna hovers watchfully, perhaps ominously and sinisterly, at Agnes's bath, Karin's and her husband's dinner, Karin's undressing, Karin and Maria's dialogue about leaving her a memento, and in the departure scene. Maria comments that "she is the kind of woman who never closes a door behind her." Furthermore, Anna suffers humiliation and physical blows from Karin's wrath when Karin accuses her of staring with sexual interest while undressing her.

After the death of Agnes, she relives the loss of her child—looking through the crib bars as in the initial view of her during the introduction of the characters—and resurrects both (Agnes in the child's white bonnet) in her dream or hallucination that begins with a child's cry. Anna tries to reassure Agnes by saying, "It's only a dream," in response to Agnes's complaint that she can't go to sleep: "Can't leave you all." "Can't anyone help me?" Agnes moans. "I'm so tired." In the story, Anna tries to reassure herself by telling Agnes that "the whole thing was only a dream." Within a dream such a protest that it is only a dream is often a last-ditch attempt to renounce an unacceptable truth of death that the censor has allowed to pass into the manifest content (Freud 1900).

In Anna's wish-fulfilling dream or hallucination, her competitive and envious feelings are apparent in having Maria and Karin flee after failing the test to respond to the beseeching, resurrected Agnes. Neither Maria nor Karin emerges from her trance when Anna approaches them. Expressing her wish for Karin and Maria to die instead of Agnes, she portrays them in a deathlike catatonic state, while Agnes's tear in the following scene attests to her return to life. Karin exclaims that Agnes's wish for closeness is repulsive and that she does not love Agnes. In her shallow style, Maria tries to sooth Agnes with affectionate reminiscences, but flees in terror when Agnes pulls her by the neck and kisses her. (As Christ predicted in his farewell speech, his disciples denied him and fled.)

Anna fulfills Agnes's needs in the pietà scene, one of seeming ultimate unity and merger. But Anna's eating of an apple identifies her with Eve—not only as the ultimate mother rather than the subjugated maid, but also as the flawed woman. (Does Bergman convey this other facet of Anna by having Agnes die after nursing from Anna's breast, as though Agnes ingests poison rather than milk?)

Is Anna's competitiveness and envy a transient episode precipitated by her acute double grief, uncertainty about her future, and feelings of being unappreciated? This question influences our interpretation of the last scene, in which Anna reads Agnes's diary about the sisters' visit. Anna retains the diary as "something of Agnes," representing her wish to be part of Agnes or fused with her in a mother-child and homoerotic union. If Agnes includes Anna—although in the role of servant earth mother, rocking the others on the swing—as "one of the people I'm fond of," then we are offered hope and redemption in the early mother-child relationship. But if in "the four of us, Anna came too," Anna is eclipsed as the servant girl, then the sisters are completely idealized. For Anna, reading this passage, then, is a final humiliation in which she is being further diminished. Bergman presents the possibility of either view. Perhaps both facets coexist in a layered complexity. This ending reasserts Bergman's view of the elusiveness and ambiguity in the effort of connecting and leaves the viewer drawn into the women's despair. Like them, one has experienced the cries and the whispers that express the frustrated and unfulfilled longings for their preoedipal mother.

> Pregnancy, a tissue of lies;
> Birth, death from the womb;
> Intimacy, isolation;
> Love, humiliation and suffering;
> Hope, tears and despair even after death.

References

Bergman, Ingmar. "Cries and Whispers." *New Yorker,* 21 October 1972. Also in *Four Stories by Ingmar Bergman,* translated by Alan Blair. New York: Anchor Books, 1977.

Blum, Harold. "Masochism, the Ego Ideal and the Psychology of Women." *Journal of the American Psychoanalytic Association* 24 (Supplement) (1976):157–91.

Cowie, Peter. *Ingmar Bergman: A Critical Biography.* New York: Charles Scribner's Sons, 1982.

Deutsch, Helene. *The Psychology of Women.* New York: Grune & Stratton, 1944.

Freud, Anna. *The Ego and the Mechanisms of Defense.* New York: International Universities Press, 1946.

Freud, Sigmund. *The Standard Edition of the Complete Psychological Works of Sigmund Freud.* Edited and translated by James Strachey. 24 vols. London: Hogarth Press, 1953–74.
The Interpretation of Dreams (1900–1901), vols. 4, 5.
"Femininity" (1933), vol. 22.

Galenson, Eleanor, and Roiphe, Herman. "Some Suggested Revisions Concerning Early Female Development." *Journal of the American Psychoanalytic Association* 24 (Supplement) (1976):29–57.

Hall, Nor. *The Moon and the Virgin: Reflections on the Archetypical Feminine.* New York: Harper & Row, 1982.

Mahler, Margaret. "Symbiosis and Individuation: The Psychological Birth of the Human Infant." *Psychoanalytic Study of the Child* 29 (1974):89–106.

Mahler, Margaret, Pine, Fred, and Bergman, Anni. *The Psychological Birth of the Human Infant.* New York: Basic Books, 1975.

Mellen, Joan. "*Cries and Whispers:* Bergman and Women." In *Women and Their Sexuality in the New Film.* New York: Horizon Press, 1973.

Rose, Gilbert. *The Power of Form.* New York: International Universities Press, 1980.

Stoller, Robert. "Primary Femininity." *Journal of the American Psychoanalytic Association* 24 (Supplement) (1976):59–78.

Weil, Annemarie. "The Basic Core." *Psychoanalytic Study of the Child* 25 (1970):442–60.

9   Chaplin's *The Kid*

Stephen M. Weissman

Like Moses among the bullrushes, Oedipus on the mountainside, or Snow White in her Disneyland forest, Charlie Chaplin's *The Kid* is a tale whose underlying archetype has enthralled audiences of all ages: the abandoned child found in the wilderness. But unlike his more privileged mythological predecessors, who at least had the good fortune to be deposited in lush, natural surroundings, Chaplin's cast-off child is discovered among the ignoble detritus of modern society. A garbage-strewn alley in the seedy Red Light District in Los Angeles's Chinatown of the 1920s serves as the shooting location, re-creating a mean street from Chaplin's feral boyhood in the slums of South London.

Ambling down the alley, taking his daily constitutional while deftly ducking the flying garbage heaved by householders from the tenement windows above, the Little Tramp appears. With fastidiously impeccable manners, he slips off his walking gloves before selecting a cigarette butt from his smoking case, an old sardine can. Pausing to note the worn condition of those shabby fingerless gloves, he tosses them away with the cavalier panache of a gentleman with a dozen other pairs of handwear at his immediate disposal. Just as he is about to surrender himself to the joys of his first smoke of the day, his tranquillity is shattered by ear-splitting distress signals from the squalling infant who has been abandoned on the garbage heap, plaintively demanding to be heard by someone, anyone.

Taking one glance at that miserable child, streetwise Charlie instinctively looks up—as if to quiz both the refuse-throwing householders and the heavens above as to just exactly where this baby has come from. But before he can even begin to explore that question, a rapid-fire series of comic interactions with a neighborhood cop firmly establishes Charlie's

183

Charlie Chaplin and Jackie Coogan in *The Kid* (1920).

predicament of mistaken paternal identity: like it or not, once he demonstrates his better nature by resisting his impulse to toss the unwanted
baby down the nearest sewer, the kid is his for life. What follows is a
series of picaresque father-son adventures for this flotsam pair of castoffs
from the Industrial Revolution in this comedy that Chaplin introduces in
his opening title card as "a picture with a smile—perhaps a tear."

Perhaps! As the lights go up, one look at the picture show audience
reveals that there hasn't been a dry eye in the house. But what is so
startling about Chaplin's comedy of fathering a lost baby is the fact that
he first conceived and immediately began to shoot this film barely two
weeks after the death of his own three-day-old, firstborn infant son.
Having turned his personal pain to such a creative purpose, he gets us to
break bread with him and take communion with his grief and loss.

By chancing upon a universal form—the myth of the lost child—to
express his bereavement, Chaplin succeeds in inviting the whole gang in.
Chinese peasants, Bantu tribesmen, European intellectuals, Cockney
tradesmen, and all the "kids" of the world can and do receive Charlie's
pantomime tale with empathy. My own three-year-old daughter calls the
film *Tarley Taplin and the Baby*. It is the only supposedly "grown-up"
video we own that she watches with the same wide-eyed fascination that
she otherwise reserves for *Pinocchio* and *Snow White*—her other two
"lost child" favorites.

But to say that grief-stricken Chaplin accidentally stumbled on the
lost kid myth is to suggest a fluky happenstance that is clearly the counterpart of his Little Tramp's nimblest pratfalls. If ballet is in Charlie's
bones, the schmaltzy nostalgia of bittersweet loss already was in Chaplin's soul—long before his bereavement over his firstborn child. Periodi-
cally left to fend for himself by his own alcoholic father and psychotic
mother, Charlie already knew what being an abandoned kid was all
about—living on the streets, dodging the bobbies and orphanage authorities, scavenging to survive.

While losing his son undoubtedly reawakened those old boyhood
memories, their artistic rendering took place with Charlie's heart, not his
head. And the idea probably succeeds because it is largely unconscious
rather than self-conscious autobiography.

A few days after his personal tragedy, tough-minded Cockney Charlie,
the professional actor who had clawed his way out of the slums, zipped
up his pain and got on with it. Back at the studio it was business as usual:
having put recent events behind him, he set out to make his latest
comedy with its hilarious motif of lost-and-found gag sequences—cast-
off cigarette butts, gloves, clothes, furniture, kids, and so forth. Taking
the lowbrow slapstick route, he quarried for bits and shticks, not arche-

types and myths. But funny things can happen on that low road to comedy, just as they do on the high road to tragedy.

Just as Oedipus and Laius—father and son—encounter each other by chance at one of life's crossroads, so Charlie the fatherless kid and Chaplin the childless father accidentally meet in a London lane. Unlike their ancient predecessors, whose hearts are filled with mistrust and hate, Charlie Chaplin and the lost child are filled with yearning and affection. And so their tale is a bittersweet ballad of love and loss. Griminess is next to Godliness in a comic universe where the disinherited can inherit the earth.

10   Being Doubted, Being Assured

Karen Hanson

A search for a proof of one's own existence might seem a mad inquiry. If the prospect of such an inquiry is indulged as an activity of philosophy, if it is thought that this disciplining of an otherwise deranged interest tames the terror of the question, then it must be remembered that even philosophy appears to insist on the certainty of one's own existence, even philosophy wants to declare that this, if nothing else, is beyond doubt.

The central declaration of this indubitability, in Descartes's *cogito*, is, of course, sometimes called a "proof," but Descartes himself, in the *Discourse on Method*, calls it simply a "first principle." The status of this claim remains a subject of controversy, however; and in the *Meditations'* counterpart of the *cogito*, Descartes does suggest the weighing of thoughts and a separate step of moving to a carefully warranted conclusion: "So after considering everything very thoroughly, I must finally conclude that this proposition, *I am, I exist*, is necessarily true whenever it is put forward by me or conceived in my mind" (Descartes 1984, 17). Individual existence is affirmed, then, not only through but also in activity—doubting, conceiving, asserting. Personal existence is in fact assured only in activity: "if I had merely ceased thinking . . . I should have had no reason to believe I existed" (Descartes 1985, 127).

If this is a solution to a problem about one's own existence, however, it begets an intensified problem about the existence of others. If my essence is thinking, if this is what I know human existence to be, then to know the existence of another human, I must know that other's thinking. But when I turn to examine the possibility of there being other beings, try to meet a like, another human mind, I see, hear, touch only what might be called human bodies. I do not know if these bodies are

187

moved by other minds, for I cannot see other minds. It is in the nature of mind, as I know from my own case, to be invisible, untouchable. I may well worry, then, that I am "alone in the world" (Descartes 1984, 29). The Cartesian certainty of self-existence produces a profound uncertainty about the existence of others.

Stanley Cavell has detected and described a yet more unsettling counterproduction: skepticism about others erodes the self. The implications of this reciprocity have been studied by Cavell, and he has mapped the moral and metaphysical transmutations of what had seemed an essentially epistemological problem. The activity in the skeptical struggle, the activity that can be regarded as the Cartesian primogeniture, is examined in his careful charts of the logic of knowing and acknowledging and is in focus in his detailed exposure of the self-destructive skepticism at the center of the terrain of tragedy.

That there is also a passive version of skepticism is suggested, though, by the very mutualities these discussions explore; and it is evident in Cavell's characterization of the private language fantasy, a fantasy usually taken to contain, among its other possibilities for instruction, some lesson about our access to the inner life of others. When Cavell reads it as a fantasy of "necessary inexpressiveness," he argues that this involves both "a sense of powerlessness to make myself known," and "equally . . . a powerlessness to make myself known to myself" (Cavell 1979, 352). With a temporary elision of, or a momentary shift from, the question of my power and its relation to action, the passive skeptical worry is then stated in its plainest form:

> The question whether there are other minds is exactly as much a question about me as about anyone else. If *anyone* is an other mind, I am one— i.e., I am an other to the others. . . . Then the question is: Do others know of my existence? [Cavell 1979, 442]

Edification on this version of the skeptical problem can be derived, Cavell claims, from a study of both the cinematic projection of, and psychoanalysis's origin in, the sufferings of women.

The idea that there is a neglected Cartesian sister or daughter, a feminine or passive side of skepticism that philosophy has mostly tried to suppress or disinherit, may provoke strong resistance. One attempt to deflect direct scrutiny of this idea would turn toward an insistence that the amplitude of Descartes's own formulation already provides sufficiently for the requirements of a passive being. If suffering is a mode of mind, then the *cogito* includes this claim to existence. Doubt and denial are, for Descartes, as much forms of thought as understanding and affirmation are. If I doubt, if I deny—I think; therefore I am. So if I suffer—I think; therefore I am.

But Descartes himself, pressed by a woman to make clearer his understanding of the relation between mentality and physical action and to say something about the substance of the soul "as distinct from its activity" (Descartes 1954, 275), declares that there are just two fundamental facts about the human soul: "on the one hand . . . it thinks, and on the other . . . being united to the body it can act and suffer along with the body"; and he admits that

> I have said [in the *Meditations*] almost nothing of this latter, and have studiously set myself to expound only the former. . . . [I]nasmuch as my principal design was to prove the distinction subsisting between mind and body, the former could serve in this design, whereas the other, if dwelt on, would have been by no means helpful. [Descartes 1958, 251]

Princess Elizabeth of Bohemia, the woman whose queries elicited this admission, continued to voice her dissatisfaction, however; and from their correspondence arose Descartes's last major work, *The Passions of the Soul* (1649).

The *Principles of Philosophy* (1644), dedicated to Princess Elizabeth, underscores the need for the later treatise, as Descartes explicitly notes what has not been clarified by the *cogito* or the *Meditations*. He maintains once again that he recognizes only two ultimate classes of real things—minds, or thinking things; and bodies, or material things. But, he adds,

> we also experience within ourselves certain other things which must not be referred either to the mind alone or to the body alone. These arise . . . from the close and intimate union of our mind with the body. This list includes, first, appetites . . . ; secondly, the emotions or passions of the mind . . . such as . . . anger, joy, sadness and love; and finally, all the sensations, such as those of pain, pleasure. . . . [Descartes 1985, 209]

Princess Elizabeth's own sense of the ultimate reality of all these "other things" and her unwillingness to turn from the problem of "the close and intimate union" of mind and body had emboldened her to confess, as early as her second letter to Descartes, that she would not find it so difficult to attribute physicality to the soul. Descartes in turn, in his reply, acknowledged that it is possible to conceive of the soul as material. But intellect alone, according to Descartes, is inadequate to grasp this conception, the conception of the union of mind and body. Even intellect aided by imagination does not suffice. What Descartes recommends for understanding here is the invaluable help of the senses—and of "conversation" (Descartes 1970, 141). With that encouragement from a surprising quarter, we should turn once again to Cavell's testimony about the testimony of cinema and psychoanalysis.

The lineaments of a supreme example of the passive version of the *cogito* can be seen, Cavell claims in the essay published in this volume, in our film experience of Greta Garbo. Her standing as a transcendent image of the unknown woman is understood by Cavell in terms of her "absolute expressiveness, so that the sense of failure to know her, of her being beyond us, say visibly absent, is itself the proof of her existence." The elements and the implications of this brief, complex characterization deserve detailed study.

To whom, for whom, is this a proof of existence? The notation of her "visible absence" directs attention to our line of sight, so that her appearance, our seeing her projection, is a proof to and for us. But, it might be suggested, if Cavell's remark is read in this way, then the cinematic proof of human existence crosses but does not adequately parallel the achievement of the *cogito*. The *cogito* gives its subject's existence. Descartes secures his own existence for himself, certifies his being to himself. Shouldn't a passive equivalent of this action guarantee to the passive object her own existence, assure Garbo herself?

Cavell's comments do in fact also convey the self-assurance in the cinematic projection. Garbo's knowledge is internally linked to her absence. Cavell has elsewhere described our, the audience's, absence from the world presented in film, and he has analyzed our desire to view the world this way, our absence mechanically effected and not a function of our subjectivity (Cavell 1971). Garbo's absence, on the other hand, *is* analyzed as a function of her subjectivity. In the essay in this volume, Cavell finds her "within a private theater, not dissociating herself from the present moment, but knowing it forever, in its transience, as finite, from her finitude, or separateness, as from the perspective of her death." Her projection is of the knowledge of separation, of privacy not as the deliberate keeping or withholding of secrets but as the acceptance of distinction and final limits. Thus, her assurance, acceptance, of metaphysical finitude cannot be taken as intellectual lack (see Cavell 1969, 263).

Moreover, the question of whose knowledge is accomplished or declaimed in these proofs can be approached from another angle. Descartes's formulation does not prove the existence of Descartes. Only the first-person articulation will do. Others' expositions of Descartes's work typically shift uneasily between the third and the first person. (When one of the first readers of the *Meditations,* Gassendi, heedlessly recapitulated the argument in terms of "you," "I," and "whatever"—"you persist with your pretence of deception, but . . . you conclude that this proposition *I am, I exist,* is true whenever it is put forward by you. . . . You could have made the same inference from any . . . of your . . . actions, since . . . whatever acts exists"—Descartes restrained the discussion by a determined and careful return, in his reply, to the first-person pronoun throughout [Descartes 1984, 180, 244].) But bearing in mind the first-person restriction can make insupportable the peculiarity of Descartes's sentences and can force one to face the irony in his writing and publishing them. It now seems that, if the Cartesian *cogito* is to be useful to us, if it is to secure human existence, we must not regard it as a proof to Descartes. It, as well as the cinematic proof, is to and for us.

The active/passive distinction remains, however. We must each assert "*cogito,*" guarantee human existence in and through our action. But we are passive before the motion picture image. Gazing at this unknown woman, we are assured of human existence, not by any action of our own, or any special action of hers, but by her passionate revelation of distance and depth.

This may, then, suggest a form of congruence in these opposing outlines of exampled existence. But details of these figures remain to be inspected. The cinematic proof, as the newer discovery, may make the freshest demands for familiarization: How can the unknown bear the burden we associate with the idea of proof? And how, as Cavell asks in his essay in this volume, can a being with an unexcelled "'psychophysical aptitude for transposing . . . large sums of excitation into the somatic innervation'" (Freud, *S.E.* 3:50), a being with "a talent for, and will to, communicate—generalized to a point of absolute expressiveness," "beyond human doubting," remain unknown?

Cavell's answer to the first question redirects our attention to the consequences of our familiarity with the older proof: if our knowledge of the human depends on our knowledge of the human possibility of skepticism, if since the time of Descartes we have found ourselves on a course of radical skepticism, then psychoanalysis is called for to provide credible proof of mind, proof of mind as unconscious, as unknown to itself. The Cartesian epistemology presents us as unknowable to others, others as unknowable to us. This would already dispose us to regard only an essentially unknown being as an other (mind). The epistemological barrier cannot, however, by itself, be taken as surety. Proof generally involves some successful demonstration. Skepticism, though, cannot be decisively refuted; so true recovery of the other should require neither denying nor dismantling the obstacles to knowledge, but repositioning these opacities.

As Cavell argues, the transparency of the self grows clouded as the Cartesian skepticism is brought home: if I am necessarily unknown to others, is it because others cannot discern my mind—or because I cannot express it? If others seem unknowable to me, is this a sign of their inadequacy or my own, my failure as a cognitive being? In this modern uneasiness, psychoanalysis appears to suggest that the obscurity of mind may be its proof, not its loss; and, in not advancing the now unbeliev- able claim that there are no obstructions to knowledge of the mind and in fact underscoring the internal barriers, it yet offers a compelling hope. Mind may be unknown, even to itself, but this does not mean that it is fixedly unknowable.

Part of what must be developed if the perimeter of the unknown is to be changed, part of what will be needed to illuminate the now darkened recesses of mind, Cavell continues, is a new attention to the human body, an understanding of it as expressive of mind. If this understanding is granted, however, we seem to face a vigorous renewal of the second question about the cinematic proof: if Garbo is a figure of absolute expressiveness—and we see that she is—how can she be, why is she said to be, unknown?

Cavell provides an answer in his studies of acknowledgement: to know the suffering of another is to acknowledge it or to withhold acknowledg- ment. We might suppose that a superlatively expressive being would challenge, might well surpass, our normal powers of acknowledgement. That the cinematic image of expressiveness is beyond our acknowledg- ment is beyond question, mechanically insured. Here the psyche is revealed—but beyond the sight or sound of us, beyond touch. We do not withhold acknowledgement, but neither do we offer it. That other remains unknown.

Still, we do not feel that there is something more we should or could find out, information yet to be uncovered that might dissolve our sense of failure. That sense is the consciousness of our separation, and here, once again, now to the credit of the viewers, metaphysical finitude is not dressed in the guise of intellectual lack.

If that seems the garb always waiting in the Cartesian closet, then it is worth noting that the *cogito*, too, elaborates a separation. Not only is the material world lost in the initial hyperbolic doubt that grounds the assertion of the *cogito*, but when, in the sixth and concluding medita- tion, it is time to determine the nature or essence of the discovered human existence, Descartes relies upon the conceivable separation of body from mind, upon distinction, difference.

There is a clear hint of death in both proofs, but the intimation is carried differently in each. Cavell is explicit about what is recorded in the film image of Garbo. She is seen by him as "a monument of memory," honoring death in honestly marking it. Her knowledge of transience is tied, he suggests, to the work of mourning, and he finds a confirmation of his suggestion in Freud's essay "On Transience." Freud's intuition that the enjoyment of beauty requires the acceptance of mourning, that love and admiration for nature and for the human face and form can be sustained only if one can submit to the facts of evanescence, of limitation, of mortality, is pictured here in the sight of Garbo, in Garbo's expression and our cinematic vision of it, of her.

Descartes's tendency is in another way fatal. He describes his drive to separate body and soul, and that is, after all, to many minds, just another description of an urge to bring death. His anxiety about his personal extinction shadows his remark that if he ceased to think he should have no reason to believe in his own existence. But the thinking, the activity, that then does necessitate his own existence does not, it seems, proceed from any general vitality. Descartes repeatedly denies that the *cogito* can be understood as a deduction of existence from thought by a syllogism. (See, for example, *Replies to the Second Set of Objections* and Descartes's letter of 12 January 1646 to Clerselier, responding to Gassendi's *Counter-Objections*.) He is insistent on the singularity of his assertion; it proceeds in the absence of a generous major premise: "Everything that thinks exists." But if this exclusive self-concern is a vice, the original sin that stains the Cartesian descendants can take a more violent form. The temptation from the Cartesian viewpoint is toward solipsism. The Cartesian separation of body and soul deprives others of life. Its crime amounts to murder.

If we move from the emblem of Greta Garbo and the details of René Descartes to a more general consideration of the passive and active grounding of existence, it may seem that the traumatic extreme to which passivity points should be discovered in the psyche of the willing victim. The unwholesome Cartesian son and daughter are then perfectly matched, made for each other, he as destroyer, she as sufferer, waiting to be destroyed. But their incestuous coupling is bound to be unproductive, for these two specimens, inbreeding having exaggerated the traits of their ancestors, are worse then sterile; they effect loss of both world and self.

The Cartesian son might at first seem, perhaps because older, more to blame for this disaster. But the daughter is equally guilty. Suffering undertaken, not resisted, may amount to self-sacrifice, and the self-denial of mortification reaches its highest pitch in suicide. Suicide is, of course, at once both action and passion. One person is both killer and victim; but, beyond that, as suicide may be a kind of revenge not just against the self but also against another, it does, then, seem to make a claim before, upon another. This claim must count as action; but as it is, more precisely, reaction, it signals the suffering it would redress. Even if suicide is understood as escape alone, this, then, denounces the world as uninhabitable. Such a violent announcement is vehement action, but, again, it is reaction; and the content of the claim is suffering.

The extreme of suicide seems to show complete passivity of the self bending back to meet, to unite with, in collapse, the extreme of activity. But this sort of vacillation in the categorization of a condition of life (or death) persists as we consider the moderations of existence, and that suggests some instability in the categorical terms themselves. The passive version is a matter of letting oneself be known, but Cavell appropriately characterizes this matter not as involving an inert capacity; it demands rather a talent, an aptitude for expression, a kind of power—capacities that are exercised and that produce effects. Knowing, on the other hand, need not be an activity, a kind of grasping. It might be a state, the circumstance of fixed possession. And thinking, the Cartesian touchstone, the basis of the active claim to existence, can certainly also be understood as a mode of passivity, an understanding clarified by Cavell's discussions of Heidegger and Emerson—on thinking as receiving—and of Thoreau—on the stillness of thought.

There is some pliancy in these notions of activity and passivity, and so the active and the passive proofs for existence tend to curve toward one another, sometimes to the point of entanglement. The activity of assertion seems sensible only if the assertion is to or for someone, if it is to be heard. And the passivity of being heard seems possible only if one has made some claim, in some way cried out. For a declaration of existence to have force, to have a point, there must be ears to hear it and a receptive silence it can fill. And, in turn, that silent listening must be antecedently known, if the declaration's import is not to be, as it were, accidental; and the declaration must justify itself before, must be adequate to that attentive listening, if both the assertion and its audience are to be sustained. Considering these mutual dependencies, these exchanges, the way in which the articulation of one version of the proof of existence demands turning to the other, we are of course reminded of Cavell's focus on the feature of conversation in the genre of remarriage comedy, and of his identification, in tragedy and melodrama, of the negation of that conversation, its baffling irony.

We are also led to a reconsideration of an earlier problem about categorizing the *cogito* and its passive counterpart. We recognized the derangement that seems to haunt the idea of proving one's existence to oneself, and we noted some attendant difficulties in the classification of the Cartesian *cogito*. Descartes himself says that it is not a syllogistic proof. It does involve the drawing of a conclusion, but that conclusion is a *first* principle and is supposed to be independent of all premises and to owe nothing to the developed standards of reasoning basic either to arithmetical or geometrical proofs or to the arguments of science. In what sense, then, is it a "proof" at all?

There is always a maddeningly vertiginous quality to the *cogito*, existence known by cogitation cognized as existent cogitation. For all its momentary lucidity, the *cogito* can also appear as a murky reflection of the dark and mysterious act of self-deception. As self-deception is said to involve both knowing the truth and not knowing it, because one is hiding it from or lying to oneself, the *cogito* suggests seizing for oneself what one must already own (in order to extend the prized object) and yet not own (in order to be enriched by the taking). Philosophers may puzzle over the correct analysis of the *cogito,* and they may try to resolve what they see as the paradox of self-deception; but we know that, in our everyday lives, in ourselves and others, we find self-deception. Perhaps, too, in our everyday lives, we and others enact the *cogito.*

Do we suffer the passive proof? Considered as a proof, this version of a response to skepticism can appear at once both more comprehensible and less certain. It is not resolutely involuted, crazily turned in upon itself, for it does not assume the fixed isolation from which the *cogito* begins. Aloneness is exactly at issue in the passive proof, and when isolation does appear, it is discovered in experience, not imaginatively contrived through method. But this allies the passive proof with experimentalism and so makes it approach a familiar, well-trodden path of knowledge, an attractive road, even when its destination is not the realm of Cartesian certainty. Like the *cogito,* the passive proof is not a syllogism. Neither does it fit any other standard deductive model; but it is crucially concerned with the business of showing, and that is clearly one way of proving.

If we think now as well about the active and passive approaches to the problem of other minds, we get another look at the relevant fluctuations in the idea of a proof. As "proof" has its roots in the roots of "probe," it does suggest an active investigation, a searching examination. Thus, in the grip of the problem of other minds, I may explore, try to know, test, prove something in or about the other. But if another is tested by me, is it my activity or the other's that would constitute the proof? What if the tests are meant to address the problem "Am I known by the other?"— the passive skeptical worry? As I move from wondering whether I know of others' existence to wondering whether others know of mine, the burden of proof, of trial, seems to shift; but it shifts unstably. And this unsteadiness—our lack of assurance about what must be established by whom to whom—may be perpetual. This is, indeed, just what we should expect: Cavell presents the active and passive versions of the problem as equivalent to one another.—For what is here at stake, the point to be proved, is the existence of *like* minds.

In the *cogito* and its passive counterpart, it is human existence that is to be proved, human existence that is, and must be demonstrated to be, both active and passive. The reciprocities involved are, then, again to be expected. They can be roughly summarized through attention to a technical stipulation offered by another American philosopher, C. S. Peirce, who claims that "*reality* means a certain kind of non-dependence upon thought . . . while *existence* means reaction with the environment, and so is a dynamic character" (Peirce 1963, 5:352); and, more precisely, "*exist* in its strict philosophical sense [means] 'react with the other like things in the environment'" (6:340). If we accept this definition of reality, we admit that humanity does not attain a real sort of stability. Whether vouchsafed actively or passively, human existence depends upon thought, ours and others', and ours of others', others' of ours. But this fits the Peircean explication of existence: reaction is possible only if there has been prior impingement, and thus it either is or involves a phase of suffering. Reaction may then appear as either a complement to action or as itself action, if oppositional and responsive. Furthermore, reactions that satisfy this idea of existence must be had by, or made in conjunction with, met by, "like things," entities correspondingly active and passive, correspondingly reactive. We see again, then, an adumbration of an essential complementarity in human beings; and we should expect to see, in each individual life, this complementarity realized in some balance of activity and passivity, and some alteration between the two.

We might also, at some times, see these phases structuring larger units of human existence, informing, for example, our sense of sexual difference, so that we call the active phase of human existence "masculine" and the passive "feminine." And if nature, nurture, or we ourselves have tended to cast women on the passive side of the human undulation, then, as Cavell says, the inventions that would help display or probe this neglected phase of the human being, inventions such as cinema and psychoanalysis, may well find deeply productive the study of the feelings and expressions of women.

In any event, any thorough study of the reciprocities, the interplay and exchanges at the base of human existence, must sometime focus on the level of sexuality and on the question of sexual difference. Whatever the initial approach to these issues—whether it is cinematic, psychoanalytic, or philosophic—when the question explored takes the form "Can I know or be known by the other?" then the obvious erotic dimension of the problem presents itself as archaic but never extinct. The measurement of this dimension is, however, a delicate business; and even the most exquisite overture risks being blocked as unseemly.

If philosophy, then, mixes a prospect of ultimate impropriety with an extravagance manic enough to motivate a worry about one's own existence, it is not altogether surprising that there should be reactions against it. The threat inherent in the invitation to philosophy received its seminal dramatization in the story of Socrates, but we do not suppose that fears about corruption, seduction, and retribution then ended with Descartes, dispelled by his attempted disguises or overcome by descendants historically removed from the situation of his personal ambivalence. The question always remains: What demon provokes a desire to think on these matters? And a refined version of this question, one sometimes posed decorously, perhaps to protect the public, asks, What should we make of the urge to communicate these thoughts, to speak or write on these matters?

In this volume, Cavell connects the violence and trauma discernible in philosophy, discernible particularly in the problems of philosophical skepticism, with the violence and trauma psychoanalysis studies and grounds in sexuality. These horrors, shown as overwhelming in melodrama and tragedy, glimpsed as contained, "domesticated," even in remarriage comedy, Cavell finds broadly instructive about the nature and power of film: our "apparently excessive response" to film discloses, he says, something of our sense of it as basically uncanny, as generally capable of "some vision of horror." Our fascination by and our fear of the objects of this discussion can easily recoil onto the discussion itself. It may now arouse suspicion—admiration and esteem, but also mistrust and uneasiness—that what is properly dark is being brought to light. The revelations at the heart of such a project as Cavell's will inspire both devotion and disgust, an incitement to denial.

This problem is obviously one crucial to psychoanalysis, and a portion of Freud's achievement rests on his not only facing this issue but also describing it and so facing it again. We can here note just one manifestation of this intellectual heroism and its attached moral bravery, but it may still, to some extent, help us begin to face this problem about the reception of ideas.

There is particular suspicion that Freud seems repeatedly to confront: distrust and resentment are evident as the attempt is made to deflect or diminish Freud's inquiry by turning back upon him and asking, with knowing indignation, "What does *Freud* want?" Cavell discusses a number of variations on this question; and two of them, not quite separate from each other, receive more detailed treatment. The first is found in some (women's) reactions to Freud's treatment of Dora. The second surfaces in a more general response to the psychoanalytic demand for access to knowledge. Cavell sees a natural stimulus for this generally wary response even in his own linkage of the psychoanalytic project with the skeptic's insatiable desire for the knowledge of another's knowledge. For if at the origins of psychoanalysis it is the woman's knowledge that is sought, then the answer to the question of who seeks it seems to be "the man." A possibility of impropriety is then suggested, as we fear that this new attempt of a man to know a woman—to have access to her knowledge, so to know what she knows—is essentially a repetition of the ancient attempts.

Cavell does not dismiss this fear, and he indeed characterizes one of Freud's achievements with Dora as an instance of Freud's "penetration of the secrets of humanity." Nevertheless, without denying the longstanding grievances that may now trigger a certain alarm and hostility, Cavell does insist that these responses—alarm, hostility, and fear—will not be wholly productive, will in fact be stifling, if they are not themselves explored. The wisdom of these reactions can only be judged if they are not allowed to preclude a full consideration of the actual character of the Freudian suggestions about access to the knowledge of the other.

Freud himself is sometimes deliberately provocative about his proposals, as when, for example, in a paper on technique, he compares the power of the analyst to sexual potency and he describes the analyst's role in treatment as akin to the impregnation of a woman (S.E. 12:130). More often, however, he defends himself against this image, and he is at pains to offer a competing representation. He finds a favorite, a recurrent, justificatory illustration in the figure of the gynecologist.

When this parallel is drawn in his preface to his report on Dora, it is with a flourish of contempt for those who would call into question the sexually frank and explicit conversations he did not hesitate to have "even with a young woman" (S.E. 7:9). The defiant assertion that he "will simply claim for [himself] the rights of the gynaecologist" (S.E. 7:9) comes, however, at the conclusion of troubled ruminations about the awkwardness of his position and after more tentative and conditional justifications of the course he has chosen to follow. He acknowledges moral problems with his publication of the case, for it involves the revelation of intimate details of a patient's psychosexual life, intimacies that would not have been forthcoming had the patient known the uses to which they would be put. Though later in the case Freud declares his conviction that "no mortal can keep a secret. . . . betrayal oozes out of him at every pore" (S.E. 7:77–8), he here presents himself as making a choice about betrayal, eventually in its favor.

How can the distress and the uncertainty of the preceding remarks be squared with the aggressive confidence proclaimed in the identification with the gynecologist? The gynecologist has access to what is customarily private, shared only in love. The medical exception to the social rule is established for the sake of treatment, for the individual patient's own good. Freud notes that the rights he demands are actually "much more modest" (*S.E.* 7:9) than those of the gynecologist—Freud asks only for talk, asks for nothing special by way of sight or touch—but he is prepared to defend the larger claim, as he evidently recognizes his truly exceptional position, and he stands on just the gynecologists's basis for his exception: his practice is for the patient's good. The misgivings he feels about publishing the case are cast in terms of a conflict between this dedication to the patient's interests and a duty to science, a duty to communicate the details of the case in order to teach and build a body of knowledge. The decision between these conflicting obligations is partially rationalized with the thought that "duties towards science mean ultimately nothing else than . . . duties towards the many other patients who are suffering or will some day suffer from the same disorder" (*S.E.* 7:8). But the idea that he has thus found a sufficient reason for publication, an excuse that shows renewed professional dedication to (many) individual patients, to treatment and the relief of suffering, is apparently not wholly compelling, even to Freud. For were he convinced, he would not persist in the belief that medical discretion would forbid publication.

He regards the gynecological precedent as exculpatory only for his practice, not his publication. But gynecologists, like other physicians, certainly do (and did in 1905) publish clinical materials and describe patients' ailments, treatments, and results in order to fulfill "duties towards science," to teach and to extend knowledge. Such writing is part of the profession of medicine, of medical science. Why does Freud declare that his writing does not conform to standard professional practice? Confident that his activities in the treatment room accord with the professional model—privacy is breached impersonally and for the patient's good—he is uncertain about the prospect of teaching from or about these activities.

The reporting gynecologist screens the identities of patients and so can produce discreet contributions to an impersonal body of knowledge. Freud proposes to disguise the identity of the woman he calls "Dora," but he recognizes the inevitably personal character of the revelations. Placing the case summary in a "purely scientific and technical periodical" helps guard against "unauthorized readers"; but the medical community itself receives no automatic authorization, as Freud indicates his appalled awareness that "there are many physicians who . . . choose to

read a case history of this kind . . . for their private delectation" (*S.E.*
7:9). There is, here, undeniable despair about finding the proper student or colleague, about teaching or building a true science. The fact of
publication, of course, suggests an eventual commitment to hope. But
Freud's prefatory remarks suggest an unrelievable difficulty for psychoanalysis, one that persists in the uncharted intimacy of both its ideas and
their communication.

Cavell claims that Freud's concern about the inheritability of his
achievement is another connection between psychoanalysis and philosophy. Freud's defensive self-analogy with the gynecologist might even
seem an updated, scientific cover for a new form of an old maieutic
engagement. Socrates likened his practice to midwifery in order to emphasize his role as an assistant, as one who helps bring forth what is
independently there, latent ideas. So when Freud retreats from the image of the analyst's treatment impregnating a woman, when he claims
instead the standing of a gynecologist, he not only faces more properly
the fact of an extraordinary dislocation of ordinary privacy; he also underscores his position as one who helps reproduction but cannot, in that
role, cause or insure it.

Nevertheless, the fact remains that the science of gynecology can be
taught, and without any special moral problems; and the standards for
its ethically exemplary practice can also be fairly easily summarized and
instilled. The mysterious moral responsibilities that pervade the communication of psychoanalytic and philosophical ideas are, however, dreadfully unclear, though they are clearly profound; thus such discussions can
inspire suspicion and deep anxiety.

That such discussions can meet their moral challenge, discern and
shoulder their own responsibilities, is empirically established. We have
evidence in, for example, the writings of Freud and the writings of
Stanley Cavell. But a version of the Socratic question inevitably unsettles
us: Can this virtue be taught? The answer remains much as Socrates
found it: The question is undecidable as long as we do not yet know the
nature of this virtue.

References

Cavell, Stanley. *Must We Mean What We Say?* New York: Charles Scribner's
    Sons, 1969.
———. *The World Viewed.* New York: Viking Press, 1971.
———. *The Claim of Reason: Wittgenstein, Skepticism, Morality, and Tragedy.*
    New York: Oxford University Press, 1979.
———. *The Senses of Walden.* San Francisco: North Point Press, 1981.

Descartes, René. *Philosophical Writings.* Edited and translated by Elizabeth Anscombe and Peter Thomas Geach. London: Thomas Nelson, 1954.

———. *Philosophical Writings.* Edited and translated by Norman Kemp Smith. New York: Random House, 1958.

———. *Philosophical Letters.* Edited and translated by Anthony Kenny. Oxford: Oxford University Press, 1970.

———. *Philosophical Writings.* Translated by John Cottingham, Robert Stoothoff, and Duguld Murdoch. 2 vols. Cambridge: At the University Press, 1984–85.

Freud, Sigmund. *The Standard Edition of the Complete Psychological Works of Sigmund Freud.* Edited and translated by James Strachey. 24 vols. London: Hogarth Press, 1953–74.

"The Neuro-Psychoses of Defence" (1894), vol. 3.

Fragment of an Analysis of a Case of Hysteria (1905), vol. 7.

"Further Recommendations on the Technique of Psycho-Analysis I" (1913), vol. 12.

"On Transience" (1916), vol. 14.

Peirce, Charles Sanders. *Collected Papers.* Edited by Charles Hartshorne and Paul Weiss. Vols. 5, 6. Cambridge, Mass.: Harvard University Press, 1963.

Index

Illustrations are indicated by italic page numbers.

Aborigines, 88, 91
"Acknowledgment of Silence, The," 114
Activity, and passivity, 8, 9–10, 193–95
Adam's Rib, 15–16, 17, 22, 29
Addams, Jane, 140
Adolescence, in Weir's films, 85–89, 90–92
Adultery, in melodrama of the unknown
    woman, 18–19
All's Well That Ends Well (Shakespeare),
    18
Amish, 101, 105
"Analysis Terminable and Interminable"
    (Freud), 40
Andersson, Harriet, *170*
Anna Karenina (film), 18
Anna O., 33, 35
Austin, J. L., 21
Australia: filmmaking in, 84; history of,
    88, 91, 94
Awful Truth, The, 14, 15, 16, 17, 19, 22

Babenco, Hector (director): *Kiss of the Spi-
    derwoman*, 8, 150–68
Bach, Johann Christian, 61 n. 9
Bach, Johann Sebastian, 61 n. 9
"Beast in the Jungle" (James), 40
Beers, Clifford, 137
Bel Geddes, Barbara, 48–49, 50, 51, 53
Benjamin, Walter, 3
Bergman, Ingmar, 60 n. 5. As director:
    Cries and Whispers, 9, 169–82; *Per-
    sona*, 172; *Virgin Spring*, 144

Bergman, Ingrid, 19, 68
Bernini, Giovanni Lorenzo, 178
Beyond the Pleasure Principle (Freud), 4,
    14, 20–25
Birds, The, 78
Blake, William, 128
Bleak House (Dickens), 23
Blonde Venus, 19, 30
Bloom, Harold, 24, 28
Blos, Peter, 92
Blum, Harold, 172
Boles, John, 19
Bounds of Sense, The (Strawson), 123–24
Boyd, Russell, 86
Boyer, Charles, 19
Breuer, Josef, 33, 35
Bringing Up Baby, 17
British Film Academy, 86
Bunuel, Luis, 60 n. 5

Cagney, James, 140
Cambodia, 98
Capra, Frank (director): *It Happened One
    Night*, 15, 17, 22; *It's a Wonderful
    Life*, 75
Cars That Ate Paris, The, 107 n. 1
Catcher in the Rye (Salinger), 138
Catharsis, 59
Cavell, Stanley, 1–5, 61 n. 8, 62 n. 15,
    102; on Freud, 197–98, 200; on Garbo,
    190, 192, 193; and *Kiss of the Spi-
    derwoman*, 162–64; and melodrama of

Cavell, Stanley (continued)
the unknown woman, 64, 78, 79, 80,
153; and skepticism, 109–36, 188,
191–92; and violence in films, 144; on
Wittgenstein, 118–24. Works: *The
Claim of Reason,* 2, 3, 21, 25, 36, 112,
119, 120, 131; *Must We Mean What
We Say?,* 3, 21, 117; *Pursuits of Happi-
ness,* 3, 13, 14–15, 16, 17, 20–22, 109,
112; *The Senses of Walden,* 3; *Themes
out of School,* 3; *The World Viewed,* 3,
112, 114
Censorship, 139–40
Chaplin, Charlie, 60 n. 3, 183–86, *184*
Chapman, Mark, 138
Chasseguet-Smirgel, Janine, 133 n. 5
Chicago Motion Picture Commission, 140
Claim of Reason, The (Cavell), 2, 3, 21,
25, 36, 112, 119, 120, 131
Cobra, 143, 147
Colbert, Claudette, 15, 17
Coleridge, Samuel Taylor, 21
Colman, Ronald, 19
Coming of age films, 92–96, 145, 146
Commonwealth Film Unit, 95
Coogan, Jackie, *184*
Corman, Roger, 143
Cotten, Joseph, *110,* 124–32
Crawford, Joan, 19
Cries and Whispers, 9, 169–82, *170*
Cukor, George (director): *Adam's Rib,*
15–16, 17, 22, 29; *Gaslight,* 19, 36,
91, 130; *The Philadelphia Story,* 14,
15, 22
Curtiz, Michael (director): *Mildred Pierce,*
19

Danto, Arthur, 134 n. 12
Dark Side of Genius, The (Spoto),
61 n. 14
Davis, Bette, 16, 19
Definition of Love, The (Marvell), 154
de Niro, Robert, 138
Derrida, Jacques, 24, 122, 133 n. 9
Descartes, René, 10, 21, 33, 112, 133 n.2,
187–92, 195. Works: *Discourse on
Method,* 187; *Meditations,* 189; *The
Passions of the Soul,* 10, 189; *Principles
of Philosophy,* 189
Desensitization, 145–46
Deutsch, Helene, 171

Developmental stages, in Weir's films,
82–108
Dickens, Charles: *Bleak House,* 23
Dietrich, Marlene, 16, 19, 30, 78
Doll's House, A (Ibsen), 16, 18
Dora (Freud's case), 29, 32, 33–35, 198
Doubt. *See* Skepticism
Douglas, Melvyn, 140
Dracula, 145
Dreams and dreaming: and film, 88; and
film viewing, 152; in *Vertigo,* 44–63; in
Weir's films, 91
Dunne, Irene, 13, 14, 15, 17, 19

Eberwein, Robert, 60 n. 1
Ecstasy of Saint Teresa, 178
Edwards, Jonathan, 134 n. 13
Eisenstein, Sergei, 46–47
Elizabeth, Princess, 10, 189
El Salvador, 98
Emerson, Ralph Waldo, 3, 21, 25, 27,
30–31, 34, 116–17, 122, 123, 194;
"Self-Reliance," 30–31, 116, 133 n. 9
Erikson, Erik, 82
Eternal recurrence, 4, 14
Eurydice, 58
Evers, Medgar, 138

Feldman, Edward, 106
Fellini, Federico, 60 n. 5
Felman, Shoshana, 23
Film: and dreams and dreaming, 47–48,
88; and philosophy, 112–15; and psy-
choanalysis, 4, 11–43; public response
to, 3, 11–13; reading, 5; and skepti-
cism, 109–36; suffering of woman in,
29–36; and violence, 7–8, 137–49
Filmmaking: Australian, 84; and primal
scene, 92
Film viewing, 5, 9, 150–53; and bearing
witness, 84; and dreaming, 152; and
passivity, 6–7, 113–14; and primal
scene, 114, 115; by projection mode,
88–89
Fischer, Kurt, 42 n. 3
Flaubert, Gustave: *Madame Bovary,* 19
Fonda, Henry, 13, 15
Ford, Harrison, *83*
Forster, E. M.: *A Passage to India,* 85
Frank, Micheline, 8–9
Frankenstein, 145

Freud, Anna, 161, 170
Freud, Sigmund, 4, 39–49, 41 n. 2, 42 n.
    3, 147–48, 197–200; Cavell's debt to,
    22–23; and *Cries and Whispers,* 171,
    172; on Dora, 32–35; on dreaming,
    44–46, 47, 59; as gynecologist,
    198–200; and *Kiss of the Spiderwo-
    man,* 156, 161, 165; and melodrama of
    the unknown woman, 15; and philoso-
    phy, 23–25, 27–28; and remarriage
    comedy, 13; and sexual differences,
    33–36; on the unconscious, 26–27.
    Works: "Analysis Terminable and In-
    terminable," 40; *Beyond the Pleasure
    Principle,* 4, 14, 24–25; *The Interpreta-
    tion of Dreams,* 23, 26; "On Trans-
    cience," 193; *Three Essays on the The-
    ory of Sexuality,* 13; *The Uncanny,* 23
Friday the Thirteenth, 147
Frye, Northrop, 17

Gable, Clark, 15
Galenson, Eleanor, 172
Gallipoli, 92–96, 99, 107
Garbo, Greta, 10, 16, 36, 190, 192, 193
Garfield, John, 138
Garson, Greer, 19
Gaslight, 19, 36, 91, 130
Gelmis, Joseph, 145–46
Gender differences. *See* Sexual Differences
Gender identity, 155, 172
Gibson, Mel, 96
"Gigantism," 114
Gilbert, John, 36
Gorton, John, 84
Gould, Timothy, 6–7
Grant, Cary, 13, 14, 15, 68, 73
Griffith, D. W. (director): *Intolerance,* 139
Gulpilil, 90–91

Hammerstein, Oscar, 19
Hanson, Karen, 9
Hawks, Howard (director): *His Girl Friday,*
    15, 17
Hawthorne, Nathaniel, 21
Hedren, Tippi, 62 n. 14
Hegel, Georg W. F., 34; *Philosophy of
    Right,* 3
Heidegger, Martin, 24, 25, 27, 28, 109,
    116, 122, 133 n. 8, 194; *What Is
    Called Thinking?,* 24, 27, 116

Helmore, Tom, 49–50, 52–58
Henreid, Paul, 19
Hepburn, Katherine, 13, 14, 15, 17, 29
Hermann, Bernard, 61 n. 9
Hertz, Neil, 23
Hinckley, John, Jr., 137–38
His Girl Friday, 15, 17
Hitchcock, Alfred: camera use by, 79; and
    melodrama of the unknown woman,
    79–80; and the ordinary, 127; relation-
    ship to actresses, 61 n. 14; signatures of,
    54, 56, 65, 67, 68, 73, 77–78, 79; on
    viewing, 5; and Weir, 92. As director:
    The Birds, 78; *The Man Who Knew Too
    Much,* 126; *Marnie,* 78; *Murder!,* 72;
    Notorious, 126, 132 n. 1; *Psycho,* 61 n.
    12, 65, 79; *Rear Window,* 126; *Sabo-
    teur,* 114; *Shadow of a Doubt,* 6, 7,
    109, *110,* 124–32, 132 n. 1; *Spell-
    bound,* 51, 52, 53, 61 n. 11; *To Catch a
    Thief,* 126; *Vertigo,* 5, 44–81, 91, 130
Hitchcock: The Murderous Gaze
    (Rothman), 65, 126
Hoffmann, E. T. A., 39
Hölderlin, Friedrich, 129
Holliday, Judy, 15
Hollywood, 84
Homesdale, 107 n. 1
Horror film, 143–46
Howard, Ron (director): *Splash,* 61 n. 10
Hume, David, 21, 112, 134 nn. 13, 16
Humiliation, 146, 147, 148
Hunt, Linda, 96
Hurt, William, 150, *151*
Huston, John (director): *We Were Stran-
    gers,* 138
Hysterical conversion, 35–36

Ibsen, Henrik: *A Doll's House,* 16, 18
Idealism, German, 27, 28
Indonesia, 96, 99, 100, 101
Interpretation of Dreams (Freud), 23, 26
Intolerance, 139
Irigaray, Luce, 165
Irony, 30–31
It Happened One Night, 3, 15, 17, 22
It's a Wonderful Life, 75

Jakarta, Indonesia, 99, 100
James, Henry: "Beast in the Jungle," 40;
    The Turn of the Screw, 23

Jouissance, 167 n. 5
Jourdan, Louis, *12, 64*
Journalists, 98
Jowett, Garth, 139
Julia, Raul, 150, *151*

Kael, Pauline, 90
Kalb, Bernard, 99
Kant, Immanuel, 27, 28, 41 n. 2, 42 n. 3
Kawin, Bruce, 60 n. 1
Keane, Marian, 64, 72, 77
Keaton, Buster, 72
Kennedy, Harlan, 143
Kennedy, John F., 138
Kern, Jerome, 19
Kerrigan, William, 61 n. 12
Khrushchev, Nikita, 138
Kid, The, 9, 60 n. 3, 183–86, *184*
Killing Fields, The, 98
Kierkegaard, Søren, 3–4, 8, 14
Kiss of the Spiderwoman, 8, 150–68, *151*
Kleist, Heinrich von, 19, 32
Kung Fu movie, 146

Lacan, Jacques, 30, 32–33, 39, 163–64,
    165, 166
Lady Chatterley's Lover, 140
Lady Eve, The, 15, 22
Lasswell, Harold, 146
Last House on the Left, 143–44
Last Wave, The, 86, 88, 89–92, 95, 99,
    100, 104, 105, 107
Leigh, Janet, 65
Lennon, John, 138
LeRoy, Mervyn (director): *Random Har-*
    vest, 19
Letter from an Unknown Woman, 11, *12,*
    13, 19, 30, 37–40, 64, 79–80, 155, 164
Lewin, Bertram, 133 n. 6
Lindsay, Joan, 87
Little Caesar, 140

McCarey, Leo (director): *The Awful Truth,*
    14, 15, 16, 17, 22
McGillis, Kelly, *83*
Madame Bovary (Flaubert), 19
Mahler, Margaret, 172
Major Arcana, 90, 92
Male bonding, 105
Maleness, in melodrama of the unknown
    woman, 16

Mann, Thomas, 134 n. 16
Man Who Knew Too Much, The, 126
Marcuse, Herbert, 165
Marnie, 78
Marquise of O, 19, 32
Marvell, Andrew, 154
Mateship society, 95
Meat inspection legislation, 139
Media, and violence, 137–49
Meditations (Descartes), 189
Méliès, Georges, 44
Mellen, Joan, 171
Melodrama, and skepticism, 21–22
Melodrama, of the unknown woman, 4,
    11–43; and separation, 154; and sexual
    differences, 30–31; and *Shadow of a*
    Doubt, 130, 132 n. 1; and *Vertigo,* 64–81
Mélusine, 50, 58, 61 n. 10
Metz, Christian, 60 n. 1
"Miami Vice," 143
Michelson, Peter, 144
Midsummer Night's Dream, A (Shakes-
    peare), 61 n. 11
Mildred Pierce, 19
Miles, Vera, 62 n. 14
Milton, John, 17
Mind That Found Itself, 137
Montage, 46–47, 59
Morgan, Helen, 19
Mother and the Law, The, 139
Mother-daughter relationship, 78, 130–31
Munch, Edvard, 171
Murder!, 72
Must We Mean What We Say? (Cavell), 3,
    21, 77

Nanjiwara, 91, 92
New York theaters, 144–45
Nicaragua, 98
Nietzsche, Friedrich, 4, 14, 25, 27, 114–
    16. Works: "On Redemption," 115;
    On the Genealogy of Morals, 115; *Thus*
    Spoke Zarathustra, 14
Night of the Living Dead, 146
Norris, Chuck, 147
Notorious, 68, 73, 126, 132 n. 1
Novak, Kim, 6, 49–58, 65–78, 130
Now Voyager, 19

Old Comedy, 17
"On Redemption," (Nietzsche), 115

On the Beach, 105
On the Genealogy of Morals (Nietzsche), 115
Ontogeny of encounter, in Weir's films, 82–108
"On Transience" (Freud), 193
Ophuls, Max (director): *Letter from an Unknown Woman,* 11–13, 19, 37–40, 64, 79–80, 155, 164
Ordinary: concept of, 21; and skepticism, 109–36
Oswald, Lee Harvey, 138
Othello (Shakespeare), 31, 33

Palombo, Stanley R., 5, 6, 62 n. 17
Passage to India, A (Forster), 85
Passions of the Soul, The (Descartes), 10, 189
Passivity: and activity, 8, 9–10, 193–95; as feminine, 196; in film, 112–15; in philosophy, 115–18; and skepticism, 188–89, 191–92, 193–94; in viewing, 6–7
Payne Foundation, 140
Peirce, C. S., 196
Persona, 172
Petric, Vlada, 60 n. 1
Pettijohn, Charles C., 140
Philadelphia Story, The, 3, 14, 15, 22
Philippines, 101
Philosophical Investigations (Wittgenstein), 24, 112, 119
Philosophy: passivity in, 112–18; professionalization of, 119; and psychoanalysis, 4, 23–29, 114–15, 197–200; and sexual differences, 31, and skepticism, 111–12; and Wittgenstein, 118–19
Philosophy of Right (Hegel), 3
Picnic at Hanging Rock, 84–89, 95, 99, 105, 107
Plumber, The, 89, 107
Poe, Edgar Allan, 21, 23
Poltergeist II, 143
Powerlessness, in violent films, 146, 147, 148
Preoedipal development, 171–81
Primal scene, 92, 114, 115
Principles of Philosophy (Descartes), 189
Professionalization, of philosophy, 119
Psycho, 61 n. 12, 65, 79
Psychoanalysis: and film, 4, 11–13, 23–29, 114–15, 197–200; and philosophy, 4, 23–29, 114–15, 197–200; and skepticism, 1; and suffering of women, 29–36; and violent films, 146–48
Psychoanalytic criticism, 22–23
Puig, Manuel, 156, 157, 159
Pure Food and Drug Act, 139
Pursuits of Happiness (Cavell), 3, 13, 14–15, 16, 17, 20–22, 109, 112

Raging Bull, 139, 147
Rains, Claude, 19, 126
Rambo, 146
Random Harvest, 19, 79
Rank, Otto, 165
Reagan, Ronald, 137, 138
Rear Window, 126
Receptiveness, 115
Red Dawn, 147
Reich, Wilhelm, 165
Remarriage comedy, 3–5, 13, 102; and education, 17; roots of, 16, 17, 18; and sexual differences, 30–31; and *Shadow of a Doubt,* 132; and skepticism, 22; vs. *Vertigo,* 59; villainy in, 16; and woman's happiness, 16–17
REM sleep, 44
Repetition: Kierkegaardian, 3–4, 14; in *Letter from an Unknown Woman,* 37–38, 39
Revenge, 146, 147, 148
Rite of passage films, 92–96, 145, 146
Ritter, Thelma, 126
Robeson, Paul, 19
Rohmer, Eric (director): *The Marquise of O,* 19, 32
Roiphe, Herman, 172
Romanticism, 21, 128–29
Roosevelt, Theodore, 139
Rorty, Richard, 7, 112, 119, 122, 133 n. 3
Rothenberg, Albert, 62 n. 17
Rothman, William, 5, 6, 61 n. 8, 126, 127, 130; *Hitchcock: The Murderous Gaze,* 65, 126
Russell, Rosalind, 15, 17

Saboteur, 114
Salinger, J. D.: *Catcher in the Rye,* 138
Salvador, 98
"Sandman, The," 39
Schelling, F. W., 26, 27

Schneider, Irving, 7–8
Schwarzenegger, Arnold, 147
Scorsese, Martin (director): *Raging Bull,*
    139, 147; *Taxi Driver,* 137, 138
Sedgwick, Eve Kosovsky, 23
Self–doubt, 2
Selfhood, 3
"Self-Reliance" (Emerson), 30–31, 116,
    133 n. 9
Senses of Walden, The (Cavell), 3
Separation, in *Kiss of the Spiderwoman,*
    153–54, 159–60
Sexual differences, 9–10, 29–36; in *Ad-
    am's Rib,* 29; in melodrama of the un-
    known woman, 30; and remarriage
    comedy, 29–31
Shadow of a Doubt, 6, 7, 109, *110,*
    124–32
Shakespeare, 31, 61 n. 11. Works: *All's
    Well That Ends Well,* 18; *A Midsum-
    mer Night's Dream,* 61 n. 11; *Othello,*
    31, 33; *The Winter's Tale,* 18, 31
Shapiro, James, 81 n. 4
Sherlock Jr., 72
Showboat, 19
Silence, The, 171, 172
Sinatra, Frank, 138
Sklar, Robert, 139, 140
Sklarew, Bruce, 9
Skepticism, 1–5; Cavell on, 109–36, 188,
    191–92; linked to maleness, 9, 10; loss
    of, 25; and melodrama, 21–22; and the
    ordinary, 21–22; and passivity, 188–89,
    191–92; and sexual differences, 31–32
Smith, Art, *12*
Smith, Joseph H., 41 n. 2
Soul–blindness, 25
Spellbound, 51, 52, 53, 61 n. 11
Splash, 61 n. 10
Spoto, Donald, 61 n. 14
Stage Fright, 78
Stallone, Sylvester, 147
Stanwyck, Barbara, 13, 15
Stella Dallas, 19
Sternberg, Joseph von, 19, 30
Stewart, James, 5–6, *45,* 48–59, 64–78,
    126, 130, 135 n. 18
Stoller, Robert J., 8, 148, 155–56, 157,
    158, 159, 162, 172
Strawson, P. F., 123–24
Studies on Hysteria (Freud), 29, 33

Sturges, Preston (director): *The Lady Eve,*
    15, 22
Subjecthood, 3
Suddenly, 138
Suffering of women, 29–36
Suicide, 7–8, 193–94
Sukarno, 96
Surgeon General's Scientific Advisory
    Committee on Television and Violence,
    141
Sylwan, Kari, *170*
Symbiosis anxiety, 162

"Talking cure," 33
Taxi Driver, 137, 138
Television, and violence, 141–42
Terminator, The, 147
Terrorism, 147
Themes out of School (Cavell), 3, 134 n.
    10
Thoreau, Henry David, 21, 194
Three Essays on the Theory of Sexuality
    (Freud), 13
Thus Spoke Zarathustra (Nietzsche), 14
Tilghman, B. R., 134 n. 12
To Catch a Thief, 126
Top Gun, 143
Tracy, Spencer, 13, 15–16, 29
Transsexuals, 155–57, 158
Turn of the Screw, The (James), 23

Ullmann, Liv, 173
Uncanny, The (Freud), 23
"Unconscious, The" (Freud), 41 n. 2
Under Fire, 98

Velez, Lupe, 140
Vertigo, 5, 44–81, *45,* 91, 130; dream
    function in, 44–63; and melodrama of
    the unknown woman, 64–81
Vidor, King (director): *Stella Dallas,* 19
Vietnam, 147
Villainy, in remarriage comedy, 16
Violence: depicted and enacted, 7–8,
    137–49; and television, 141–42
Virgin Spring, 144

Warshow, Robert, 3
Wayne, David, 15
Weil, Annemarie, 172
Weir, Peter: and aborigines, 91; entry into

filmmaking, 95; and witnessing and bearing witness, 82–108. As director: *Gallipoli,* 92–96, 99, 107; *The Last Wave,* 86, 88, 89–92, 95, 99, 104, 105; *Picnic at Hanging Rock,* 84–89, 95, 99, 105; *The Plumber,* 89; *Witness,* 82, 101–7; *The Year of Living Dangerously,* 55, 61 n. 13, 82, 94, 95, 96–101, 105
Weissman, Stephen, 9
We Were Strangers, 138
Whale, James (director): *Showboat,* 19
What Is Called Thinking? (Heidegger), 24, 27, 116
Wilden, A., 164
Williams, Linda, 143
Williams, Tony, 143
Winer, Robert, 6
Winnicott, D. W., 8, 152–53, 159–60, 165–66
Winter's Tale, The (Shakespeare), 18, 31

Witness, 82, 83, 95, 101–7
Witnessing, and bearing witness, 6, 82–108
Wittgenstein, Ludwig, 2, 6, 21, 24, 25, 28, 34, 42 n. 3, 109, 112, 134 n. 16; Cavell on, 118–24; *Philosophical Investigations,* 24, 112, 119
Woman, melodrama of the unknown. *See* Melodrama of the unknown woman
Wood, Robin, 143
Wordsworth, William, 21, 129
World Viewed, The (Cavell), 3, 112, 114
Wright, Teresa, 7, 124, 126, 129–30

Year of Living Dangerously, The (film), 55, 61 n. 13, 82, 94, 95, 96–101, 105
"Year of Living Dangerously, The" (speech), 96

Zweig, Stefan, 40